Writing Short Films

Structure and Content for Screenwriters

2nd Edition

Linda J. Cowgill

 lone eagle THE REPORTER

WRITING SHORT FILMS
Structure and Content for Screenwriters, 2nd Edition
Copyright © 2005 Linda J. Cowgill

WATSON-GUPTIL PUBLICATIONS, an imprint of the Crown Publishing Group, a division of Random House, Inc., New York
www.crownpublishing.com
www.watsonguptill.com

Printed in the United States of America
10

Cover design by Lindsay Albert
Book design by Carla Green
Edited by Steve Atinsky

Library of Congress Cataloging-in-Publication Data
Cowgill, Linda J.
Writing short films : structure & content for screenwriters /
    by Linda J. Cowgill. — 2nd ed.
        p.   cm.
    Includes bibliographical references and index.
    ISBN 1-58065-063-5
    1. Short films—Authorship. I. Title.

    PN1996.C815 2005
    808.2'3—dc22   2005044185

Books may be purchased in bulk at special discounts for promotional or educational purposes. Special editions can be created to specifications. Inquiries for sales and distribution, textbook adoption, foreign language translation, editorial, and rights and permissions inquiries should be addressed to: Lori Horak, Watson-Guptill Publications, 770 Broadway, New York, NY 10003, 646.654.5462 or send e-mail to: lhorak@watsonguptill.com.

Distributed by Watson-Guptill, 800.451.1741 x153
Lone Eagle Publishing Company™ is a registered trademark.

To David and Clea,
who make everything worthwhile.

CONTENTS

PART TWO - INTERMEDIATE STEPS

PART FOUR - KEEPING FOCUSED

APPENDICES

Acknowledgments

The new edition of *Writing Short Films* would not have been possible without the help of numerous people, who I am happy to thank here.

Jeff Black at Lone Eagle and Hollywood Creative Directory, whose encouragement and aid has been instrumental to keeping me focused and on track.

Joan Singleton and Beth Wetzel, for originally recognizing the value of this book and putting it into motion.

Hilary Ripps at Chanticleer Films and Bryan Gordon, for the use of the screenplay to *Ray's Male Heterosexual Dance Hall*.

Michael Kelly, at *Vidiots* in Santa Monica, along with the owners: Cathy Tauber and Patty Polinger, for having such a great selection of short films on video.

Ed Carter and Fritz Herzog, at the Academy of Motion Picture Arts and Sciences, for help screening several Academy Award winning live action shorts.

Geoff Grode for starting me on this path at AFI, Richard DeBaun for helping me prepare, and Steve Sharon for being there all these years.

I have to thank my students at the Los Angeles Film School who have appreciated my ideas and allowed me to learn from them.

Introduction

"Today in Hollywood it's far easier to get an agent, producer or production executive to view a short film than it is to get them to read a feature length screenplay. (Short form screenplays go virtually unread at studios and agencies.) The reasons are obvious. It takes less time to watch a short film than to read a script, and if it's good, it's far more enjoyable."

If those words were true eight years ago when I first wrote *Writing Short Films*, they are even truer today. *South Park* creators, Trey Parker and Matt Stone, launched their careers with a short done as a video Christmas card for a Hollywood executive. Christopher Nolan's short film *Doodlebug* announced a new talent. Stephen Daldry's short *Eight* got him ready for *Billy Elliot*. Joe Nussbaum's *George Lucas in Love* introduced him to studio execs and landed him *Sleepover*. Billy Bob Thorton wrote and George Hickenlooper directed *Some Folks Call It a Sling Blade*, the film that preceded the feature *Sling Blade*. Tom DiCillo wrote and directed the short *Living in Oblivion*, and then found financing to turn it into a feature film. The list goes on.

The short film, whether made on a university campus or independently financed, continues to be a well-traveled road into the film business. Steven Spielberg, Martin Scorsese, Francis Ford Coppola, George Lucas, John Carpenter, to name a famous few, all started this way. Lucas and Carpenter expanded their student films into low-budget features; the others used short films as calling cards to production executives and producers who championed them and launched their careers. Sidney Sheinberg recognized Steven Spielberg's talent from his short film and hired the young director for an episode of Rod Serling's anthology series *The Night Gallery*.

These days short films are everywhere: on the internet, on television and in theaters at festivals specializing in shorts that are popping up all over the world. With low cost digital media, simple home DVD duplication and the internet, it's never been easier to produce and distribute short films.

However, just because it's easier to make a short and get it seen doesn't mean there's an ocean of great films out there waiting for you. The problem of story still exists. So while everyone is making shorts (from elementary school students to professional screenwriters aspiring to become directors), the search for good ones, great ones, the best ones continues — because mastering story is still the essential art. Every other aspect of filmmaking in the narrative form exists to serve the story. If the story isn't sound, the film can't be. A film may be fantastic visually, but if the story doesn't work, the film won't serve you, the director, to the extent it should. Strong visual images are found on the reels of many cinematographers and editors; well-acted scenarios make up the reels of many actors. But your job as a filmmaker — a screenwriter, director, producer, or some combination of all three — is to deliver a film that makes sense as a *story*.

THE DESIGN OF THIS BOOK

The focus of *Writing Short Films* is on writing the screenplay for the synchronous sound narrative short film. This is not a manual on filmmaking, geared in any way toward production other than providing the best outline possible of principles and techniques for constructing the short screenplay. This book is designed specifically for those wanting to make a narrative-driven short film, and who recognize that before production can begin a completed script must be in hand. (Experimental, non-narrative films are not dealt with.) Though most of the examples I have selected derive from narrative sync sound shorts, these same concepts can be applied to non-sync sound short films. I use examples from Albert Lamorisse's *The Red Balloon* and Robert Enrico's *Occurrence at Owl Creek*, both essentially non-sync sound films, throughout this book. The reason is simple: even without a synchronized soundtrack, these films are *story*-driven.

I've laid the book out in four sections. Part One introduces the concepts the beginning writer must know to develop an idea; provides an overview of screenplay structure for the short film; and covers the principles of plot. Part Two considers structure in depth — the set-up, rising action and conclusion — emphasizing the tools the screenwriter uses to construct a plot. Part Three covers the writing process, with discussions on scene construction, dialogue and subtext. The final section deals with ideas for keeping a story focused. Appendices cover information on proper screenplay format, computer screenwriting programs, and more information on the referenced films.

A major shortcoming I've found in other books on writing the short screenplay is the lack of examples drawn from easily available sources. Without concrete examples to illustrate the principles of characterization, construction and theme, the discussion becomes elusive. The reader depends upon a description of events, sometimes problematic if the memory of the author fails him. Even if student screenplays are included in an appendix to the book, it is not the same as seeing a finished film.

I believe it's more important to see a film than to read one. Wherever possible, I have tried to use examples from films that are on video, several of which can be found in major video chains, while others can be located in more eclectic stores, libraries or through outlets like NetFlix and Facets Media. Many are now turning up on the internet for viewing, or for purchase at Amazon.com or FacetsMedia.com. Internet sites such as iFilm.com, Atomfilms.com, TriggerStreet.com, BMWFilms.com and more, all have short films available for round the clock viewing.

The numbers of domestic and international film festivals increase annually, and short films make up growing portions of their programs. Each year Hollywood pays greater attention to the festivals, both as a source of new talent, and for short form product, which is in demand from major cable channels and those specializing in independent film. (The Sundance Channel, IFC, HBO and Showtime all acquire shorts for programming needs.) Many new filmmakers emerge from these forums, if not with production deals then often with interested agents, producers or production executives.

Every short film begins with a screenplay, even if it's only the director who reads it as he picks up his camera. Just as the short story writer envies the novelist's freedom to leisurely establish mood and story, the short film writer has a difficult job in structuring his story so that the characters, theme and plot all prove satisfying in a shorter framework. This book is designed to impart a set of skills to master the craft of screenwriting for this shorter medium.

A NOTE ON THE REFERENCED FILMS

If you watch only one film while reading this book, make it *Life Lessons*, written by Richard Price and directed by Martin Scorsese. It is the first segment of a trilogy of films in *New York Stories* (Touchstone, 1989). Every major video chain should have a copy of this film. Examples taken from *Life Lessons* are used throughout the book because, in addition to being readily available, it is expertly written and directed. The film is a real amalgam of Hollywood's best, working in an unusual short film format. (The other two segments of *New York Stories* are worth seeing for how Woody Allen and Francis Ford Coppola work in the short film arena, but are less successful than the other films referenced.)

Also strong and available on DVD is Billy Bob Thornton and George Hickenlooper's *Some Folks Call It a Sling Blade*. If you watch this film, remember that when it hit the festival circuit in 1994, Billy Bob Thornton's face had never been on the cover of a supermarket tabloid. You'll appreciate the construction of the story that much more. Recently available on DVD is the *75th Annual Academy Awards Short Films*, a compilation of both the live action and animated short nominations and winners that year.

Both *Occurrence At Owl Creek* and *The Red Balloon* can be found in many video stores and libraries. *The Red Balloon* won an Academy Award for Best Original Screenplay in 1955, and *Occurrence at Owl Creek* won for Best Live Action Short in 1963.

A list of all the films discussed in this book and their video distributors is in an appendix at the end of this book. It may take a little digging to find them, but it's definitely worth it. Almost all have been commercially released, and are good examples of short films made for commercial markets, a presumed goal of all writers reading this book.

PART ONE

THE FUNDAMENTALS

1

Before We Start – The Principles of Drama

Stories are how we understand the world. An encounter with a surly bus driver that we relay to a friend at lunch, a fairy tale we read to a child in bed, Tolstoy's epic historical novel *War and Peace* — all these are narratives that explain some part of our world to ourselves, that help us define the struggles of a daily commute, the unseen forces a child confronts, and the tribulations of war in a Russian winter. To more completely understand these events, we may even have to invent details that make the story "work better." The bus driver is a true sadist; forests feel alive because of unseen spirits; armies are driven to folly the same way lovers are. We'll invent whatever we have to in order to make our stories make sense. Only if stories make sense can we make sense of our world. Telling stories may be an essential existential act. We tell stories to define our world in causal, temporal terms we can understand. And maybe, at some level, we have to tell ourselves stories to prove to ourselves that we exist.

Stories are told in simple jokes, oral sagas, ancient texts, live performances and visual recordings. But stories aren't always transferable across different media. Just because a story can be "told" or written or acted out in a dance or pantomime doesn't mean it lends itself to a filmic telling. Every day filmmakers start shorts and features that are misconceived and doomed because writers don't understand the underlying principles of drama. These filmmakers believe assembling a string of incidents — a character does this and goes here, then meets another character, and something else happens — will somehow create a dramatic story. This *may* be the case in *writing* a short story or novel because incidents can be shaped and framed by the author's voice in the narrative. But even in filmic stories where narration is fundamental to the storytelling, drama requires more than the sum of a number of incidents.

So before we start, let's take a moment to consider these principles of drama up close, define them and understand their application in creating a story that will work in film. By drama, I mean it in its broadest and most inclusive sense: works written for performance, serious or comedic, on stage, film or television.

THE PRINCIPLES OF DRAMA
Drama relies on two important rules. There must be:
1. A character (the protagonist), who will take action to achieve something
2. This character will meet with conflict

The character must act, and the level of conflict can be subtle or strong as long as it's apparent. If film stories do not have a basis in these two fundamental rules, they will not work.

Drama needs characters who desire, who want, who need, and who will act (even if the action is reactive, or centered around avoidance of action or reaction). This kind of character will drive a story forward and provide an understandable framework for the story's action. Conflict builds the tension that keeps the audience interested in what happens next. These two ideas work together to create a context for the story's information so an audience that is <u>seeing and hearing a story *instead* of reading it</u> will understand what's going on.

This is the key point. The audience is *viewing*, not reading — a completely different mode of understanding. Film, as with theater and music, is a temporal art form. It communicates its content within a precise time span. The audience must be able to process the information and make meaningful connections to understand it. Drama drives home its information differently than narrative prose. The obvious example is how in a book an important thought in someone's mind can be written for the reader. In film, especially if voiceover narration isn't used, screenwriters must externalize what characters feel and think, and this can be extremely difficult. As film has become more naturalistic, it has left behind most theatrical conventions such as asides, monologues, chorus, etc., and instead relies on authentic behavior to convey the sense of realism the audience expects.

Reading is an "active" activity while viewing is a passive one. The bookworm actively reads the words on paper, making the decision to keep turning pages or not. Stories can be picked up and read at will while films play out in specific duration (though DVD viewing may eventually alter how we watch drama). With film, viewers sit and watch as action happens before them and screenwriters have to work harder to hold their interest with the activity itself. With a book, the voice of the narrator can lead readers through the material, making leaps and connections through what is really a commentary on the action. Tension and meaning can be created by what the writer tells the readers. And if readers don't understand a passage, they can re-read it until they do. But in film, the action must develop in a way that is clearly understood as it happens, and builds tension so the audience stays attentive.

This is where a character's desire and conflict come in. Screenwriters use specific actions growing out characters' wants and needs — objectives — to keep the audience clued in to the story line — the plot. On the most superficial level, every story is about the quest to attain a goal and whether a character will achieve it or not. Conflict casts doubt on the character's ultimate success and increases our interest. Conflict creates stress and trouble we want to see resolved.

If we have no clue as to what a character wants and where a story's heading, we tend to lose interest because we don't understand the primary connections between the actions enough to assign meaning. If the action is mere activity or characters simply talking about their ideas, feelings or what's going on, little tension develops and again the audience's attention dwindles.

PRACTICAL APPLICATION

But let's not stay in the theoretical. Let's get practical. Anyone who has ever directed a scene will tell you the first things the director and actors must find in the material are what each actor wants (in the scene and overall) and the source of the conflict. Without scene objectives and conflict, tension never develops, the scene falls flat, actors flounder and the audience yawns and heads for the doors.

Try this simple directing exercise with the dialogue below and find out yourself. Corral two actors for the parts of A and B, and read the lines.

A: Hey.
B: Hello. Do you know what time it is?
A: No. What time is it?
B: It's one AM. Where have you been?
A: Out walking... walking and thinking.
B: Thinking about what?
A: About what happened.
B: What about it?
A: I don't know. G'night.
B: Good night.

Without any context, the lines are flat and not very interesting. But if you create a dramatic framework, find the conflict between the characters in contradictory objectives the lines will come to life. Say, A and B are lovers who have had a fight. B has to go home because his father is very sick. A wants to go, too, but B doesn't want her/him along because of a troubled relationship with the family and he's unsure of his feelings for A. B wants A to accept his decision without laying on the guilt. A senses that B is pulling away, but wants B to take her/him along. A is hurt and suffering, and isn't going to make it easy on B. Now have the actors read the lines and see what happens.

If you've done this right, you should see that once purpose and conflict have been added to the scene, it becomes more interesting. You can take this further by delving into the emotional subtext of the scene and giving the actors specific actions and emotions for each line that then demands an emotional reaction from the other actor. B might be dismissive and condescending to A's real pain and suffering, provoking A to deeper pain or anger.

The point is the lines take on greater meaning when given direction and conflict that allows for emotional response. Narrative films need action and conflict to frame the important ideas the writer is concerned with and make them compelling to the audience. By understanding the special properties of film — this visual medium of images and sound — and using these dramatic principles of action and conflict to evaluate an idea and shape a story, writers can save time and energy in choosing which stories to develop into screenplays.

REACHING THE AUDIENCE – EMOTION!

Every successful film, short or long, gives the audience an emotional experience. It makes us laugh or cry (in great films we do both, and a lot more). You must understand your audience craves this emotional experience. Emotion takes us out of ourselves and connects us with others, and brings more deeply into ourselves. It's a paradox. More importantly, emotion makes us feel alive, and when a film gives us this experience, it has us. We connect with it.

How do you give the audience an emotional experience? One tool is your characters and their emotional responses. We understand or empathize with characters who have recognizable emotional reactions. Emotion is the quickest way to expose a character to the audience (more in Chapter 3). Another tool is humor. Laughter is a wonderful emotion; it makes us happy (and causes the brain to release those amazing endorphins). Surprise and suspense are tools to build tension by creating anxiety, and to keep us wondering what will happen next in the story (more in Chapter 7). The key is to make them feel *something*. The worst thing is when you watch a film and feel nothing.

I've heard it said that books use ideas to get to emotions (to provide the emotional experience we readers demand) and films use emotions to get to ideas. The truth of this lies in the power of cinema — a visceral art form that uses images, language, music, psychology, technology to communicate its message. It's the immediacy of the medium that makes emotion so pivotal. So as you plot out your story, a great writer thinks not only of what the character would do and feel, but what he wants the *audience* to feel. (Chapter 3 will continue this discussion, in more depth.)

ACTION VS. DIALOGUE (WORDS, WORDS, WORDS!)

Another distinction worth noting here is the one between action and dialogue. Many beginning screenwriters mistakenly think you tell the story with the dialogue. Characters tell us what's going on in their hearts and minds, and fill in all the important details, leaving nothing for the imagination.

What the best screenwriters know, however, is that action drives 99 out of 100 film stories and the dialogue is subsidiary to it. They know that telling the audience everything in words lessens a story's impact, reduces its tension and ultimately creates a boring tale. The best writers conceive their stories so that characters' actions are at the heart of them. Dialogue supports the plot movement and doesn't supersede it. What these writers know is that the audience likes a little mystery, to figure things out along the way. Your audience is already in a passive relationship with the work, and if you tell your audience everything, it leaves them little to do. By giving the viewer just enough so that he understands what's going on, and then allowing the characters to reveal themselves through their actions and reactions, the audience follows along putting the information together and making sense of it. Chapters 10, *Dialogue*, and 11, *The Subtext of Meaning*, talk about this in more detail, but it's an important point to think about at the start. You want to show your story, not tell it.

On the practical end, when we overuse our dialogue it tends to feel forced once it gets into actor's mouth. Good actors don't need a lot of explanation to tell us what's going on in them. They convey the inner life we writers so desperately want to get across with their feelings and expressions, actions and reactions. Good writers must learn to be good actors, too, so that they understand what must be said and what can go *unsaid*, and then figure out how to effectively communicate that on the page.

THE ENDING

If you are serious about writing a short you wish to film, or even as an end in itself to teach yourself about screenwriting, I urge you as early as possible to start thinking about an ending for your story. You want a strong finish or pay-off for your film. Too many feature film screenplays and shorts build to — well, nothing — to endings that are flat and unsatisfying because nothing definitive happens. They follow a character around and the story just sort of peters out and concludes. The protagonist doesn't make a choice that means anything, doesn't take action that plays out to a conclusion with real consequences for the characters, or doesn't respond to the earlier events that lead us to believe they have had any meaning in his life.

Students sometimes tell me they use passive protagonists (though they rarely call them that) because these kinds of characters are more modern and/or more representative of real life. It may be real life, but in fiction (film or otherwise) we want and expect more. The wonderful thing about how art functions in our lives, especially in literature — film, theater, novels, short stories — is that it gives us what often eludes us in real life — a meaningful emotional experience of the world. This is what your audience wants and deserves from your film. Robert McKee in his book *Story* describes this desire as "aesthetic emotion." He writes, "In life, experiences become meaningful *with reflection in time*. In art, they are meaningful *now, at the instant they happen*." That's the power of a story; it gives us meaning we can understand now. In great art, we are able to relate to the story so that it resonates and affects us in a deep way.

The ending is what you leave your audience with, and the stronger it is the more clearly you reach them. And that has to be your ultimate goal — to reach the audience in some fundamental way.

THE DISCLAIMER: COMEDY

Now let me contradict myself. A short film, particularly a funny one, can get away with breaking these rules. Humor can be an end in itself (though generally, it works best when it's fraught with conflict as a character goes after what she wants, and that's what makes it so funny).

But there is a danger with comedy or parody. The longer a short film lasts, the more the audience wants it to be a story. They want it to mean something. Sketch comedy, like what's on

Saturday Night Live or *Mad-TV*, can be very effective — in smaller sizes. Have you ever noticed when watching these shows that the longer a sketch goes on, the more it seems to run out of steam? Unless the comedy is downright hysterical, keeping us in stitches one moment to the next, our minds try to find the meaning of the events — how they will wrap up into a cohesive whole we can relate to. And with skits, this is rarely the case. When we can't make the connections and find meaning even on a basic level, we tend to get frustrated and bored.

So the rule here is, if the script's truly funny, from start to finish, with the biggest laugh at the end, your film may work regardless of many of the rules of drama. But if it lags in the least, if transitions reduce the effect of the humor and your story stretches out past five or six minutes with no real point, you may find your audience deserting you. (I've sat through films no longer than seven minutes checking my watch and wondering when they will ever end?) If this is the case with your script, try applying the basic principles of drama to your comedy and see if it doesn't help you to develop a more cohesive plot line.

THE DIFFERENCE BETWEEN SHORTS & FEATURES

Is there a difference in form between a short film and a feature, apart from running time? Many writers approach their shorts with stories that are just too big. They want to *do* too much in their short films, cover too wide a territory than can be effectively managed for their budgets and skills, and don't understand the primary differences between a short and a feature. A short film differs as much from a feature as a short story does from a novel.

Many of the concepts for the short film screenplay (1 to 40 pages) are the same for writing a feature (90 to 130 pages), but there are major differences. Not only do shorts differ from feature films in the size and scope of the drama, but in plot structure, too. A five-minute short might start with an inciting incident that happens off screen and before the movie starts while a feature needs to show that development. A requisite for success in a feature is a sympathetic protagonist. A short film, however, may succeed primarily because it examines an unsympathetic protagonist who is fascinating. The reason this works in a short and not a feature is you're asking the audience to invest a shorter amount of time in your character, not the traditional 90 minutes to two hours. It's difficult to maintain interest in characters we don't care about past the half-hour mark.

Short films can focus on the conflict in one incident to great effect, but features focus on any number of incidents, and usually in less detail. For example, both Pepe Danquart's *Black Rider* (*Schwarzfahrer* in the film's native German) and Sam Karmann's *Omnibus*, two Academy Award-winning live action short films, explore incidents on a man's commute. Both are less than ten minutes long and very satisfying.

Short films can effectively deal with difficult themes longer mainstream feature films avoid for fear of alienating the mass audience. Academy Award-winning shorts have dealt with are racism (*Black Rider*), homelessness (*The Lunch Date*, written and directed by Adam Davidson), and childhood homosexuality (*Trevor*, written by James Lecesne and directed by Peggy Rajski). These films weren't afraid to make us squirm in our seats. Released from concerns with commercial success, they were free to follow their plots to their strongest conclusions. People in the industry appreciate filmmakers who aren't afraid to take risks, and a successful comic tale can open many doors in Hollywood, even if its bleak or black, as long as it's short.

EXERCISES

Take a moment to think through these concepts presented above. Now try and come up with a simple story that can be told with no dialogue, something you might even be able to film with a home video camera and edit on a home computer. Your tools are desire, action and conflict. Create a character who wants something specific, give him/her conflict to make it difficult to attain, and then find a climax and resolution that are unexpected. Write the story using an active voice (use active verbs that describe what the character does, and don't dwell on explaining why he does it), telling us what we would see and hear.

Once you have something, try and shoot it, staying on the action and reaction of the character. If video equipment isn't available to you, show your short script to people who will be honest with you, and ask if they can follow and understand it.

Were your readers interested in finding out what happened at the end? If they didn't understand what was going on and why, ask for specific feedback on where they got confused. And learn to love that criticism, especially when it's specific, because it will make your rewrite much easier.

2

Starting Out – What's It About?

If you've picked up this book, chances are you either have an idea for a short film you want to develop, or you are in the process of coming up with one. Either way, the start of the process can be both exciting and daunting. Inspiration stimulates ideas and they tumble in. Then the inner critic steps up and sends everything crumbling.

Writing is a process. Rarely if ever does a script come out perfectly produced, ready to roll before cameras without need of rewriting — like Botticelli's Venus on the half-shell emerging fully formed from the sea (although even she needed the help of the wind god to push her to shore!). The key to creation is to create, then evaluate, improve and complete, and not be waylaid by fear and uncertainty. The best writers know this, and do rewrite after rewrite after rewrite, until the characters, plot and theme come together to effectively tell their stories. It's hard work, but it can be fun and illuminating. The wonder of writing isn't what you know, but what you discover along the way about your characters, your ideas and values, and ultimately yourself.

Making a good movie, a great one, short or long, is no easy task. There isn't a surefire recipe for success, no matter what anyone says. People work differently. Ideas come in various ways. But however we work, we must understand the form. Let's use this as our starting point to get the process rolling by describing the characteristics of a good short film, examining its basic ingredients and defining steps you can take to develop an idea and discover its underlying meaning.

Storytelling is an age-old art. The first men and women to sit around the fire tried to make sense of their world by telling stories. Their myths and legends, which have been passed down and recorded, form the earliest record we have of mankind. In them we find all the elements we still use, to this day, in drama.

- A *hero*
- who *wants* something
- takes *action*
- meets with *conflict*
- that leads to a *climax*
- and a *resolution*

From the first creation myths to the *Lord of the Rings*, from Looney Tunes to *Lawrence of Arabia*, these elements endure: <u>Hero</u>, <u>want</u>, <u>action</u>, <u>conflict</u>, <u>climax</u> and <u>resolution</u>. Stories are about characters in conflict. They are told through action. Conflict results because the hero wants something he doesn't have or must solve a problem in the environment. At the most basic level the story tells us how the hero overcomes the conflict or how the conflict overcomes him.

THE CHARACTERISTICS OF
A GOOD SHORT FILM

What makes a good idea for a short film, or any film for that matter? A good idea for a short film needs to be focused and specific. It doesn't have time to leisurely explore more than one topic. An idea should be fresh, something we haven't seen before. The characters should engage the audience emotionally in some way, even if they don't gain our sympathy. The story should hold a few surprises for us as well as tell us something.

These are very general considerations, to be sure. What makes a good idea and how we come up with them is really a complex process that depends as much on who we are as our understanding of the medium of film. But there are a few peculiar distinctions worth looking at to help evaluate and develop an idea.

Simplicity

The best story ideas for short films are relatively simple. They can often be told in a sentence. They focus on one main conflict, sometimes only one incident, which is developed from inception to climax. A film may be framed by secondary conflicts but the main story is most effective when it establishes or hints at its conflict early and then sticks with it. The less it veers into incidental material, the stronger the film will be. (More on this in Chapters 4 and 5.)

In the Academy Award-winning live action short *The Lunch Date*, the mere act of eating a salad becomes the central conflict on which the whole film is based. The idea is simple enough. An elderly woman believes a homeless man has taken her meal. The action she takes in relationship to her assumption develops the conflict and the story.

The Academy Award-nominated *I'll Wait For The Next One* (*J'attendrai le suivant...*), written by Thomas Gaudin and Philippe Orreindy, directed by Philippe Orreindy, starts with a dumpy young woman on her way down into the Metro. As she descends, she passes a couple riding the escalator up, locked in an embrace and watches longingly. She's barely gotten on the subway train when a man hops into the car. He begins his pitch. Tired of the single's scene, he's looking for a woman between the ages of 20 and 55 who shares the same ideas and values as he. In spite of jeers from the other car's occupants, the man sincerely lists his good points and asserts his belief in love. All the while, the woman watches him, bemused and taken. Then he gets to his point: any woman interested in trying a relationship with him should discreetly get off the train at the next stop. He's looking for love, he says, not just an affair. The train pulls in and the doors swoosh open. The woman hesitates and then jumps off, waiting expectantly for him. But the man stays put and reveals this was only an actor's skit. She looks at him, hurt and shocked, and we fade to black as his voice asks for a donation from the car's occupants for the show.

Interesting Characters

Characters become interesting in various ways. Sometimes the nature of the conflict the character faces creates enough tension to stimulate our interest. We know nothing about the protagonist in *405*, other than he's trapped on the freeway with a huge jet bearing down on him and he's got nowhere to go. This predicament is strong enough to hold our interest for the length of the film (just under 3 minutes). However, if the film were to go on longer, we'd want to know more about him.

Often in short films it's a character's behavior that makes him the most interesting. How the protagonist responds to conflict, what actions he takes and the consequences he faces will define him more to the audience than anything he says or other characters say about him. You need to understand what makes your character interesting to the audience then find ways to demonstrate those qualities or traits in action. (More in the next chapter.)

Conflict

In the opening chapter, I spoke about conflict and its importance in dramatizing a story. The role of conflict is so important to grasp that we'll review it again and again. Let me add here that good story ideas for short films contain more than just the seeds of conflict: they expose a situation where conflict already exists. Conflict can be inherent in an abstract idea, a situation, an arena — but must be realized in a conflict involving characters. Characters can be animate or inanimate but they must take on human dimensions in order for us to understand the story.

The best characters are ones who commit to trying to accomplish something. Their want/desire/need/goal draws them forward and they meet with problems/conflict. The opposition can come from a single character or many, a physical barrier, an irritating complication, or even an inner doubt. Whatever the opposition, it must be externalized and show the conflict in relation to your main character, the protagonist. This opposition establishes immediate tension and interest, and creates the conflict that drives the plot.

Conflict for a short film can be subtle or definite. In *The Lunch Date*, the conflict is subtle, already existing in the class distinctions between the two characters and making them opposites. In *Life Lessons* (the first segment of the film *New York Stories*, written by Richard Price and directed by Martin Scorsese), the conflict between the two main characters is direct; they're opposed in every way.

Emotion

Every successful short delivers emotional content — whether it's a joke we laugh at or an incident that moves us to tears. If you aren't touching your audience in some way, you're not doing your job. Great filmmakers consider how they want the audience to feel about their stories, and not just how they want them to feel at the end. Throughout the film, as they plot the action, they are plotting an emotional arc for the audience, too.

Originality

The best films, short or features, are always fresh in some way. We may feel we've seen every iteration of action film, fish-out-of-water comedy and family drama but a fresh set of characters dropped into even the most familiar arena will reinvigorate a familiar genre. Think of Axel Foley in the first *Beverly Hills Cop* or Riggs' suicidal quest in the first *Lethal Weapon*.

Content based on ideas never before explored on film will give a decidedly original quality (*The Crying Game*). A new point of view toward an old subject may create the feeling of freshness (*Unforgiven*). An innovative filmic style can do the trick with a familiar plot line (*Raising Arizona*). The combination of genres, a comic western (*Blazing Saddles*) or a murder mystery raised to the level of tragedy (*Chinatown*) can make us look with new eyes again.

The arena or setting of your film can by itself add an element of originality. We've seen countless buddy comedies set on the American road (from *Huckleberry Finn* to *Dumb and Dumber*) but *Sideways* feels new and original just by having its duo explore California's central coast wine country. A revisionist look at an old cultural arena can be original too; for example, a covert, upscale world in 1950s America (*Far from Heaven*) or the overt, Midwestern counterpart (*Kinsey*).

Considering the originality of an idea up front can save hours or reworking later on. The question to ask is "What's new and different about my story?" Only you can discover your original vision.

Filmic Qualities

It should go without saying that all good films must be filmic. They have to be more than talking heads. They must be visual. This means a good narrative film takes advantage of the remarkable properties that distinguish it from other narrative media. Novels, short stories, journalism, plays, situation comedies, radio and theater rely on the written or spoken word to communicate story and express meaning. The real power of film lies in it using both sound and image to tell a story.

Film differs from these other forms in several important ways. First, I can't stress enough the power of images. What we *see* strongly affects us all, consciously and unconsciously. The old saying "a picture is worth a thousand words" is constantly renewed through the proliferation of images and icons in our world (think especially of the computer screen). Our brains process visual information much more quickly than verbal data. Though we have to write a script first and make sure the story tracks and builds, when we get into the editing room we often find information that needed detailed explanation on the page is immediately digested in visual form. In script form, the pathos of a story about an old man dealing with the death of his plant and his crumbling world might be missed, but when we see that elderly man, frail and alone, on screen, his suffering comes into the foreground.

Films allow us to get close to our subject. Films tell stories in much greater physical detail, in a shorter period of time, and recreate a sense of reality on screen rather than simply suggest it. A filmmaker can define an environment as completely as his talent allows. When his choice of images transfers a believable universe onto the screen, the audience becomes more available to him and the story he tells. If we're shown a world that mirrors our reality, or truly creates its own, we are more apt to accept the story that inhabits it. This helps us enter "the world of the story" because it creates a sense of a "real" backdrop for the experience.

In *Franz Kafka's It's a Wonderful Life*, another Academy Award-winning live action short, writer/director Peter Capaldi uses what is clearly a model of a towering cluster of gothic apartments. As the camera ascends the model, toward a lighted window at the very top, foreboding music plays. Inside the cold, austere room, Franz Kafka perches at his desk, pen in hand, paper before him, struggling to compose the first line of his book.

"Gregor Samsa," he says as he writes, "awoke one morning from uneasy dreams and found himself transformed into a gigantic... a gigantic... what?" he pleads. Clearly upset, he casts about the room, at the furnace vent, the clock, the window. His gaze falls upon a bowl of fruit. Suddenly, his eyes light up. The film cuts to black and white, showing a man wreathing beneath a blanket until uncovered. He's a gigantic banana! By the time we return to Kafka's room, he's already crumpling the paper, tossing it to the floor where it joins a host of other aborted attempts.

The world created by Capaldi is clearly at odds with our own. But through the effective use of humor and the attention to every detail, the audience accepts the "reality" of it and enjoys the story that examines and pokes fun at the creative process.

Another key factor that distinguishes film is its fluidity or movement. Movement can be understood in three ways: The movement of character (action), movement through space, and movement through time.

On film we record the actions of characters. In order for characters to be interesting to an audience, they must <u>do</u> something — take action, which has consequences the audience can understand. What action a character takes defines who he is, and this is paramount to understanding narrative-driven filmmaking. In a novel we can be told what happens in a story, but in film we see it happening. It becomes a record, in a way a truth. (And when this "truth" becomes suspect, as in Kurosawa's *Rashomon* or Cronenberg's *Spider*, we immediately feel lost — giving filmmakers another powerful storytelling tool.) The story in a narrative film unfolds through time. We see it, not merely hear it being told. Watching it unfold through the actions and counter-actions of the characters involved in a good film makes us take an active interest in the story. We wonder what will happen next? Our minds try to figure it out without our even knowing it. We ponder the open-ended question, until we hear a satisfying answer. Watching the characters struggle to find what they want, we become more involved with them. We root for those trying to accomplish something, and are disaffected by those who don't.

Movement through space and time is also a specific property of film. Unlike narrative painting that is also organized around a dramatic idea shown in space, narrative film shows the whole story, not just one static moment of it (i.e., The Last Supper vs. *The Last Temptation of Christ*). In film, we the audience occupy the place of the camera and see what and how the filmmaker wants us to see specific events. As the filmmaker moves his camera, we move through the story, encountering character and plot in ways that play as vividly upon our senses as engage our intellect in our search for meaning. Camera position and movement (and the changing perspective of what we see in the scene, or *mis en scene*) significantly enhances our perception and experience of screen events, intensifying emotions such as alarm or elation. Expressive motion can draw us into a scene or pull us out of one. It can express exaltation and freedom, or indicate danger or confinement.

Take, for instance, the Academy Award-nominated live action short *The Dutch Master*, written by Susan Seidelman and Jonathan Brett (and directed by Seidelman). On a chance visit to New York's Metropolitan Museum of Art, Teresa — a working class dental assistant with repressed pre-wedding jitters — becomes fascinated with a 17th century Dutch painting. Every day, she goes to look at the painting, enraptured by the sensuality of the scene, and a young man in it. As her friends, boss, fiancé and parents all become increasingly baffled by her behavior and recount their versions of events as on-screen commentators and off-screen narrators, we discover why her fascination has taken hold: the painting has come alive to her and she is able to enter it. Through the use of expressive camera movement, lighting and music, we share the wonder and the reality of Teresa's experience.

How the filmmaker uses his filmmaker's tools — space, light, color, sound and time — again depends upon his talent. But the original blueprint — the screenplay — must include ample opportunity for the filmmaker to capitalize on his visual expertise. The filmmaker's tools are similar to those of the painter. He uses space, light and color to create affective images. With the addition of time and sound, he expands the reach of those images to tell a narrative story. The ability to intercut between geographical locations in an instant as well as time frames (past, present and future) opens up a film editorially to endless possibilities. The dynamic created by juxtaposing present and past, or jumping from city to city, can keep a film unexpected and compelling. Again, we move *through* a film, sharing with the characters a wide range of experiences and feelings. When we suddenly shift between time periods or locations, we experience something the characters do not; we experience a storyteller's point of view. The ability to share both character emotion and the point of view of the filmmaker can produce startling results. (Of course, characters *can* share this dual experience themselves in a personal memory or flashback.)

If the plot of your story requires a great deal of explanation in dialogue, the idea may be better suited to a play, short story or book. Even in a short film, the story must be told through *action*. What are the characters doing? What actions do we see them take which further the story? The oft-quoted rule is "Show — Don't Tell," and the screenwriter and filmmaker must take this to heart.

The short film *The Red Balloon*, written and directed by Albert Lamorisse, mixes the real and fantastic with Academy Award winning results. (The film won an Oscar for Best Original Screenplay in 1955.) With virtually no dialogue, it tells the story of a young boy who finds a red balloon on his way to school and what happens because of it. Actions and conflict carry the content and convey the magical odyssey Pascal takes because of the balloon.

The same is true of *The Lunch Date*. It has little meaningful dialogue. The story grows out of the class distinctions between the two main characters, a wealthy dowager and a homeless black man. The woman misses her train in Grand Central Station. She's lost her wallet and now, killing time and without any cash, she buys a salad with her last change, sets it and her packages down at a table, then goes back for a fork. When she returns a black man is sitting in her booth and eating her meal! "That's my salad!" she says indignantly. The man laughs at her, Yeah, right.

She sits down and tries to take it back, but he won't let her. Piqued, she attacks the salad, spearing lettuce with her fork as if skewering him. He doesn't bat an eye; he even chuckles at her. When the salad is just about gone, he gets up and she gets ready to go. But before she does, he returns with *two* cups of coffee. Surprised, she accepts the coffee and they share a friendly moment. Then her train is called and she leaves suddenly. The man appears sad. Walking through the station, she remembers her packages and hurries back to the cafeteria. The table is un-cleared, but the man is gone and so are her packages. Terribly upset, she paces, trying to decide what to do, and as she does, she passes by the next booth where *her* untouched salad and bundles still sit. When she sees them, she breaks out in laughter. She can't believe what she's done. The film ends as she makes her train, her demeanor changed by her encounter. The conflict is based on her assumptions, and her aggression is demonstrated through her actions.

This short film doesn't rely on dialogue (indeed, it could work as a silent piece) but stays on the characters' actions and reac-tions to drive the plot. Through editing, it withholds crucial infor-mation (the salad at the next table) until the filmmaker wants to reveal it to make his dramatic point. Told from the woman's point of view, the simple story (and short at ten minutes) exposes our assumptions about people and how wrong they can be. The meaning is communicated visually, not through dialogue. This brings us to:

The Deeper Meaning

All great films, whether short of long, have a broader subject mat-ter than just the story line the writer wants to illustrate. This is the theme, the underlying unifying idea. Themes are concerned with universal concepts, issues and emotions. Love, honor, identity, compromise, responsibility, ambition, greed, guilt, etc., are all experienced and shared worldwide. The universal quality of these ideas and emotions helps insure the audience will relate to the material on a level deeper than just the plot.

Without a theme, a film's an aimless story, having little signif-icance for the audience. Without this unifying ingredient, there's no purpose or meaning to the work. The theme is the ultimate subject of the film. Good triumphs over evil, love conquers all; though broad, these themes tell someone's point of view about the world.

Life Lessons in *New York Stories* tells the story of a successful New York artist at the end of a love affair with his assistant. The broader subject of the film concerns romantic self-indulgence and artistic self-absorption.

In the Academy Award-winning collection of shorts, *Yesterday, Today and Tomorrow*, the *Mara of Rome* episode (written by Cesare Zavattini and Billa Billa, and directed by the great Vittorio De Sica) is ostensibly about a prostitute's encounter with a young seminarian. The ultimate topic, however, is the power of faith and love.

Jane Campion's short film, *PEEL*, is a tale about what happens to a man, his sister, and his son on their way home from viewing a property. Its real significance has to do with our inability to communicate even within our families.

Milcho Manchevski's *Words*, from the feature *Before the Rain*, a film told in three parts, shows the uncompromising nature of war as it ravages the lives of the unsuspecting, and forces the innocent to take sides.

It isn't essential to have the theme completely worked out when you begin but it must be by the final draft. Themes often emerge or change in the process of writing. You may take several drafts before you discover your theme. But whenever your theme emerges, it's best to let it help unify the story. The closer your story stays to its theme, the easier other choices related to it will be.

Themes grow out of who you are and what you believe. The best come from your emotions, experiences and insights about people and the world. For a theme to be compelling to an audience, it must first have compelled you in some way to understand, believe or share, to tie your individual beliefs to a collective ethic. It must be important to you. You must believe in it; if you do not, no one else will.

A few questions can help define and clarify a theme. Ask yourself:

1. How does the story speak to me?
2. Does it represent my best dreams or worst fears?

3. Is there something innately universal themes suggested in the material?

4. Are there archetypal relationships in the material, i.e., mother/daughter, father/son, mentor/student, whether the characters are related or not?

If you know the story's ending, even only conceptually, then put it together and see what it says to you. Ask:

5. Who is destroyed?
6. Who grows?
7. What causes the destruction or growth?
8. If the hero wins, what special quality enables him to overcome the opposition?
9. Did he have it at the beginning?
10. If not, then how does he get it?

If the protagonist falls in love and spends the rest of the screenplay trying to capture the object of her affections, then your story's about love. But what kind of love? Is it a romantic infatuation that may deepen over time? Is it an obsession that will lead to disaster? Be as specific with your theme as you will with individual plot considerations.

The topic of theme is always controversial. How it comes into being, when and who defines it, whether it is important at all, have all been debated. Films are first and foremost entertainment. But even in comedies, whose purpose is to make us laugh, the best ones always comment on our condition. Stories are always about something and the more conscious the writer is about what she's saying the more powerful the pull of the message and the more effective the film. But don't beat anyone over the head. A good rule is to think of your theme as another writer's tool, to keep a story on track and not a message to be conveyed by your work.

WHERE TO BEGIN?

Depending on how you work, ideas for short films evolve in different ways. Actual events from TV or the newspaper might provide inspiration. A person you've met or just a situation can spark an idea. A dream I had one night was the source for a film I made at UCLA that won the Jim Morrison Award.

Beginning can be difficult if an idea doesn't jump right out at you because the choices seem limitless. But let's examine six areas that can provide the rich source material for ideas.

1. Character. We've all met people who in one way or another fascinate us. Maybe it's what they do or how they do it that interests us; maybe it's what they know. Something in their personalities draws us to want to understand them. Human action forms the core of drama. Because human behavior fascinates, people are the most obvious starting point for a writer.

Most short films are, in fact, "character pieces." They focus on a character by allowing his behavior to show who he really is (*Life Lessons, Mara of Rome*). "Character piece" is a term used to describe a story that is thought to have little plot. But all the best stories in every genre are character-driven, and not plot-driven. Your idea for a short film may not be originally propelled by the need or desire to study one or more characters. But no one element of your screenplay's success is ultimately more important. Think about your characters as soon as you come up with your idea. They'll help you as much in developing your idea as in telling your story.

2. Environment. Certain human behavior tends to occur in specific places. Different places attract different people. Stock car races take place in one environment, a game of croquet in another. Place also relates to mood. Because environment contains specific activities and actions, writers can use place to generate ideas.

3. Incidents. An incident is a rapid change in circumstances for one or more people. It usually has to do with actions and events; someone does something to others, or something happens to him. Although incidents can be gentle or violent, for a writer the most productive are life changing. The change in circumstance should involve highly contrasting conditions. The feature film *Trading Places* is a perfect example of this in the extreme. But many short films explore a strong incident, as in *The Lunch Date, Black Rider* and the Academy-Award nominated *Gridlock*

(*Fait d'hiver*), written by Johan Verschueren and directed by Dirk Beliën, developing it in detail and in unexpected ways.

4. Abstract ideas. Using philosophical or thematic ideas as the starting point for a screenplay does not necessarily mean the film will be didactic, although this is always a danger. The beginning thesis can be suggestive of the other elements, such as character and plot, and these must be fleshed out to bring the film to life. Think twice, though, about using themes that have been overused and overworked by other writers. If you must use a common theme ("love conquers all"), be sure to look for unique characters and a novel way to illustrate your idea.

5. Situations. Let's define a situation as a relationship placed within a certain set of circumstances. One example might be the prostitute and her pimp. Relationships that are locked together on an emotional level deliver the best potential material for writers. Thus, a prostitute and pimp who need each other emotionally and form a kind of family could make a stronger story than two characters who aren't emotionally involved. Contrasting individuals within these circumstances makes for colorful situations.

6. Informational Area. This consists of subjects you want expose and write about. Homelessness, terrorism, the Holocaust, all can provide rich backdrops for stories. Research follows in painstaking detail. Current and past historical material can be a great source of ideas for writers.

Once the idea emerges, you must shape and expand it with elements that will contribute to the story and screenplay. Asking these questions will help you begin:

1. Who are the main characters?
2. What are their main relationships?
3. What do they want?
4. Where is the conflict?
5. How does the conflict erupt?
6. What drives the action of the story forward?

Sketching out the motivations and back-stories of the main characters helps make the idea concrete. Describing time and place lends specificity to the world of the story. Writing down your initial thoughts on the arrangement of the material will aid the process of organizing scenes later. Compiling a mass of miscellaneous notes will support the whole endeavor. Remember, for the writer, ideas remain abstract until written. Just writing down incidental notes to yourself will start the process of putting ideas to paper. You will have already begun your script.

RESEARCH, BELIEF & THE WORLD OF THE STORY

The world of the story is not just the setting or backdrop in which the characters act and the film takes place. It's the feeling that the space delimited on the screen extends beyond what we actually see; that the lives of the characters inhabiting this world continue when they're out of view, that the world created and shown is part of a larger world. This world outside the camera lends the work a feeling of authenticity.

At the same time, it is important to understand that the world in the screenplay or film is not a real world but a representation of one. Though this distinction is obvious, it needs to be pointed out time and time again. What happens on the screen is a portrayal of characters and events, not real life. Your audience knows this, but desires nothing less than to lose themselves in the events happening up on the screen. To achieve this, the audience must willingly suspend disbelief. This willingness of viewers to suspend doubt about the "real truth" (that what they're watching is fiction) makes it possible for them to fully accept imaginary creations during the time span of the film. But it's only possible if what they see happening on the screen feels true and credible.

Achieving truth and credibility in drama is a multi-dimensional task. It starts by making sure you understand the arena you're writing about. If one of your characters is a gourmet and your idea of cooking is opening a jar of readymade pasta sauce, it's obvious you need to do a bit of research in order to bring this character and her world intelligently to life. If you're writing about an abusive relationship, read the latest literature. If possible, interview therapists, victims, and perpetrators. Delve deep into case studies, which offer a key to how characters create a situation, conflict and push a story. If your story is set in the coldest reaches of Antarctica and you've never been there, research it.

Read books, rent documentaries, try to find people who've been there and can tell you about it. Go if you can (or maybe find a place a little closer to home).

Research is a writer's best friend. Out of it comes twists and turns, obstacles and complications impossible to imagine, little details that give a screenplay authority and an authentic feeling. It only comes from knowing the material. If research is skipped over, the work often seems superficial, familiar or, worse, phony. The screenplay and film must <u>feel</u> real or it won't succeed. Researching it well is the first step toward making that happen.

TURNING AN IDEA INTO A GOOD FILM STORY

The evolution of ideas into screenplays has as many routes as there are screenwriters, and every writer must find his own best approach. But no matter how different, ideas generally develop through these stages: concept, character and conflict.

Concept, Character & Conflict

The initial concept or idea for a film usually yields either a character or a conflict. Whichever it is, the other must be supplied before any real development can take place. If the idea revolves around an interesting character, you must invent a problem or conflict in order to reveal what makes this character interesting. The same is true if the starting point is a conflict. You need to create a character who will take action and best exploit the conflict of the story.

Sometimes the beginning concept is not developed enough to produce either character or conflict. In this case, you can do a couple of things to get moving. You may research the backdrop of the concept, hoping to discover in the process a springboard to either a character or a conflict. Or, after researching the area, you may want to ask questions about what interested you in the first place about the idea, hoping to find any tension around the concept to expand into a conflict. If nothing occurs, you may want to look for a new idea.

Short films and features depend upon conflict to work. It is primarily the struggle between opposing forces that holds the audience's attention. Without tension, audiences lose interest. Conflict equals drama.

Five Questions That Won't Go Away

To develop the story, key elements need to be defined. The following five questions will help you monitor your story and keep it focused. Think about the answers to these questions as steady feedback — information you need in order to know how you're performing as a writer. As the story evolves, don't be afraid if the answers change. These mutations usually signify greater development and deeper meaning.

1. What's it about? Initially, the answer may involve only the subject matter of the story. But as the writer works with the material, a broader subject should emerge. This is the theme, the underlying meaning of the screenplay, what you are saying about your world.

2. What's the genre? Basically, there are five types, though these can be subdivided endlessly:

    a. Comedy

    b. Farce

    c. Drama

    d. Tragedy

    e. Melodrama

In comedy (*Mrs. Doubtfire*, *Tootsie*) and drama (*Erin Brockovich*), the central motif is the triumph of the hero over adverse circumstances resulting in a happy ending. In comedy the story is humorously told. Farce is ridiculous, exaggerated comedy based on broadly humorous situations (*Ace Ventura: Pet Detective*, *The Nutty Professor*). It's only intent is to be funny.

Parody makes fun through humorous imitation of another, more serious work. *George Lucas in Love*, the short film that launched Joe Nussbaum, parodies *Star Wars* and *Shakespeare In Love* to tell the story of how the young George Lucas conceived his franchise in film school.

Tragedy refers to any work dealing with somber themes, leading to a disastrous, catastrophic conclusion (*Chinatown*, *Glory*).

Melodrama intensifies sentiment, and exaggerates emotion, action and plot over characterization (*Twister*, *Cliffhanger*).

There are numerous sub-genres: film noir, westerns, murder mysteries, sci-fi, fantasy. Most fall under the heading of melodrama, though a few may be considered dramas or comedies in their own right. Most short films fall into the first four categories. Time considerations do not usually permit the development of a complex plot usually found in melodrama. Also, as we'll see in Chapter 3, the best short films rely on effective characterizations.

Defining the genre usually implies finding the right tone of your film. If it's a comedy, is it dark and satiric like *War of the Roses* or more rooted in reality like *Tootsie*? Is it a romantic fantasy like *Pretty Woman*? Satire creates a distance between the viewer and subject. Realism tends to bring us closer to the characters.

3. Who is the protagonist? This is the main character who pushes the action of the story. The next chapter will discuss this character in greater depth, but for now think about the protagonist in this way:

    a. Who is this character fundamentally and why is he involved in this story now?

    b. What does he want and why?

What the protagonist wants relates to the plot of the screenplay. To plot an interesting story, we must know what the main character wants. "Why" the character is involved in the story relates to his motivation.

4. What is the driving action of your story? The driving action originates in an event or incident that serves as a catalyst for the story. The catalyst focuses the protagonist on a course of action, toward his goal, what he wants or needs. What the protagonist wants to accomplish draws or pulls the character forward, why he wants it (motivation) pushes him. The structure for the story comes from its driving action.

5. Who or what opposes the protagonist? This opposition provides the main conflict of the story. The main conflict is the primary obstacle or obstacles that stand in the protagonist's way. If a person (the antagonist) represents the conflict, you should answer the same questions for her as the protagonist. What does she want and why? If the antagonist is as committed to her goal as the protagonist, the conflict will be stronger and the audience more interested in sitting through your film until the last frame.

Many beginning writers resist personifying the antagonist. Either they don't want to commit to one specific antagonist or they don't see a person in that role. In a short film, the antagonist doesn't have to be "evil" or "mad" as he often is in so many feature films. The antagonist in a short film is generally the character opposing the protagonist in the pursuit of his want.

You cannot have a story without conflict. Action and conflict are the starting points of plot construction. If you have a character who has no problem, wants nothing, doesn't take action, you don't have a story. People may try to make a word game out of this equation but it all comes down to: drama is conflict and conflict is drama. How you get there depends on each writer's process. But until you do, you won't have a story.

Development

The basic formula for a short or long film is:

- A *hero*
- who *wants* something
- takes *action*
- meets with *conflict*
- that leads to a *climax*
- and a *resolution*

This incredibly broad plan for construction can be amplified or modified in many ways. But because it's so broad it becomes a generous starting point.

Once the key elements have been defined, the writer may start developing a rough, overall story plan. Using the formula above for reference, the plan should break into three simple, rudimentary parts: the beginning, middle and end. The beginning sets up the story by introducing the protagonist and establishing the dramatic problem or conflict. In the middle, the protagonist faces progressive complications as he attempts to reach the goal. The end focuses on how the conflict is resolved.

Most stories flow from the clear goal of the protagonist. The tougher the obstacles he encounters in the quest for this goal, the harder the protagonist must work, and the more interesting the story will be.

31

ENTERTAINMENT & INSPIRATION

Stories, films, features and shorts, fiction in general, must succeed first and foremost in earning and holding the audience's interest. To be successful, they must entertain on some level. To entertain means to hold your attention, to divert, to amuse. Entertainment does not always have to be happy or amusing. But it must be potent. Entertainment succeeds when it removes you from your own life and involves you in the story you're watching.

All writers must determine what's interesting about the stories they want to tell, and what has the potential to grab viewers. A strong film needs to be fresh, unique and different, so audiences won't feel they've been here before, even if the basic tale has been told a hundred times. How many different ways are there to make a romantic comedy? The basic ingredients are almost invariably the same (boy meets/loses/wins girl), but original-thinking writers continue concocting stories that keep the genre alive and audiences laughing.

Guy de Maupassant put it this way when discussing the purpose and effect of a story:

> *The public is composed of numerous groups who cry to us [writers]: "Console me, amuse me, make me sad, make me sympathetic, make me dream, make me laugh, make me shudder, make me weep, make me think."*

This is our job: To entertain, inform, move and inspire. We entertain through amusement and surprise; we inform by having something new, relevant or important to say; we move by arousing the emotions; and we inspire by showing a character's ennobling action. Remembering these story goals helps when we begin to create and develop the plot. Just as the protagonist has a goal, you have one, too: To stimulate the audience's curiosity about the character or situation, and then engage their emotions.

EXERCISES

Screen *Life Lessons* from *New York Stories*, or another film, preferably short.

1. Identify the underlying concept of the film.
2. Identify the main conflict for the protagonist.
   a. What does the protagonist want?
   b. What stands in his way?
3. Jot down a few sentences to describe the basic story conflict as that conflict progresses from its inception to its climax and resolution. Make it a very general description of the basic story idea, not a detailed account.

Now, take *your* idea and jot it down in a few lines or a few paragraphs. You might start by defining a backdrop or situation or character. Examine the idea with an eye to turning it into a workable concept. Focus on the main character and the central conflict (problem) this character faces.

For example: You're interested in dance and you want to use this backdrop for a short film. You have an idea about a young tap dancer who admires a beautiful ballerina at his dance school.

Here you have the germ of an idea. The tap dancer admires the ballerina, but how does she feel about him? Does she know about his feelings? Does she even know he exists? If the tap dancer secretly admires her, too shy to declare his feelings, and the ballerina is so beautiful as to seem unapproachable, we have now described a problem for the protagonist. Implicit in this is the action the protagonist must take: To somehow connect with her. How and what happens becomes the plot, dictated by what you are trying to say.

Now, remember that formula? <u>Hero</u>, <u>want</u>, <u>action</u>, <u>conflict</u>, <u>climax</u> and <u>resolution</u>. Using this, determine what action the hero takes, what resistance (conflict) he or she meets, and how the action builds to an unexpected climax. You don't have to have all the specifics yet; think in broad terms. And jot a note or two as you go. The process of writing will reward you in its own special way.

3

Character & Emotion – Who Does What and Why

Depicting characters in film differs greatly from that in prose fiction and theater. In novels and short stories, the author can describe the protagonist and other characters in minute detail, telling the reader everything important about them. The omniscient voice most novels use helps to establish exactly who the characters are in the reader's mind. In theater, playwrights follow a structure somewhat analogous to the screenwriter. But dialogue plays a proportionately greater role on the stage because the proscenium arch limits the action. The characters describe action and themselves, and because the world on the stage tends to be more symbolic and artificial than in film, we accept it.

But in film, where the principles of drama tell us that stories must take the form of characters in action (and where we can get so close to our subjects that the audience expects a certain amount of authenticity), the emphasis is on *showing*. The screenwriter must rely on action and behavior to *show* the audience who the character really is.

Creating characters that ring true is probably one of the more difficult, if not most difficult, tasks screenwriters face. If characters don't feel authentic, the audience is less likely to accept a film on the basis of the story alone. The audience must willingly suspend disbelief and enter the world of the film. The strongest, fastest way into this fictional world is through the characters who act and behave in ways we accept as real. The best writers create characters we can relate to and identify with, or at the very least, ones we're intrigued by and want to know more about, to bring us along in the story.

What makes effective screen characters and protagonists who drive stories forward? How do we make them compelling people the audience accepts? These are really two separate areas, intimately connected, whose intersection forms the key to creating workable characters in film. On the one side are the specific concepts that have to do with how characters function in drama; on the other are the creative considerations we use to design the characters who inhabit our stories.

But before we define what characters have to have to function effectively in film and delve into the creative process, let's examine the lifeblood of all characters.

EMOTION

In the first chapter, I spoke about emotion as the way to reach the audience. True emotion is the source of our connection to other people. We see someone in pain and it elicits feelings of sympathy. We watch people celebrating and their joy makes us smile. Emotion is one of the great universals, connecting human being to human being despite sexual and ethnic differences. We all feel. We've all felt love, joy, hate, jealousy, anger, fear, humiliation, regret, etc. One might argue this is what it means to be human, to feel. And because we feel, emotion is at the basis of the audience's identification with your characters. When we see a mother, desperate and worried, defending her young — whether she's the Vietnamese woman in *Platoon*, the Anglo prostitute in the play *Les Miserables*, or the wolf roaming the Canadian wilds in *Never Cry Wolf* — our response is the same. We feel and root and hope for her. We become involved in her crisis.

When we see people feeling the way we would feel if we were in similar situations, we can identify much more quickly with them. These recognizable responses make them appear true to us. If characters don't respond emotionally, and walk through a script or film like an automaton, they don't seem real and render the story false. Our already tenuous connection with the make-believe world breaks and the story fails.

Screenwriters, regardless of experience, often neglect the emotional aspect of characters. This oversight is particularly interesting to me because I know screenwriters and filmmakers want to make movies because of how movies have made *them* feel. They want to be part of this process because movies move them. But when it comes to working on their own scripts and films, they often forget this side of their stories, glancing over their characters' emotional reactions or totally ignoring them for fear they slow the action of the plot. Often when emotions are expressed, they come in tears or anger, with little range in between.

But in many ways emotion *is* the story. Believable emotion, besides creating connections, makes scenes more interesting and compelling. We see someone in the grip of an emotion and we're forced to watch to find out what happens. How characters respond emotionally to the story often is the way we develop meaning and understand the importance of those events. We understand motivations better if we see the emotional component to them.

We screenwriters must conceive characters whose emotional lives are available to them, and so to us. We find those emotions not only in the basic makeup of a character, but also in how they respond to the conflict they meet. As you think about your story, you need to think in terms of how your character is affected by what happens to her, the incidents and events and changing circumstances.

Another thing about emotion to remember is this: stories are best when told in terms of relationships, which are matrices of emotions we share with others. If a character pursues a goal and affects no one, he can't affect the audience. He must relate to other characters, positively or negatively, in order to stir and sway the audience. Relationships on the screen (and in our lives) have meaning only to the extent they engage and arouse our emotions. We love or hate, and in drama, these emotions cause us to respond one way or another. We care for or disdain someone, and this colors how we react. Great writers — screenwriters, novelists, playwrights — understand that emotional reaction is the source of a character's true motivation. They find actions that are both logical and surprising but clearly represent the emotion.

Emotional Progression

Incorporating a progression of emotions into the plot of the screenplay helps us better understand the character and her motivations. A profound disappointment to a pragmatic character might lead to depression and ultimately a spiritual crisis. Demonstrating mercy to a criminal could lead to a painful reassessment of life and a spiritual rebirth. Including emotionally varying scenes increases the depth and complexity of the story and helps insure the audience's involvement.

In *Some Folks Call It a Sling Blade*, written by Billy Bob Thorton and directed by George Hickenlooper, we see Teresa's anger and anxiety at the beginning of the film. The misunderstanding with the hospital administrator makes her angrier and reinforces her resolve to get a story for her paper. Her anger turns cynical and is then matched by the administrator who removes her photographer (and ally) from the interview with Carl. But as she hears Carl's story, we watch as her emotion changes from anger and skepticism to empathy and concern.

In *Mara of Rome*, Mara's anger burns deeply when Umberto's grandmother scorns her. Then when her client Rusconi arrives, this anger consumes her. She can't deal with him and his lust. Her anger drives him away, and he vows never to return. Yet the next day, after she has reconciled with Rusconi and they are finally going to bed, Mara is interrupted by the old woman. Her first reaction is trepidation (after all the old hag has threatened to get a petition signed against Mara to throw her out). Mara chains the door and opens it an inch, coolly rebuffing the old woman. But when she sees the old lady break down, Mara melts and invites her nemesis inside, wanting nothing more than to assuage the old woman's pain. It is a marvelous moment, which tells everything we need to know about Mara's character.

One emotion audiences generally understand is fear. Many writers believe that the most important aspect to know about their characters is what they fear. In a sense, if you know what the character is most afraid of, then you know what he needs to face. This is true for the characters populating short films and features. Think of Lionel in *Life Lessons*. What does he fear? That Paulette will leave him and he won't be able to paint anything worthwhile. He must keep Paulette around so he can paint. This explains the neurotic way he pursues her, as if everything else in the world counted on her staying. Unconscious fear often drives a character.

But fear can also be more fundamental. It can come in a character's reaction to an alarming situation, and in this way lead the audience to a deeper empathy with him. In *Words*, from Milcho Manchevski's *Before the Rain*, a young ethnic Albanian girl hides from Christians hunting her for the murder of one of their own. Her panic and desperation make us sympathetic toward her, hoping somehow she will find a way out even though we're unsure of what she's done.

THE FOUNDATION OF DRAMATIC CHARACTERS

According to the principles of drama, for the protagonist to function effectively, he must take action to achieve something. John Howard Lawson writes in *Theory and Technique of Playwriting* that drama cannot deal with "people who are weak-willed; who cannot make decisions of even temporary meaning; who adopt no conscious attitude toward events; or who make no effort to control their environment." In drama, characters, specifically the main characters, must be active. If they are not, the drama (film or play) will fail. The protagonist must be committed to something and forced to take action because of that commitment.

As I explained in Chapter 1, a protagonist's want drives the story and allows the audience to better understand the flow of information and make basic connections between the scenes to grasp the meaning of what's going on. Let's look at this more closely now.

Want & Need

For a protagonist to operate successfully in a story, the screenwriter must answer three important questions about her character.

1. What does the character want?
2. Why does he want it?
3. What does he need?

The *want* refers to the story goal, what the protagonist is after; it creates the action of the story and gives the plot direction. The *why* relates to the protagonist's conscious motivation; these are the reasons he understands and gives for the pursuit of his goal. The protagonist's *need* differs in many cases from what he wants (although in some cases it can underscore the character's want). Need refers to an unconscious, inner force that compels a character to act without understanding the real reasons why.

A protagonist's want (goal) helps define the parameters of the plot. It gives a basic direction the audience can clearly grasp while allowing a writer to explore other issues or themes he finds important. It draws or pulls the character toward something. In *Some Folks Call It a Sling Blade*, Teresa wants to get a story. In *Life Lessons*, Lionel wants Paulette to stay. In *Words*, Father Kiril wants to help the Albanian girl. The "want" is so important that actors will tell you when they understand what a character wants moment to moment in a film then they know how to play the character.

A "need" also can give direction to a plot. But instead of pulling the character it pushes him. A need is used to create more character dimension. This is what compels the hero to act often in irrational ways. The need can also oppose the character's stated goal so that part of the conflict results from the disparity between the stated aim and the subliminal need. (Knowledge of basic psychological principles can help you here.) Another way of understanding the character's need is to think of it as what he unconsciously needs to become whole but will have difficulty achieving.

If you haven't seen *Life Lessons* now is a good time, because it is a perfect example of want vs. need. The protagonist, Lionel Dobie, is a successful artist living and working in Manhattan. At the beginning of the film we learn two things: he has no new paintings for a big exhibition in three weeks, and his assistant Paulette, whom he loves, is leaving him. What does he want, why, and what does he need? Spoilers below, so beware.

Want: Paulette
Why: He loves her
Need: Emotional turmoil in order to paint

Let's look closer. Lionel states his goal at the beginning of the movie. He doesn't want Paulette to leave New York and he tells her this. His conscious reason is because he loves her, and he tells her, and the audience, this time and time again. But what he really needs is turmoil in his life in order to paint. He uses this turmoil to fuel his art. Is he conscious of his need? Not in the least. How do we know Lionel needs this conflict to paint? The film shows us in Lionel's response to every disagreement, dispute, and battle with Paulette. After each fight, Lionel throws himself into his painting, with wondrous results.

In Jane Campion's *PEEL*, a father (Tim) wants to prove a point to his son (Ben). Because Tim is already upset with his sister Katie at the beginning of the film, he overreacts to his son's behavior. His regressive action causes Ben to run off. Now Tim's conflict with his sister really heats up because they're stuck out in the boondocks and Katie wanted to be home by a specific time. What are Tim's wants and needs?

Want: To prove a point
Why: Ben is acting up (Tim's really mad at his sister)
Need: To free himself from his rivalry with his sister

The rest of the film tells us whether it is possible for him to achieve his need or not.

In *Ray's Male Heterosexual Dance Hall*, an Academy Award-winning short written and directed by Bryan Gordon, the protagonist, Sam, desperately wants a job. In order to find one, he must disregard his ideals to kiss up to self-appointed big shots and stuffed shirts. But he needs his self-respect, which is constantly assaulted as he hunts for a job lead at Ray's. Given his situation, his want and need are at odds. Finally, the brown nosing becomes too much for him, and after a snub from a past co-worker, Sam's self-respect wins out, and in the process, wins him a job. What does Sam want, why, and what does he need?

Want: A job
Why: Because he needs one
Need: To maintain his self-respect

Features and short films use the answers to the questions of "want," "why" and "need" to define a protagonist and build a plot. Characters who want something definite and go after it are clearer and more active, and therefore more interesting than passive characters. Most successful feature films are driven by an active protagonist, committed to achieving his goal, in order for him to last a feature's ninety-minute to two-hour length.

These rules, however, can be bent to some degree and still succeed.

Character Need Driving the Story

If the protagonist's want doesn't drive the story, his need must. We see in feature films and shorts that sometimes protagonists don't have an apparent "goal" that is drawing them forward. But if the film is working, holding our interest and building tension, we'll see that underlying needs provide the power to push the story forward.

Casablanca is famous for having a protagonist who proclaims his neutrality. "I stick my neck out for nobody," Rick says, and when he says it he means it. A lot of people say Rick is active in pursuing his neutrality. But I disagree. What drives him once he sees Ilsa at the end of act one (about 30 minutes into the film) is his need to know why she left him. If you look carefully at act two, the action isn't focused so much on him looking out for himself (though he's doing this) or getting ready to leave Casablanca (which he might be setting up with those Letters of Transit). The action is really about his pursuing Ilsa, driven by his need to know what happened. He can't come out and ask her because of his bitterness. But the longer she's around, the more he softens and his real need comes to the surface. At the end of act two, she finally gives him his answer, and this frees him to act in act three and bring the story to its conclusion.

I use this example because the movie's easily available and perfectly illustrates this point. Other films use a protagonist's need similarly, but often with less success because the need isn't as specific, and so the characters seem passive. In films such as *Salaam Bombay* and *My Life as a Dog*, children with no real control over their destinies carry the stories. At the beginning of *Saalam Bombay!*, Krishna works at a circus, is sent to fetch something from a village and when he returns the circus has left him. Though he doesn't tell us what he's trying to accomplish, he finds his way to Bombay and gets work, living as a street child. We know he needs to survive and this provides tension. Nearly 35 minutes into the film, we find out he's trying to save 500 rupees to go home and repay his mother for something he destroyed. The story isn't so much about how he works to get the money, but how hard life is around him. In *My Life as a Dog*, when Ingemar's mother gets too sick to care for him, he's sent away to relatives. Though we know he wants to go home, he takes no action to get there. He wanders through this new world, needing a family and trying to fit in. His need to find meaningful connections and the conflict with the real world provide the tension and direction.

When the need is something specific, like Rick's, it becomes apparent the further along in the story you go. When the need is more amorphous and less defined, the conflict the character faces must be definite and clearly present obstacles for him, making the need more apparent.

An interesting attempt at this for a short film is in Frederic Raphael's adaptation of Mary McCarthy's short story *The Man in the Brooks Brothers Shirt*. Set in the mid-1930s, the story begins on a train bound for California. The protagonist, a cynical young New York journalist with leftist sympathies, is on her way to tell her father she is getting married — for the second time. An encounter with a traveling salesman, though, forces her to face the fact that she does not know what she believes in or wants anymore. "What do I want?" she asks herself, "Mr. Right — or Mr. Left?" When the film starts, the cynical heroine thinks she has all the answers, which is what leads her astray. Through her sexual encounter with the older man, she discovers she has none. The film dramatizes her conflict: bourgeois security or the bohemian excitement of the "good fight." Her uncertainty about her upcoming marriage, her goals, and her future in general, is what she needs to face.

The Man in the Brooks Brothers Shirt uses a very goal-driven antagonist, Gerry Green, to give the film focus. He raises the questions: can the heroine, Vicki, resist him and what will happen if she can't? He makes the protagonist *reactive*, not passive. Her reason for accompanying him to his cabin, because there might be a "story in it - 'Sex and the Modern Working Girl'" - gives the illusion she knows what she's doing. Her heavy drinking, however, unmasks her unconscious motives. The alcohol enables her to check her good intentions at the door, and allows her unconscious mind to take charge. It is only at the end, after her confusion has surfaced, that we understand why she put herself in such a psychically dangerous situation in the first place: Because she is unsure about her marriage and life. What does she want, why, and what does she need?

Want: Initially, to exploit him and get a story
Why: She's bored and it's hot
Need: To face her confusion over her conflicting desires

The heroine's need drives her to compromise herself so that she might wake up and look at what she's doing with her life.

Finding the answers to these three questions of want, why and need isn't as simple as one may think. Often a character's real need is as elusive and impenetrable to the writer as those of actual people. Yet if you keep digging and thinking about the character, trying to discover this psychological key, you'll be rewarded. A clear understanding of the character's need will usually increase the story's intensity and deepen the meaning of the conflict. It may take several drafts of a screenplay before the need of the protagonist begins to emerge truthfully. But it's worth the time and effort.

If you are having difficulty answering the question "What does my character need," it can help to ask three other questions about your character that may lead you to an answer. The first is, "What does my character want out of life?" The second is, "What does my character dream of?" and the third, "Why isn't my character achieving these?" The answer to any or all of these questions can lead you to the character's basic need in terms of what he needs to do to achieve his life goals, or in determining what he must address, overcome or accept in himself to find success or peace.

CREATING THE CHARACTER

Once you have a basic understanding of these questions you have the structural key to what drives the plot. But unless the characters are conceived in three dimensions, the audience won't fully relate to them or the story. Your characters must have emotions, attitudes and beliefs, and actions that represent them. They need a history, personal traits and quirks, to come alive. How do we create these? Where do we start?

Personal Experience

A good place for you to begin is to draw from your whole background of experience to create the people who live in your scripts. Good characters often come from actual models. Basing characters on people we know well gives us an indication what a character's response might be in a particular situation. How a character deals with conflict or the lack of it can be very telling, and helps shape the audience's opinion of him one way or another.

Somerset Maugham, though, said in his autobiography, *The Summing Up*, since we really know very little even of the people we think we know the best, we can't just transfer them wholebody to our work "and make human beings of them. People are too elusive, too shadowy to be copied; and they are too incoherent and contradictory. The writer does not copy his originals; he takes what he wants from them, a few traits that have caught his attention, a turn of mind that has fired his imagination."

Your characters are just that, your characters. They have to serve the themes and story you create and come from you. We use people we know as models for behavior, but you still must shape them. A perceptive writer is observant, watching people for interesting and entertaining features, mannerisms and reactions, then trying to figure out why they are that way. Writers use these clues to reveal the character on the page and in the movie. A character's idiosyncrasies and unusual behavior encourage the audience's interest. We wonder, "Why did she do that?" and we follow along hoping to get the answer.

Character Biography

Many writers use character biographies to define the character and keep actions consistent with who he or she is. A character biography is a description of the relevant information of the character. Whether your protagonist looks like Quasimodo or Prince Charming, appearance plays a part in defining who he is. What part of the world he's from and his social class are also factors. Psychological make-up, too, will affect how he acts. It's important to know as much as possible about all aspects of your main characters to make them come alive, whether you write it all down or not.

Below is an outline of what you might want to cover in your biography.

Physical Appearance
1. Sex
2. Age
3. Race
4. Physical Attributes
5. Physical Defects
6. Heredity
7. Bodily Care

Sociology
1. Class
2. Education
3. Occupation
4. Home Life
5. Religion
6. Nationality
7. Political Affiliations
8. Amusements

Psychology
1. Sex Life
2. Moral Standards
3. Personal Ambitions, frustrations
4. Temperament, attitude toward life
5. Complexes: Obsessions, inhibitions, neuroses
6. Extrovert/introvert
7. Abilities: Talents, IQ
8. Qualities: Imagination, judgment
9. Unique traits

This brief outline of topics, qualities, attributes and peculiarities, is not meant to be solely a fill in the blanks questionnaire. These headings should be developed with the idea of understanding your story better through understanding your character and her motivations.

It is through our physical appearance that we first meet the world — or how the world first meets us. People are judged by the clothes they wear, the cut of their hair, whether they are clean or dirty, and if they are normally healthy, athletic or deformed. How someone looks has a definite effect on how he acts, as well as on the way other people react to him. Think about the Hunchback of Notre Dame and how his appearance influenced his behavior. The same process works in the audience, too, as they meet your characters. Physical characteristics can be very important.

The sociology of your character is a study of his or her environment. Where a woman is born effects who she'll become and how she'll behave; East LA is very different than Manhattan's Eastside. Were her parents nurturing or oppressive? That will determine if she's healthy or scarred. Knowing her education, social status, ethnic background, religious teaching, etc., all help create a rounded character.

The psychology of the character is not just the product of the other two categories, although you can first grasp it this way. Personality development is far more complex. Numerous theories try to explain it, and a study of any of them will help you. All writers have to be amateur shrinks at some level, analyzing and understanding characters. The more you know about what motivates people, the better.

In order for a character's biography to be effective it needs to address not only what motivates the character to behave as she does overall, but also why she's in the predicament she's in now in your story. Without providing a clear understanding of these questions, the biography becomes merely a list of interesting but not especially helpful information.

Again, the essential things the writer must know about the protagonist are: What does he want and why, and what does he need emotionally? The character biography must lead to the answers to these questions. An excellent example of this approach can be found in Lajos Egri's *The Art of Dramatic Writing*, in his section on character.

46

Back-story

Back-story and character biography aren't identical but they are similar. Both deal with the character's important history. The crucial difference is this: Back-story focuses on specific past events that directly affect the protagonist's emotional involvement in the plot as it unfolds. In a sense, all else is irrelevant. This is what defines the character in the story. This is why he or she is here. Often it's connected to the protagonist's need. Many writers feel this is all they need to know to begin writing. Though a detailed character biography would include this information, these writers don't use one.

In *Life Lessons*, the most important piece of Lionel's back-story isn't given fully until the end, though we get hints along the way. This revelation of character is indeed the point of the film. Though Lionel has said he loves Paulette, this claim is finally cast into doubt when he meets the young and beautiful painter serving wine at his art opening. Clearly taken with her, he offers her Paulette's job. As we watch their interaction, we sense that Lionel is about to start a new version of the cycle he just completed with Paulette. This is what he does. He's incapable of true love with a person. His true love is his canvas.

Sometimes understanding the back-story is made an explicit goal for the audience to attain. Only then will the protagonist's plight be comprehensible. *Memento* (written and directed by Christopher Nolan) and *The Machinist* (written by Scott Kosar and directed by Brad Anderson) are two examples where the question of what's going on in the main story only makes full sense when we find out what happened to the protagonist in his back-story. *Memento* is an interesting ride, but because we're never really sure of the veracity of the information we're fed along the way, and because the back-story is never made fully clear even in the last scene, the plot device of unfolding in reverse time, however much tied to a unique, short-term memory impaired hero, really remains a plot gimmick. We've experienced something new with *Memento* — and in the world of feature films that's important — but *The Machinist*, while perhaps not as innovative, offers a more complete back-story explanation of what's made its protagonist go without sleep for a year and emaciate himself to the point of death.

All the information in the character's biography or back-story won't necessarily come out in the screenplay. What specifically does come out should provide us with insight about the past that helps us make sense of the character's present. Why is a character afraid to feel or to love? Why is she angry or cynical? It's important to remember that these emotions must impinge on and push the screenplay one way or another. They must be addressed in the film.

The back-story should not get in the way of the current story. Giving too much only weighs down the present situation. What we need to know of the back-story is this: How is the character's current behavior related to his past life? In many cases we don't need to know all this information; we just need to feel it's there.

ATTITUDES & EMOTIONS

It's not enough just to think about who the character is, where she comes from, and what she wants, to create a full-blooded characterization. The character comes alive when she has emotions and attitudes. The *action* of the screenplay must illustrate these emotions and attitudes.

Emotions & Identification

At the top of this chapter I talked about emotion, so I won't go on at length here. Let me just reiterate that the emotional life is generally what makes a character available to the audience. Through recognizable emotions that we find believable, we accept behavior based on them. Actions may be dramatic and surprising, but if we don't feel they're rooted in a true emotional reaction, we won't accept them.

Attitudes, Beliefs & Values

Everyone has a point of view or toward the world. It can be sentimental or cynical, positive or negative, happy or sad. What's great about an attitude is that it can be interpreted and played by actors. It can be shown visually in actions and supported by dialogue. It doesn't rely on words to tell the audience, but can be sensed and felt.

Often a writer conceives or "gets" the character first through the attitude. The hard-boiled cop, the cynical politician. To avoid stereotypes, you need to show this as the persona or outward face, and include another side to the character. Perhaps the hard-boiled cop meticulously cares for his fingers because he plays the violin. The cynical politician may still love the idea of democracy, but no longer believes in it. The key is finding the other side of the person to give the character complexity.

Attitudes are based mainly on our beliefs. In film we don't want to hear a character explain his philosophy. Instead we rely on his attitude and actions to show us what he believes in and values. Everyone believes in something, and knowing what it is for a character brings new dimensions to the story. The over-worked secretary: will she fight for women's rights or sit at home and whine about them? The tough longshoreman: will he support his son's pursuit of an education or be threatened by it? In our own lives, too, actions more than words tell us who someone is. No matter what people say, a person is truly defined by what he does. A character's beliefs influence his attitude and actions. The stronger the belief is, the more definite the attitude and the action.

Values tell us what someone holds dear. Values are important because, along with beliefs, they tell us what a character will or won't fight for. This can be translated into action.

Opinions also help define the character. They let us know what the character thinks about people or the action in the story. If viewers share the character's opinion of what's happening on the screen, it can increase their identification with the character and their involvement in the story. If the audience has a radically different view of events on screen it can distance them from the character.

Attitudes & the Psychological Life

It is important to understand that at a deeper level, our emotional and psychological life plays a large part in determining our attitudes and beliefs. Constantin Stanislavski, author of *An Actor Prepares*, said, "First there is the emotion, then the thought," and most psychologists would agree. An individual may have specific talents, be predisposed toward extroversion or introversion. She may be naturally inclined to deal with the world through feeling-based reactions or intellectually based efforts to understand. Intuition may be her primary guide or she may be led by her senses. Whatever the case — cynic, optimist, realist, romantic, neurotic — these attitudes are to an extent all rooted in the past's emotional/psychological experiences. Positive interactions with the world produce positive attitudes; negative interactions produce negative ones.

REPRESENTING THE CHARACTER

Drama depends upon action and conflict. Character is represented in the context of action, and this is, or should be, most of what we see on the screen. Characters aren't defined in description by the writer or in dialogue (which is description by the characters of themselves or others). Characters, just as real people, are defined by their actions, by what they do and what they don't do. What you know about the characters has to be translated into actions.

Decisions, Choices, Commitments & Actions

Generally, before someone can take action, a choice or decision must be made. That choice forms the basis of a commitment for the protagonist, and this decision to commit to something starts the story. As the commitment continues and/or is altered, the story develops.

The best stories are on some level about choices and commitments. A character determines what he or she wants and decides to pursue it. The story shows the protagonist's commitment, the consequences of taking action, and the sacrifices made because of that commitment. The choices a character makes tell us who he is. How the audience comes to know your character is fundamentally through what he does on screen.

Character Is Action

In order for your protagonist to demonstrate who she is to the audience, you must incorporate action that shows us the qualities central to understanding her. Any important character quality or trait must be worked into the action of the plot for it to have any meaning for the audience.

Writers often want to take short cuts and *tell* us a character's qualities or back-story through description, eschewing the more challenging task of *showing* us who is protagonist is. If we never see a demonstration of his/her important qualities in the story, how do we know they're true? In the feature film *The Clearing*, written by Pieter Jan Brugge and Justin Haythe, directed by Pieter Jan Brugge, Robert Redford plays Wayne Hayes, kidnapper Wilhem Dafoe's victim. We are told Hayes is a "great man" time and again, ostensibly because he's rich, a self-made man, and his kids love him. But does Wayne ever demonstrate his greatness anywhere in the film? He cheated on his wife, was caught, resumed the affair again, and always lied to her about it. What we learn through the action of the film is a more negative portrait of the man. His kids love him, but he seems disconnected to his children, especially his daughter. Yes, he had a successful business but its success seems more the result of fortunate timing than business acumen. Furthermore, his second big business effort went bust. What's so great about him? The only real affection he demonstrates is with the family dog. Later on, Wayne has a chance to kill his abductor and flee to safety. But he can't deliver the coup-de-grace and must face an unfortunate fate. Even this action spells weakness, or equivocation, or a subtle death wish, or something other than greatness. The argument that Wayne is a nice guy because he engages his kidnapper on a human level doesn't make sense. We've known at least since the development of the Stockholm Syndrome that hostages naturally bond with their tormentors; more likely, Hayes wants to entice his kidnapper to let him go.

In *Life Lessons*, we know Lionel is important by the way other people treat him and the work he creates. Throughout the film, he tells us he loves Paulette, but by the end of the movie we know he's incapable of love, not by what he says but through actions demonstrated in the film.

In *The Dutch Master*, Teresa's family and friends tell us all about her. But by watching what she does and seeing how it contrasts what they say about her, we, the audience, have a better idea of who she is and what's going on.

If a character is kind and this is important to the story, then he needs to demonstrate kindness in the plot action. If a character has a hot temper, we need to see the short fuse ignite and watch her deal with the consequences. If a character is supposed to be great and admirable, we have to see the significant action that shows us. Otherwise these assertions are meaningless, and, if unproved in the case of a central character, will lead to unsatisfying drama.

But understand that a character's "plot action" is not about merely showing a character *doing* something. Character isn't revealed by seeing Jane studying or helping an old lady cross the street when the light is green and Jane has nothing better to do.

Character Is Revealed In Action Under Stress

Conflict strips away our masks and defenses. The *only* way a character shows us who he *really* is, what his *character is made of*, is how he deals with conflict.

Sixty years ago, Lajos Egri wrote in *The Art of Dramatic Writing* that only in conflict do we reveal our true selves. "Even an illiterate knows that politeness and smart talk are not signs of sincerity or friendship. But sacrifice is."

Conflict, stress, and pressure strip us down to our core. (Vince Lombardi said, "Fatigue makes cowards of us all.") How we react to trouble tells us about our essential selves, and this is really what the audience is interested in, the stripping away of artifice to the essential person. In the face of misfortune, do we fall apart or buckle down and work harder? Do we sweep our problems under the rug or chin up and face them? When trouble comes calling, do we run in fear or stand up and fight for what's right? Is our perspective "what will happen to me?" or "what can I get done?"

Character, the kind that excites readers, actors and the audience, is not the list of qualities and traits, a biography of where they grew up and whether mommy loved them or not. This is the psychology of the character. (Don't get me wrong, all this is important to know as the writer, but little of it is important to the audience if they "get" what the character is about on an emotional level.) Character, in the dramatic sense, is shown in the strengths and weaknesses of the personality that we see *dramatized in action* on stage or screen.

What the really good screenwriters know is stories aren't about a situation or a series of actions; they're about characters caught up in conflict reacting to the situations in ways that the audience finds compelling, understandable and surprising. A character has a (*back*)story but he is *not* that (*back*)story. He is the personified action of the main story you are dramatizing.

Indeed, we could argue that the purpose of drama is to demonstrate how (heroic) people take action that is outside the realm of their personality. We show how people change or alter their basic psychology when they realize their usual patterns of behavior don't work — and may even get them killed. (Comedy, of course, or wistful drama like *Forrest Gump*, or fantasies like the *007* series, is often built around the premise that a "hero" will change his circumstances despite never having to undergo change himself.)

What do we know of Lester Burnham (Kevin Spacey) in *American Beauty*? He's a frustrated middle-aged man who hates his life. We don't get a life history that tells us why; we see it demonstrated in his actions and through his conflict with his wife, daughter and the external world. He's so sexually frustrated he obsesses on his daughter's friend Angela and this raises the stakes of the story. Yet how and why do we connect with him?

Even as we squirm while Lester makes a fool of himself with Angela and things worse with his daughter, we admire his courage for confronting the job he hates and turning a bad situation to his advantage. We see his regret over angry words he exchanges with his daughter. We feel his longing and frustration with his wife who can't give an inch. And in the end, as he recognizes Angela's vulnerability, we see in his actions his core humanity of putting someone else's needs above his own desires. And this is why Lester is a great character and an Oscar-worthy role.

In short films we see the same thing: how the characters deal with conflict tells us what we need to know about them. In *Franz Kafka's It's a Wonderful Life*, Kafka at one point wants more than anything to stop the noise in his building that's disturbing his concentration. Finally, he goes to confront the people in the downstairs apartment. He marches up, bangs on the door, and tells Miss Cicely she must stop the music at once. Remarkably, she agrees. Only this is a fantasy. A moment after it plays out we see we're still standing in the hallway with Kafka, staring at the door, frozen. When he finally walks up, he taps ever so lightly. Miss Cicely answers and pulls him into the party; he's so shy he can't even resist. He can't muster the words to object, but we sense it's not just because he's shy but he doesn't want to ruin the fun.

Character is revealed in action, what the characters do. The stronger the pressure on the character, the clearer look we get at his real nature in his response to the challenge from that pressure. The clearest look into a character's heart is when the pressure is on and the character is confronted by a hard choice.

Character Is Revealed Through Choices Made Under Stress

This is perhaps the most important dramatic concept surrounding character and plot, and the least understood. Great stories capture characters in situations where they are called on to make difficult choices. Spiderman, Lester Burnham, Jerry Maguire, Will Turner and Elizabeth Swann (*Pirates of the Caribbean)* are all characters faced with difficult choices. We know what's in their hearts from exposition or ancillary action. But we learn the truth of their hearts, by the choices they make, even if it breaks those hearts. (For instance, Spidey refuses love that might jeopardize his girlfriend.)

In the Academy Award-winning short *Election Night*, written and directed by Anders Thomas Jensen, idealistic Peter realizes he's forgotten to vote when he stands up to a friend who is making racist statements in a bar. Even though there's very little time left, he races out to "mark the ballot." He hails a cab and seems on his way until the driver starts making racist comments. Peter tries to ignore the man until he can no longer take it and tells the driver to shut up. The driver refuses, saying he can do as he likes in his cab. Suddenly, Peter (who earlier with a friend has said "Silence gives consent") finds himself in a moral dilemma. He makes his choice and tells the taxi driver to stop: he's getting out. He makes a moral stand, but it gets him no closer to voting, his ultimate goal. As the short plays out, we see him tested over and over, until he reaches a surprising result.

In *Words*, from *Before the Rain*, Father Kiril faces the choice of helping hide the girl at the monastery or telling his superiors about her as he's required to do. His actions show us the compassion in his heart.

The really great writers understand that making a choice is a dramatic action and they use it. They dramatize the situations that place the character at the blazing crossroads of choice, then rake them through the coals to turn their actions into significant moments of the plot. A dramatically effective choice offers characters radically different outcomes arising from autonomous decisions. (It's too easy if Superman has no choice but to save the school. But if he has to choose between the lives of many children and that of Lois Lane, things get tougher.) The best way to frame these choices is in moral terms, but not in terms of moral absolutes.

New and even advanced writers often offer characters choices between something positive and something negative. But this isn't really a dramatic choice unless the character chooses the negative and gives up the positive consciously. Unless it's Luke Skywalker choosing between the good on the side of the rebels or standing with his father and the evil Empire, it is dramatically ineffective because the negative doesn't represent something the character truly wants.

Often, feature and short films glance over the act of deciding or choosing for fear it will slow or stop the action. But the process of coming to a decision *is* an action. Seeing someone consider and reflect on what to do can help increase our understanding of that character. We see the weight of the decision. Watching someone rashly push ahead without thinking reveals a different kind of character.

In *Life Lessons*, Lionel is not a man who stops and thinks. He doesn't decide. Lionel acts, without thought of the consequences. He will say and do anything in his nearly irrational pursuit of Paulette. This tells us he is a man in love. But by the end of the movie, we have a different picture of what love means to him when he impulsively decides to offer Paulette's job to the aspiring painter. On the other hand, Paulette can't decide what to do. One moment she is leaving, the next she has allowed Lionel to change her mind. Her indecision defines her. Her actions also help us sympathize with Lionel's frustration dealing with her. Yet as we watch her move from one choice to its opposite, we sense the depth of her conflict, and begin to glean its source. She is in the grips of a major identity crisis, and Lionel is totally oblivious. (Consider the way she asks Lionel whether or not she has talent. As Lionel indicates to her, such an important question goes to the core of who she is, and only she can answer it.)

The decisions and choices at the beginning and the end of the story are the most important and revealing about the character. The beginning decision is made when the protagonist decides what he wants and commits to pursuing it. In a sense the film becomes a test of that commitment and the price he will pay for maintaining it. Usually well before the end of most feature films, there is a moment where the protagonist recommits to his or her goal. In a short film, the choice at the end often leads to the revelation of character on which the story is based.

One last point: the strongest moral choices or decisions have consequences. When the action costs the character something, it deepens the significance of these choices and commitments. In *Mara of Rome*, Mara vows to sacrifice a week's income if Umberto returns to the seminary. In *Election Night*, Peter gives up the taxi ride he desperately needs in order to exercise his right to vote because of his commitment to stand up against bigotry. Personal loss is best expressed in terms of relationship. In *Life Lessons*, Lionel loses Paulette because of his commitment to art.

TRANSFORMATION

Characters only change under the force of conflict. In successful feature films, the change in one or more of the main characters is dramatic. In a short film, character transformation isn't generally as pronounced. The same distinction exists between novels and short stories: The former allow heroes a complete reexamination of the human condition; the latter usually detail one incident that offers a challenge to an accepted orthodoxy. Sometimes in features the protagonist doesn't change himself but causes profound change in those around him (this is especially pronounced in comedies). This lack of change in the hero is more often than not the case in short films. But even though the protagonist doesn't always change, his action changes others, as in *Life Lessons*, *Mara of Rome*, *Anna of Milan*, and *PEEL*. Mara doesn't change in *Mara of Rome*, but Rusconi and Umberto do. Lionel's basic nature hasn't changed in *Life Lessons*, but his circumstances have (i.e., Paulette's left him, but he's created the art work for a successful show).

But main characters *can* change in shorts, too. Look at Teresa in *Some Folks Call It a Sling Blade*. She goes from angry and nervous about Carl's impending release in the beginning to calm and concerned for his welfare at the end. In *The Powder Keg*, one of the BMW Films *Hire Series*, written by Guillermo Arriaga and Alejandro González Iñárritu, story by David Carter, the driver (Clive Owen) is cool and in control at the beginning, but is clearly affected by the tragedy by the end of the story. In *The Dutch Master*, Teresa moves from being quietly uncertain at the beginning of the story to totally withdrawn from the world at the end.

Sometimes short films effectively chart a progression, as from bad to worse. In the Academy Award winning short *The Appointments of Dennis Jennings*, written by Steven Wright and Mike Armstrong and directed by Dean Parisot, the protagonist Dennis is clearly disturbed at the start of the film: He is stalking a man in the woods with a hunting rifle. The story then flashes back three months and shows through a series of funny encounters with an unfeeling psychiatrist (Rowan Atkinson) just what led the hero Dennis to attempt murder. The film climaxes when Dennis shoots his shrink, and ends with him in police custody ironically about to be interviewed by a court appointed psychologist.

The same thing is true with *PEEL*. The characters don't change for the better but disintegrate and prove they're incapable of change by the end.

Some films show the protagonist becoming aware of some hidden aspect of his or her personality. This coming to consciousness, or recognition of a "new" reality represents real growth for the character. *The Man in the Brooks Brothers Shirt* is a good example of personal growth through the protagonist's interaction with the antagonist.

As a writer and filmmaker, you need to recognize that the best short films often have an interesting and forceful protagonist who does not change in the course of the story, but forces another major character to change. If you are blocked with your story by an inability to perceive the lesson learned by your protagonist, ask instead what lesson your protagonist could teach another character (and us). Even if your protagonist comes to no new awareness of her lot in life, she should be so compelling that her behavior gives us new insight into ourselves.

THE IMPORTANT CHARACTERS

We've talked a lot about creating and building characters. Although all the characters need loving attention, the ideas and concepts presented above must apply most to your main characters, because in all screenplays with the exception of the most obviously melodramatic, it is the main characters who carry the story.

The Protagonist

The most important character in the screenplay is the protagonist. He or she is the focus of attention. Even in feature films considered ensemble pieces, one character usually emerges out of the group as the true protagonist. In a short film, one protagonist carries the story line and forces the action. She has the decisions to make and the task to accomplish. The protagonist takes the film to the climax.

Effective protagonists drive the story by having something they must do. I've seen countless films die on the screen with protagonists who are unable to act, to commit to something, losing the audience when they lose patience with the character. Often writers understand their characters' flaws and shortcomings, but because the film is so short they don't have time to effectively communicate them to the audience.

In feature films, we say that strong protagonists must appeal to your audience. They don't have to be physically good-looking, but must have traits or virtues the audience considers admirable or entertaining. The protagonist must be intriguing, sympathetic or empathetic, to keep the audience caring and interested in what happens in the movie.

Many successful shorts, though, don't emphasize the positive traits of the protagonist but instead focus on the negative. The filmmakers find humor, menace or creepy apprehension in the characters to build tension, and this keeps the viewer interested in the short term.

Attractive traits are generosity, good will, humor, courage, honesty, responsibility or even the consummate skill of a master assassin. Whatever generates respect or admiration holds our interest, at least initially. A protagonist is considered entertaining by his ability to amuse the audience. A character who makes us laugh easily gains our sympathy. A protagonist may have all sorts of flaws and weaknesses but will maintain the audience's sympathy as long as we see she is in some manner funny or virtuous. Artist Lionel impresses us with his real talent for the canvas, even though we suspect early on he would be a bear to live with.

A protagonist's commitment to his goal can serve a protagonist if she will struggle with the conflict and not give in and admit defeat easily. Active protagonists grab the audience's interest and hold it. Even an unsympathetic protagonist can keep our attention for quite a while if he is struggling valiantly for his goal.

To create a first rate characterization the protagonist needs something genuinely unique and something archetypal to separate him or her from the group. In *Life Lessons*, Lionel is an extremely successful artist. Being an artist puts him in a limited group, and his success separates him even further as does his sexual success with a pretty live-in woman. Indeed, Lionel is a particularly rich character because he carries all of the following archetypes: Artistic mentor, spiritual advisor, father figure, initiator into the sexual world (older man, younger woman), sponsor/patron (he supports Paulette's art, at least financially), and bon-vivant.

Finally, contrasting what makes the protagonist unique against what makes him universal will help bring the characterization to life. Again, using *Life Lessons*, what connects Lionel to other people is his love for Paulette, which isn't returned. Who hasn't felt unrequited love? We admire the successful artist but *identify emotionally* with the man losing the girl.

The Antagonist

The antagonist is the principal adversary of the hero. The antagonist can be one person or a group of people who oppose the protagonist's pursuit of his goal. The antagonist doesn't have to be a "villain" to be effective. In feature vehicles he's often conceived that way, and the more despicable the better. But in a short film, the antagonist is more often the character who initiates the problem for the protagonist or who stands in the protagonist's way of reaching her goal. A strong antagonist is as committed to his goal as the protagonist is. The more this goal directly conflicts with the protagonist's, the more tension develops.

In many shorts, the protagonist/antagonist connection is the primary relationship explored. Giving the same amount of thought to this character's wants, motivations (conscious and unconscious), and needs, in opposition to the protagonist's, will strengthen the overall conflict, plot and story. The more believably drawn this character's wants and needs are the better he will play against the protagonist. The antagonist needs to be drawn with emotions and attitudes, and given actions to represent them, the same as the protagonist. Also, understanding what is unique as well as archetypal and universal about the character will help the audience understand him and perhaps empathize with his problem. The grandmother in *Mara of Rome*, though thoroughly disagreeable when we meet her, is understandable in her attitude toward Mara. When she swings from being an adversary to ally, she moves from being the archetypal wicked witch to a fairy godmother in relationship to Mara. Paulette, the antagonist in *Life Lessons*, isn't an evil, remorseless woman. Though flawed, she's struggling with her own problems and this motivates much of her bitchy behavior. She opposes Lionel because she doesn't want him in the same way he wants her.

The best way to explore the protagonist is in relationship to the antagonist. What would we know about Lionel without Paulette for him to obsess upon in *Life Lessons*? What would we know about Tim without Katie in *PEEL*? If you try to see this opposing force as fully as the protagonist, then she can emerge as a full character in her own right, instead of a cardboard cutout moved around solely for plot reasons.

Supporting Characters

A catalyst is the character who causes something to happen and involves the protagonist in the conflict which becomes the plot. In *Life Lessons*, Paulette becomes the catalyst once she declares she is leaving. In *Mara of Rome*, Umberto is the unwitting catalyst who causes the conflict between Mara and his grandmother.

Often in a short film, the catalyst and the antagonist are the same character.

The confidant is a close friend of the protagonist. He or she allows the protagonist to reveal sides of his or her nature that are not apparent on the surface. Protagonists act differently with confidants than they would with others.

Confidants permit the protagonist to show vulnerability, doubt, emotion, etc. But when confidants are used for expository purposes, they can slow the story down with talk. Though the audience needs a certain amount of information to understand the story, and sometimes the best way to get this across is through expository dialogue, the tendency is for new writers to explain everything, and this can be deadly. The best way to use a confidant is to conceive this character with wants and needs, too. If these characters have minor conflicts with the protagonist, or other characters, getting information across can become more fun and feel less expository. In *Life Lessons*, consider Lionel's art dealer Philip Fowler. He is used to get a lot of information across, but he has a conflict with Lionel. He wants to see Lionel's "work" in the studio. Lionel has nothing to show and won't even let him in. Look at how the conflict is dramatized between them. Philip is locked in the elevator, behind the cage wanting to get in, and Lionel won't open the door. In segment entitled *The Gambler from The Gold of Naples*, written by Cesare Zavattini and directed by Vittorio De Sica, the butler fulfills the role of confidant for the Count.

In the feature film *Sideways*, screenplay by Alexander Payne and Jim Taylor (novel by Rex Pickett), the confidant character is the actor who enables us to see what our protagonist, the writer, is up against. Of course, the actor is also an antagonist who uses what he knows about the protagonist against him; for example, in determining that both men should get laid before they must return home by the weekend.

EXERCISES

The obvious place to start building a character is with writing a character biography of one or two of your main characters. But before you try this, look at another film and analyze the main characters. Determine what you know about one or more of the characters from what you see in the film. Start with their goals, what they want and what they need. Then, using what the character says about himself, what he does, and what others say about him, ascertain who the character really is. Are there hints about a deeper background for the characters that never really come into play? Is there information given that fills in the details of a life that makes it feel true?

Now, look at your own characters. Consider who one is and how she became this way. You probably already have an idea of what your character wants. Why she wants it and her need may still be unfocused. So ask about her psychological make-up. Where was she born and how did she grow up? What kind of person is she today? All of this information is especially relevant if it is leading to explaining why the character is in her present predicament.

Now focus on:

1. What does the character want (in this story)?
2. Why does the character want it?
3. What does the character need?

Remember what he *wants* will be stronger if it is something specific, something the audience can easily understand and relate to. *Why* gives us his conscious motivation for wanting it. The *need* tells what the unconscious wants from the character. It is often the true motivation for him. Sometimes it is what the character needs to learn in order to succeed. Keep these answers handy and consult them often. As you do, you may find the answers changing. That's okay. It should signify you are getting closer to the real truth about your character.

To fill out your character, determine which emotions generally rule her life. Is she someone who is in touch with her emotions in a healthy way or unable to deal with them? Consider her anxieties, how does she handle them? Does she deny, suppress, escape, or face and assimilate them? Ask what she's afraid of?

What's the character's attitude towards life? Does he think it's as good deal or a bad one? What do his beliefs and values tell you about him?

Another good question is what does your character want most out of life? This is not the want/plot goal of your film, but a question which when answered truthfully defines whoever answers it. Is she consciously pursuing this long-term goal or unconsciously undermining it because of self-destructive patterns within her personality?

These are only a few questions that can provide insight into your characters. Ask the same questions of your characters that interest you about people generally. The answers should provide you with ample information to build a story.

4

The Three-Part Nature of Film Structure

"A script is more architecture than literature," Elia Kazan writes in his autobiography *A Life*. Kazan means by this that a script provides the structure of a story that is only truly complete when the actors, production design, cinematography, music, editing, etc., all come together to create the finished product — the film. The script is the blueprint, the plan that provides the planners, the filmmakers, with the means to bring all the ideas together.

However, the script a writer constructs has to be as close a facsimile of the film on paper as he can make. He must imagine how to bring all the elements of his story together to make sense, build tension and move the audience. Because a script and its meaning are communicated by actors, information must be presented in clear relationships the audience can grasp from viewing the story. Structure focuses the organization of the material to best tell the story.

Your basic materials revolve around the protagonist's and other characters' individual wants and needs. They are what force the characters to take action and that leads to conflict. Obstacles and complications — the crises characters face — are tools to be used in conjunction with reversals, reveals and surprises to construct a plot that conveys your ideas and satisfies the audience.

Plot structure can be viewed as a two-part process. First is the overall form the story takes. Second is the actual plotting of the scenes, the order and arrangement of specific events that creates specific meanings. The overall structure focuses on the relationships between beginnings and endings, on the development of conflicts in the middle, and how these parts hold all the elements of your story together. Plotting finds the connections in the specific scenes.

The ultimate plot structure of a story depends on many things — genre, your point of view, even your true purpose for writing it. These particular considerations contribute to making your work unique. But even as we strive for originality, we must realize that good structure, whether in features or shorts, tends to follow basic rules. The beginning of a film must set up a dramatic problem the audience understands. The middle builds the story's rising action, which then intensifies to the final climax and resolution. This "formula" is simple enough in theory, but in practice, keeping the characters on track, the story moving ahead, the theme meaningful, and the audience from becoming bored can be an infuriatingly difficult task.

STRUCTURE IN GENERAL

Much depends on the length of a short film in understanding how best to structure it. If a film runs under 3 minutes like *405*, you must set up the problem quickly, develop the conflict and then hit your pay-off climax with no time to waste. If you're developing a 10 to 20 minute or longer film, then the overall plot structure tends to become a little more complex.

If you know something about typical three-act construction, you can relate it to the short like this: Act 1 encompasses the set-up of the problem for the protagonist, but your inciting incident serves as the Act 1 climax; Act 2 develops the action and conflict to a final crisis point; and Act 3 builds from that final crisis to a main climax and resolution that resolves the story situation. Often there is a strong midpoint that helps support the story in the middle of longer pieces. This midpoint advances the action or conflict in some significant way to keep the story interesting.

These key points are where you play specific obstacles, complications, decisions, or choices — actions that further your story line and theme.

Structure and plotting go hand in hand. So in this chapter we look at overall structure, break it down into its components and define each. In Chapter 5, we discuss the principles behind how you put the individual scenes together to create a compelling plot for a story.

IN THE BEGINNING – THE SET-UP

In a short film, the set-up functions much the same as in a feature film. Its goal is to orient the audience to the characters, backdrop, time frame, mood, as well as give them a clue as to the direction of the film and theme, and present the conflict. It provides the important information the audience *needs* to get the story moving. But instead of taking ten or fifteen pages (minutes) to set the tone, characters and action, the short film must accomplish all this right up front.

This is where countless short films and scripts fail. Writers often spend too much time "setting up" *all* the elements of the story when they should focus on only what's *essential* for the audience to know to go along with the action once the conflict or problem engages. The audience can learn other important information as the story progresses, but we must get to the conflict to pique our interest and we need to understand the basis of it. These essential elements come in the form of the main exposition and the inciting incident. Remember, the main point of the set-up is to establish the conflict, or basis for that conflict, that the protagonist faces so the audience can clearly understand what follows.

The Main Exposition

You must determine what is primary and vital for the audience to know at the start of the story about the hero and the conflict. In a feature film, this information can be developed more naturally, but because of time constraints in a short, we must get it across more quickly. The main exposition grounds the audience in the basis of the story. Sometimes it's given in dialogue; sometimes it can be shown in action; sometimes in shorts we get in exposition printed in cards. Regardless, audiences need this information so they can orient themselves to the plot and understand what's happening and what follows. Generally, it takes a couple of scenes to get this information across, but it may be as brief as a quarter of a page if that does it.

In *Life Lessons*, we see immediately that Lionel Dobie is a successful artist. We know he's an artist by his paints, brushes, canvases and studio. The expensive cognac the director shows us tells us he's successful, as does the enormous studio. His paint-coated fingers and the manic look in his eyes tell he's totally dedicated to his craft. All this is shown under credits.

The first scene introduces Lionel's art dealer, Philip, who comes to the studio to see Lionel's new work. But Lionel won't show his work, and through dialogue we learn he has three weeks until a big exhibition. Lionel's nervous, scared, and depressed. "I'm going to get slaughtered," he groans. When Philip suggests lunch, Lionel tells him he has to pick up his assistant at the airport. This scene, primarily all exposition and given in dialogue, establishes the possible story problem (the art show) and drives the plot to a second piece of exposition in the following scene.

Franz Kafka's It's a Wonderful Life starts with a shot traveling up a stack of books. At the top the only title we can read says *Metamorphosis* by Franz Kafka. A still photograph of Kafka (really the actor playing him, Richard E. Grant) is shown next, and then a book opens showing text that then isolates the first line from *Metamorphosis*: "As Gregor Samsa awoke one morning from uneasy dreams he found himself transformed into a gigantic insect." This line is given a musical sting before fading into a shot of a towering cluster of gothic apartments, and then we find Kafka trying to compose this first line. However, he's blocked and can't quite get it.

All of this exposition is focused on setting up the dramatic problem. In a short screenplay, every word, every line must advance the action and reveal only what is necessary for us to understand the characters and the story. There's no time for incidental information. Every word has to be to the point, especially at the beginning. Other insights and information about the hero or other characters can be revealed as the story advances, and as the audience needs it in order to understand the progressive actions of the protagonist.

The Inciting Incident

For most shorts, the set-up is complete once the inciting incident starts the story's forward motion in earnest. The inciting incident is like a catalyst. It forces the conflict into the open and demands the hero respond and take action. This action puts the protagonist on the path toward his goal.

The second scene in *Life Lessons* functions as the film's catalyst. At the airport, Lionel waits anxiously for his assistant Paulette. Everything is in slow motion to emphasize both his impatience and his total concentration on her. When she gets off the plane, what he lives for has arrived. He absent-mindedly crushes his cigarette into the carpeted floor and he starts for her. But when Paulette sees him she hisses in disgust. She tells him their affair is over and she's leaving New York.

Now we understand why Lionel was so depressed. And now there is conflict. Lionel wants Paulette, wants her to stay and she wants to leave. In a couple of scenes, we'll see him convince her to remain in New York, but the price will be a platonic relationship instead of a romantic one, and this is the real end of the set-up. The question raised in the audience's mind is — "How will this ever work if he's in love with her?" The story reverses itself when she decides to stay. But the sides have been drawn and the problem is clear. The action (and themes) can develop from here.

The inciting incident doesn't always have to be action we see take shape. In *Franz Kafka's It's a Wonderful Life*, once we understand that Kafka is blocked, we understand the story's conflict. There isn't a new action that develops this problem. The problem is there before the movie opens, but writer/director Capaldi has to show it to us, and the conflict develops from this point forward. Short films often play the catalyst off-screen so that the characters are already in motion when we meet them. Through exposition we learn what exactly the problem is.

What to Set Up?

What has to be set up depends on your unique story. Every story is different. *Life Lessons* sets up Lionel's character as a depressed and blocked artist, the coming art show and the fact that Paulette's leaving as the reason for his creative impasse. Once she agrees to stay, he can paint, but the question is can he keep her there?

However, for the ending (and theme) to resonate, other information must be worked into those opening scenes. The film shows how artists use people and relationships as creative material. Screenwriter Richard Price expertly uses Lionel's art dealer Philip to set up this information. When Philip tries at the beginning to coax some indication of when he might see the work, he reminds Lionel gently that, "The show's in three weeks." Lionel panics. He slams the down button on the elevator, sending Philip away in the cage. Exasperated, Philip hollers up at him, "You can pull off, Lionel, you always do! Now, get to know yourself a little better!"

These wonderful lines set up how we'll understand the climax and resolution. Philip here lets us know that whatever Lionel's going through, it's part of a pattern, a cycle. Then at the end, when Lionel uses the same lines on the young painter, we are completely convinced that the whole story has been about his creative process.

The full-length film *Living in Oblivion*, written and directed by Tom DiCillo, began life as a short film people loved so much the filmmakers were able to raise money and complete it as a feature. It's filmed in three segments, the first of which was the original short film. Its set-up is simple and direct. The film starts out establishing the location of a micro budget film set, with craft services setting up early in the morning. Next we meet the actress (Catherine Keener) who has the scene they're shooting. Then we meet the director and the producer (Steve Buscemi and Danielle Von Zerneck) on the set getting ready with the director of photography (Dermot Mulroney) discussing how the director wants to shoot the scene.

Within each of these scenes writer/director DiCillo sets up specific information that will resonate at the conclusion of the plot. With craft services, the PA's argue over milk that could be bad, but isn't replaced. We see the DP complain about his coffee, and we learn he's cut it with the milk. And we get more exposition setting up the scene titled, "Ellen talks to mom." Everyone thinks the actress, Nicole, is really good.

Next we meet Nicole (Keener) on her way to the set. Through her driver's questions, we learn she's nervous about the scene because it hits close to home with her own mother. She tells the driver that her mother died before they could reconcile.

After they pick up Cora, the actress playing "Mom," we meet the director, producer and DP discussing the scene. Director Nick (Buscemi) feels he compromised the day before. This is an important scene today and he won't settle for anything less than what he wants. Nick describes the shot to the DP, how he wants it all in one take, and thus sets up the basis for the story. He wants his shot and he won't compromise.

Now everything is set up. We know what the director wants; we know the actress is nervous about her scene and why; we understand the background of the story. The conflict that follows springs from the simple principle that whatever can go wrong *will* go wrong, challenging Nick's goal of getting the shot he wants.

But the specifics of the early scenes pay off at the end, making the conclusion extremely satisfying. After unforeseen problems have mangled each take, Nick breaks a few moments to run the lines with his actors, Nicole and Cora. As Cora empathizes with Nicole over the trouble, the two connect in a startling way. Cora tenderly pushes Nicole's hair back behind her ear, and Nicole freezes. Using a flashback, DiCillo sends us hurdling back to the moment when Nicole's real mother while in the hospital did the same thing. When Nick has them run lines, Nicole is so raw and real he can't believe it. Nick whispers for the DP to start rolling, only the DP isn't around; he's in the toilet puking from the milk — yet another obstacle to Nick getting what he wants. The moment Nick's been waiting for is gone and he knows it won't come back, so now he decides to compromise the shot and do it in two set-ups instead of one long shot.

What makes the pay-off so satisfying is that the key pieces of information, the milk and Nicole's feelings about her real mother, are worked into the early scenes naturally. The lines, though clearly there to set up the pay-off, don't tip the writer's hand but function as background conversation until needed to make the filmmaker's points.

In the much shorter *Gridlock* (*Fait d'hiver*), the film opens with a man stuck in a terrible traffic jam. Impatient, angry, he fiddles with a new cell phone he takes out of the box and calls home. He reaches his daughter and asks to talk to "Mama." The little girl tells Daddy Mama's upstairs with Uncle Wim. Surprised, because there is no Uncle Wim in the family, the man concocts a plan and sends the girl upstairs to spring it. The ending pay-off, set up right at the start, comes from when the man realizes he's dialed the wrong number, as could logically happen with a new phone.

THE ORDER OF THE SET-UP

The structure of the set-up doesn't have to follow any particular arrangement. The inciting incident can come before the protagonist and main exposition are introduced, or after. In *The Powder Keg*, someone is taking photos of a massacre in a Latin American country as the film starts. In the next scene we meet newspaper photographer Harvey Jacobs (played by Stellan Skarsgård) and see he's been badly wounded. The people tending him want him out; it's dangerous with him in their home. The driver (Clive Owen) arrives in his BMW to get him across the border to safety. The situation is the problem and the driver comes to remedy it.

If you are working within the confines of a thirty-page screenplay, the set-up really ought to play out in the first five or six pages. If your movie is ten minutes (i.e., a screenplay length of ten to twelve pages), you need to establish your main conflict through the main exposition and inciting incident in the first couple of pages. The goal is to set your story in motion as quickly as possible.

THE RISING ACTION – DEVELOPING THE CONFLICT

Once the set-up is complete, the main action begins. In dramatic terms, this is called the rising action. The protagonist has expressed his want, the goal is clear and generally the conflict has been set up. The ensuing action is what the protagonist does to achieve his goal, the conflict he meets (as well as support), and how this action affects him along the way.

By definition, rising action requires an escalation of tension in the plot. We structure that escalation by using a variety of increasing conflicts confronting the protagonist. This keeps the story building and provides new developments to help flesh out the characters and the plot. If conflict doesn't build, the audience loses interest in the story. If the conflict isn't varied, a story will feel repetitive.

Before tension can really increase, we first must know what the character intends to do about the problem. Once the conflict is set in motion, the protagonist must respond to it in some way, and the audience must be able to understand reasonably well the character's intent in dealing with the problem.

The Plan

Once the problem has surfaced, the hero usually formulates a plan of action and starts implementing it. Often the protagonist's actions give us the indication of his plan. In *Life Lessons*, Lionel acts desperately to convince Paulette she must stay in New York. He promises her their romantic relationship is over and she won't have to sleep with him anymore, though by seeing how he looks at her we wonder how this will ever work out.

Action can communicate the protagonist's intent, but sometimes it isn't clear enough to fully orient the audience. A plan or simple declaration of what the character intends often finds its way into dialogue to help the audience understand the direction and meaning of the action. In *Life Lessons*, Lionel tells Paulette, and us, what he wants — for her to stay — in dialogue.

Plans may be conscious or unconscious, carefully thought-out or spontaneous. The "plan" also allows the audience to see how the protagonist initially grasps the conflict and anticipates the results. As the story progresses, the gap between the protagonist's anticipated results and reality (the main conflict) produces story surprise and leads to greater struggle. As the protagonist perseveres, he reveals his true character, and the audience gains insight into the meaning of the story.

In *Life Lessons*, Lionel's plan is arbitrary. He will say or do anything to convince Paulette to stay. He will plead, promise, lie, cajole, scare, threaten, whatever occurs to him in the moment he is confronted with her leaving. In *Mara of Rome*, Mara first decides she'll write the old woman a letter and tell her how she feels, but this won't do her much good. Later, after she and the old woman make peace, she makes a sacred vow and promises to help the grandmother convince Umberto to return to the seminary. In *Living in Oblivion*, Nick's plan can't be any more specific: to get his shot.

In films like *The Lunch Date* and *Election Night*, the protagonist's plans take the form of simple declarations so we know exactly what the characters are trying to do. In *The Lunch Date*, the protagonist tells the man she's bumped into "You're making me miss my train!" This lets us know, if we didn't already, that she's trying to catch a ride somewhere. In *Election Night*, Peter runs out of the bar declaring, "I have to vote!" and flags down a taxi. We know exactly what he's trying to do and how he's going to do it.

Obstacles

If the protagonist hasn't already encountered a true obstacle in the inciting incident, the rising action is the place where these obstacles come. An obstacle is the clearest form of conflict. It opposes the protagonist as he attempts to achieve his immediate or overall goal in the story. It stands in the hero's way. The best obstacles incite the most action from the protagonist and other characters, and once they become apparent should aim a direct threat at the protagonist achieving his goal. When obstacles are properly conceived and presented, they force the major characters to make decisions. Such decisions produce dramatic action. Dramatic action creates compelling stories.

Traditionally, obstacles are man, society, nature, and the character himself. But we can break them down a little more specifically and use the terms: antagonist, physical obstructions, inner or psychological obstacles, and mystic forces.

1. The Antagonist

The clearest obstacle is the antagonist. This character opposes the protagonist. The antagonist holds opposing goals to the protagonist's. Though not necessarily evil, this character personifies the protagonist's difficulties. Frequently, the antagonist initiates the protagonist's (and the drama's) crucial problem that engages the plot at the inciting incident.

The antagonist's primary function is to oppose the protagonist. In psychological terms, he may represent those everyday forces that keep heroes behind desks in jobs they hate instead of fighting the battles they should. In a sense, the antagonist represents a real break for the protagonist. At last our hero will fight. Keep this in mind when thinking about motivating your protagonist. What will get him to put on his gloves and fight? What will get her mad enough to draw the line in the sand?

Though a film can exist with only an inner problem or physical barrier as the main conflict for the hero, a specific antagonist lends clarity and power to the dramatic structure. The opposition of these characters clearly defines the conflict for the audience. The battle of wills influences the action, and because the characters counter each other, tension rises. It's not an inanimate object the protagonist faces but a person who consciously acts against him.

In *Life Lessons*, Paulette is the antagonist. She no longer loves Lionel nor wants him, and this conflicts directly with Lionel's desire for her. In *My Generation* (from *Strange Frequency*, written by Joseph Anaya, Steve Jones, Dale Kutzera and Dan Merchant and directed by Mary Lambert and Bryan Spicer), Bob (Eric Roberts) is an aging hippie and serial killer, cruising the rock festival circuit and preying on grungers he perceives as ruining rock music. His antagonist is a streetwise hitcher (Christopher Masterson) whose own goal is to rid rock of aging hippie-types — just like Bob. In *The Appointments of Dennis Jennings*, Dr. Schooner (Rowan Atkinson) is Dennis' antagonist. Dennis wants and needs help but the shrink isn't the least bit inclined to provide it.

2. Physical Obstructions

Physical obstructions are just what they sound like, anything physically preventing the hero from reaching or moving closer to his goal. These are concrete barriers the protagonist faces. Dangers such as river crossings, desert journeys, mountain climbs or urban jungles are all obstacles if they stand in the way of the protagonist moving toward a specific goal. A dead end at the end of an alley stopping the hero from pushing forward or a dead battery in a car that won't take the character where he wants to go both serve as obstacles.

A good obstacle forces the protagonist to take action, either to confront the obstacle straight on, or to take a different tack. In the Academy-Award winning short *Occurrence at Owl Creek*, based on the short story by Ambrose Bierce, written and directed by Robert Enrico, the gallows, river and Union soldiers are good examples of physical obstacles confronting the protagonist Peyton Farquhar. At the beginning he's about to be hanged. He wants to live but he's going to meet the end. The rope breaks and saves him from his fate, and this allows him to take action, swimming like hell to escape the soldiers on the bridge trying to stop him. But then he gets caught in the river's rapids and he must negotiate them. He does and winds up on a shore, only to realize the army is approaching, which forces him to run again.

3. Inner Obstacles

Inner obstacles are intellectual, emotional or psychological problems the protagonist must overcome before being able to achieve his goal. Fear, pride, and jealousy fall into this category. Lionel's jealousy in *Life Lessons* is an inner obstacle he needs to confront in his relationship with Paulette (or the energy of envy must be harnessed in another way). Teresa in *The Dutch Master* can't face the fear of her upcoming marriage. In *Franz Kafka's It's a Wonderful Life*, Kafka suffers from writer's block. In *The Appointments of Dennis Jennings*, Dennis' neuroses provide the conflict. In fact, we could understand the whole story as an outer experience of Dennis' inner fears and complexes.

These inner obstacles are often connected to what the character needs and oppose what the character wants. These are the aspects of the character he must deal with or overcome in himself in order to get what he wants.

4. Mystic Forces

Mystic forces were once seen as a way of describing appearances in theater of the gods and goddesses who controlled the fates of man from above. Today we use this category for obstacles coming from the paranormal and supernatural worlds because these can't be fully defined under the other headings.

Mystic forces can also enter stories as accidents or chance, as well as moral choices or ethical codes, which create obstacles for protagonists. In *Election Night*, Peter is faced with a moral conflict. He can keep his mouth shut and continue to the polls, or he can stand up for what he believes and get out of the cab.

Crisis

Each time a protagonist confronts an obstacle, he encounters a crisis, and a crisis is a definite point of conflict in the action. The action may be an attempt to reach a goal or capture a stake, but because there is an obstruction, the hero cannot prevail — at least at this moment. The screenwriter dramatizes a crisis because it creates tension until the immediate action is resolved. Because the ultimate outcome remains uncertain until the end, crises arouse suspense. Through this, viewers should be pulled deeper into the story, wondering what's going to happen and how the characters will prevail or not.

Dramatizing a crisis and how the characters respond to it helps define them as well as demonstrate their commitment to their goals. A crisis also necessitates decisions. The protagonist and antagonist must decide whether or not to fight, and if so, how to do it. Crises involve some combination of physical, verbal, emotional and intellectual activity on the part of one or more of the characters. A crisis can be a physical fight, a verbal argument or an introspective search.

Crises build crises, and these escalate and intensify the action until the climax is reached. As the confrontation is in progress, the outcome of the crisis is in doubt. *Life Lessons* is full of crises because Lionel and Paulette are in constant conflict. The first crisis arises when Paulette announces she is leaving and Lionel clearly wants her to stay. The next crisis is Paulette's personal one. After Lionel critiques her work and shaken what little confidence she had, she calls her mom and asks about coming home. This crisis is more muted, but difficult just the same.

Complications

Complications are factors that enter the world of the story and make things tougher for the protagonist. The strongest complications cause a change in the action. This means they enter the plot and divert the protagonist from pursuing his goal — temporarily. Complications differ from obstacles in that they don't pose an immediate threat to the protagonist achieving his goal; but they make it more difficult to attain. A great complication can become an obstacle later in the story.

Complications are a staple of feature films where they contribute to story extension, character development and surprises. They work best when they're unexpected, and add tension because we know they're taking the hero away from his real concern. Typically, complications arise in the form of a character, circumstance, event, mistake, misunderstanding or discovery.

In short films, because of time, we find more development around the obstacles a character faces than in complications. But if we look at a film like *Some Folks Call It a Sling Blade*, we see that the story is structured not so much with obstacles standing in Teresa's way of getting her story, but as a series of complications (the hospital administrator was expecting a man and doesn't think Carl will talk to a woman, no photos because Carl doesn't like to be photographed, etc.). These serve to annoy Teresa more than divert or prevent her from carrying on and getting what she came for.

In *Life Lessons*, you could look at the young men Paulette is attracted to as complications for Lionel. They don't stand in the way of him getting her — her feelings have already taken care of that — but they do make things harder for him because of how he feels about her. In *Mara of Rome*, Umberto is the complication that leads to the conflict Mara has with both the old grandmother and her client.

The Midpoint

The period of rising action can be the longest segment of the film and consequently liable to drag. A strong midpoint can make this section easier to manage, and keep it moving by focusing the action of the first half on whatever happens at this point. Here something significant happens that affects the protagonist. He might confront an obstacle he can't get around, or encounter a complication that turns the action in a new direction. But whatever happens here must have consequences, and these consequences will drive the action toward the main climax in the second half.

Action at a good midpoint surprises us. It might come in the form of an obstacle, reversal or complication; the dramatic problem might even appear solved, for the moment. In *Life Lessons*, the midpoint comes when Paulette's anger turns to awe as she

77

watches Lionel work, resulting in her decision to stay. As she reconsiders her decision to leave New York, Paulette tells us something about herself. It is Lionel's art, not the man that keeps her. Can that be enough to hold a woman to a man? This question leaves the climax in doubt.

In *Franz Kafka's It's a Wonderful Life*, Kafka overcomes his writer's block with creative inspiration — only to be overcome by guilt — at the midpoint, and the story proceeds in a completely unpredictable manner. In *Mara of Rome*, the grandmother comes to Mara's house to ask Mara to help stop Umberto from leaving the seminary. Before this scene, the two women are enemies. By the time the scene is over, they are friends. It reverses the direction of the story, at least temporarily.

Even in films under 10 minutes we often see expert use of the midpoint. In *PEEL*, the brother leaves the car to retrieve his son who's run off to appease his angry sister. However, he takes his car keys in a passive/aggressive action so she can't listen to the car radio, and in so doing further angers her.

In the Academy-Award nominated *Ernst And The Light*, written and directed by Anders Thomas Jensen, cleaning supply salesman Ernst is about the only person on the planet not to have noticed the worldwide appearance of light emanating from Denmark (his home country). On his way home to his wife after a business trip, he passes a hitchhiker twice before his car mysteriously stalls. The hitcher appears and Ernst agrees to give him a ride, and then miraculously his car starts up again. It turns out this is Jesus, returned, and he expects Ernst to be his first disciple. However, Ernst will have none of it, and thinks the guy is crazy. At the midpoint, he stops his car and tells the man he must get out. But Jesus miraculously disables his car and won't let him start it again until Ernst will accept that he's the Son of God. When Jesus starts the engine again, Ernst begrudging acknowledges the possibility of the savior's return. They start driving again, but Ernst now goes to work on Jesus and effectively convinces him people don't want to be saved any longer and there's no reason to return. The action of the first half is on Jesus convincing Ernst who he is; the action of the second is on Ernst convincing Jesus there's no need for him.

The Main Crisis

In order to reach the climax, the conflict must intensify and increase, causing the action to rise for the last time. The struggle between the protagonist and the antagonist comes out into the open. Now there must be a definite solution to the problem.

After the midpoint in *Life Lessons*, the conflict heats up again. Unable to leash his jealousy, Lionel embarrasses Paulette at a tony New York art party when another man shows interest in her. (Young men are Lionel's complications with Paulette, revealing his jealousy and insecurity — which are, in turn, obstacles Lionel faces.) To get even, she brings the man back to the studio and sleeps with him there, escalating the conflict. The audience wonders what Lionel will do? He paints, and paints with a vengeance.

Next Lionel apologizes and gives Paulette advice on how to handle the performance artist, Gregory Stark (Steve Buscemi), who dumped her at the beginning of the film. When she tries to retreat from her proposed plan and stay in to paint, Lionel admonishes her not to use her painting as an escape. "Your work is sacred," he says. So Lionel accompanies Paulette to see Stark's new piece at a club. Paulette's plan is to congratulate him and show him there are no hard feelings. She barely gets out a "hi" before other people interrupt and distract him. This only makes her feel worse and causes another crisis for Paulette. Lionel, trying to comfort her, declares his love again But she blames him for making her feel foolish and insignificant. She dares him to kiss a policeman to prove his love for her and then ditches him. Now he's the one who feels foolish.

Returning to his studio, Lionel finds Paulette making tea. Barely clad in a robe, she is clearly teasing him. The conflict now takes a dark turn: Lionel threatens her. He could rape her or murder her. He could do anything because "I'm nothing to you," he says. She only smiles, sphinx-like, and goes off to bed. Lionel throws himself back at his canvas.

The last straw comes when Paulette meets a girlfriend for a drink, coincidentally, in the same restaurant as Lionel and his art dealer. Who should present himself but Stark, the performance artist. He invites her to see his new show, the one she just saw.

Before she can respond, Lionel breaks in and tells the kid off, embarrassing Paulette again. She exits and Lionel punches Stark.

All of these incidents between the two characters dramatize their conflict. The scenes build to a breaking point, to the climax of the film.

THE CLIMAX & RESOLUTION

The climax is the highest, most exciting point in the drama. The conflict must finally be resolved, one way or the other. The climax involves a discovery or realization for the characters, or at least the audience. In film, the best climax is visual and emotional, not internal. It can be one scene or unfold over the course of several.

In *Life Lessons*, Lionel finds Paulette back at the studio. She is angrily knocking over her paintings. Apologetic yet again, Lionel tries to stop her. "Don't do that," he says. "Are you trying to punish me?"

"Am I punishing you?" she incredulously responds. He entirely misses the point; her actions are directed at herself. They have it out. Her frustration with her art and herself is what's fueling her crisis. His needs, demands, self-absorption are all secondary. "Am I good? Will I ever be any good?" she wants to know. And Lionel can't tell her. He confesses he is the problem; he indulges himself, his passion, his art. He melodramatically offers to give up painting for her and become a "nice person," asking pointedly if that's what she wants. This is the breaking point. Paulette screams she doesn't care what he does. She can't take it anymore. She's going home, and must threaten and physically drive him from her room.

In the next scene, Paulette comes in to say good-bye. Her brother has arrived to help her move out. She again watches Lionel paint, still clearly awed by it. If only he'd just once told her, she says, that she was a terrible painter and should get a job she might have believed he really cared for her. Lionel angrily spins from his work. "You think I just use people," he says. "Well, you don't know anything about me. You don't know how involved I get or how far down I go. Hell, I was married four times since before you were born, so don't you tell me."

Paulette backs away and leaves as Lionel angrily returns to his painting. He mumbles to himself about chippies. "You know why they call 'em that? Because they like to chip away at you, man. Take a little chip at your art form, at your talent. Chip, chip, chip." And then suddenly he realizes what he's said. More than anything else before, this reveals his feelings for Paulette and women in general.

The Resolution

At the end of the film is the resolution, the falling action. The problems not resolved in the climax are taken care here. This final part of the structure realigns the parameters of the screenplay's world as a result of the climax, fixing the fates of the main characters involved in the struggle, especially those the audience might be most interested in. The best resolution bestows a final insight or revelation on the story, which puts everything into context by elucidating the theme. All of this happens in the last couple of pages. In a very short film, the resolution need be one scene, or even only a part of one. More often than not, the resolution in a short film is included in the climax.

Life Lessons ends at Lionel's exhibition. It's clearly an event and his paintings are a big success. Even he is impressed and satisfied with the work. As he admires one of his paintings, he gets a glass of wine at the bar. A lovely young artist touches his arm for luck. As it turns out she is struggling to make ends meet. Smitten, he winds up offering her Paulette's job. In this final moment, the audience learns the whole affair with Paulette was "nothing personal" and Lionel is into the cycle again.

EXERCISES

Screen another short film. Look at the structural considerations first.

1. Identify the underlying concept, the story idea and the dramatic problem.
   a. Who is the protagonist?
   b. What does he or she want?
   c. How is this established?
   d. Where does the main problem (the conflict) stem from?
   e. How is it introduced (the inciting incident)?
   f. How long does it take for the problem to surface?
   g. Does the protagonist's need come into play in defining the conflict?

2. Does the main conflict escalate?
   a. What are the main obstacles the protagonist encounters?
   b. Are there external and/or internal obstacles for the protagonist?
   c. Does the protagonist face any complications? Do they impact the protagonist in a positive or negative way?
   d. Is there a distinct midpoint to the plot? What happens there? How does the action change or develop as a result of what happens? Is it a reversal?

3. Is there a main crisis?
   a. Is it fully realized in terms of the screenplay's basic conflict?
   b. Is the film's dramatic problem crystallized in the main crisis?

4. Does the main crisis lead to the climax?
   a. Is it the peak (strongest) emotional experience?
   b. Does the climax solve the film's dramatic problem?
   c. What happens to the protagonist as a result? Is he changed? Is someone?
   d. Does the climax sum up the meaning of the film?

5. Is the resolution a result of the basic conflict?
   a. Is it purposeful?
   b. Does it comment on the problem?
   c. What does it say?

6. Finally, what is the theme of your film?
   a. Has it been motivated by the central idea?
   b. Is it valid, true?
   c. Is this theme implicitly or explicitly stated?
   d. If it is implicit, how do we know it?

5

Plotting –
The Twists & Turns

Once you have an understanding of structure and the purpose of each section of the story, you can begin to think of the actual step-by-step plan for constructing the plot. Structure gives you the basic plan, the framework, but plotting is the real nuts and bolts construction of your story. It orchestrates the action and conflict, designs the sequences, and creates the story line so that the progression of events makes sense, builds suspense and moves your audience.

Constructing a believable, exciting plot is never easy. Plot isn't a complex structure that drops complete from thin air to the writer and then is handed over to a group of characters to act out. Plot develops as you turn the general theme and the characters into specific details — actions, dialogue, circumstances, time and place. Good plot evolves organically from the reaction of a particular character in a particular situation.

The plot of your story depends on the protagonist pushing the action forward, whether from her own design or as a reaction to the situation. *If the protagonist isn't committed to the drama, the audience can't commit to the story.* If the plot is a mere natural sequence of incidents, with no real orchestrated rising action, it'll be ineffective as well. The incidents may reveal your characters, but if they don't advance the plot a step further towards the crisis, if they don't lead to a big situation, they'll be of no dramatic value. Plot is made interesting by the obstacles standing in protagonist's way. The audience watches with anticipation, in suspense, waiting to see what the hero will do, if he'll succeed or fail. If the attainment of the goal is too easy or unrealistic, no one will care. But if the struggle is fierce and the suspense intense, the audience will feel satisfied at the end of the film.

The simplest form of plot is one in which the screenwriter places the protagonist in a predicament, keeps him there as long as suspense is maintained, and then extricates him in a surprising but logical way. This goes along with what the seasoned screenwriter once told the novice: "Get your protagonist up a tree, then throw rocks at him, and then get him down in a unexpected way." It's good advice, but keep in mind that in addition to the bare predicament, you must provide interesting and logical reasons for the character falling into the predicament, logical causes for his inability to get out, and finally a logical but unforeseen escape.

In the last chapter we discussed the overall structure of a short film, and illustrated various forms of conflict the protagonist can face. Now we focus on the process of selecting and ordering the scenes that develop the conflict and create the plot, the blueprint for the drama. But before we do, let's define exactly what we mean by "plot."

WHAT IS PLOT?

Many people confuse plot with story. Story, as defined in the *Concise Dictionary of Literary Terms*, is a sequence of events designed to interest, amuse or inform its audience. It doesn't need conflict or desire, but most stories make use of these factors to some degree.

Plot, however, refers to the overall organization of your material that makes it coherent and compelling. Creating a strong plot is dependent on three important factors. First, plot refers to the arrangement of events to achieve an intended effect. A plot is constructed to make a point, to reach a climax that produces a specific result at the end. It isn't a string of events that arrives at a simple conclusion. A plot is always aimed at the point it makes in the climax and resolution.

Second, plots are based on causally related events (and this is the basis of all plot construction as we'll see later in this chapter). It isn't "a" happens, then "b" happens, and then "c" happens. It's "a" happens and *causes* "b" to result, which in turn causes "c" and so on. These cause-and-effect relationships between the scenes are instrumental in creating continuity of action while also developing the conflict, characterizations and the overall meaning of the work.

Third, a plot must have enough conflict to awaken the audience's desire to see what happens next. Depending on the story, conflict can be strong or subtle — but there has to be enough to arouse your audience's interest. More importantly though, conflict can't just be conflict for its own sake; it must be significant to the characters to be meaningful to the audience.

Plot is a series of interrelated actions that progresses through a struggle of opposing forces to a climax and resolution that defines the meaning of the work. The use of such factors as conflict, suffering, discovery, reversal, tension, suspense, etc. in the plot's overall arrangement builds momentum and arouses curiosity. Films that don't have a clear plot often feel aimless. They seem like a mere sequence of events that never leads anywhere. Story is the starting point, but an effective plot made of scenes with strong cause and effect relationships is the goal.

Defining Your Plot

Sometimes your material gives you a plot almost ready made. More often, you need to create one where none exists. Once you know your protagonist and his goal, a good starting point is to establish exactly what forces are in conflict with him. Ask yourself, who is trying to accomplish or decide something? What does he wish to do? Who or what opposes the main character? Consider both internal and external forces. What will the result of the commitment, action, struggle be?

Next, determine the moment when conflict begins. This is the initial action or, as defined in the last chapter, the inciting incident. Then find the moment the character succeeds or fails in his effort: the climax. Both should grow from the character's basic nature and situation.

Now focus on the active moments in your material, the moments of conflict, change, growth, and discovery. These moments are usually the most dramatically significant. A clear understanding of them will help organize the material around the points which will be the most effective to emphasize. These are the moments that should be prolonged within the drama. It can be helpful to list possible scenes, but an actual scene-by-scene outline can be done later.

Think of your film in terms of broad blocks of movement. For example:

- A balanced situation (main exposition)
  - Some force unbalances the situation (inciting incident)
- The character's reaction (or his decision to act)
  - Consequences of the character's action's (obstacles & complications)
- Re-establishment of balance (main climax & resolution)
  or
- New Balance
  or
- Degeneration into chaos

Determine which scenes fall into which categories. Scenes that have to do with the initial conflict belong near the beginning. Scenes that dramatize the protagonist's struggle probably belong in the middle. Scenes that show growth or change in the character will most likely go in the second half of the story. The most dramatic crisis point undoubtedly relates to the climax that will then result in either the re-establishment of balance or the creation of a new balance or chaos.

This is only a general plan from which to work. Don't be afraid to change, reorganize or even delete scenes as you move ahead. Once a general plan is laid out, creating a more specific scene-by-scene outline of the plot will provide the connections between these broad story beats. Change and growth in the characters need to be shown. Complications, obstacles, surprises have to be incorporated into the line of action. Remember to always keep the conflict front and center in your mind.

THE ROLE OF CONFLICT

It should be obvious by now that conflict is integral to narrative driven filmmaking. Action in drama and fiction depends on it. Without conflict a story sits on the page (or screen) static, immobile, and the audience (reader or viewer) goes along for a little while but finally gives up on it because it hasn't kept their attention. Conflict engages the audience's initial interest by getting them to wonder what happens next with this problem? A film might be about the selflessness of true love, but unless it emphasizes a strong conflict for the characters to face, the audience isn't really going to care.

The role conflict plays in dramatizing a great story is not limited to engaging your audience's interest. Conflict plays a key role in revealing your character to the audience. As we mentioned in Chapter 3, a character reveals his true nature under the stress of conflict. It forces him to choose between the easy and the hard, and in his response his essential nature is shown. In *Life Lessons*, each time Lionel faces a conflict with Paulette over another man, his actions show him as desperate and capable of almost anything. In *Election Night*, Peter stands up to the racist tirades even though it gets him no closer to his ultimate goal. In *The Powder Keg*, Harvey, facing death, admits to regrets about his life. Conflict brings the characters face to face with reality and makes them show themselves.

Conflict also forces emotion out into the open. Again, from *Life Lessons*, Lionel's passions animate each scene, from one to the next making them rich and expressive. In *Election Night*, Peter's emotional responses motivate reactions that push the story toward its climax. In *The Powder Keg*, both Harvey and the driver respond to the looming threat with powerful emotions. These scenes come alive, becoming more intense and interesting. When characters express emotional reactions, the audience generally feels them too, creating a deeper connection between them. This strengthens the effect of the work as well as making for stronger scenes.

Positive & Negative Conflict Development

In order for conflict to really be effective, it has to develop and affect the protagonist and other characters. This means conflict can't be conceived as merely a series of hurdles your protagonist has to get over as she moves from her desire to her goal. Problems press down upon the protagonists making their journeys that much more difficult (and so more interesting). In *Election Night*, Peter has to get out of three cabs before he decides just to try to make it on foot to the polling place. All three racist taxi drivers succeed in driving him off; he doesn't overcome any of them in his quest to vote. This drives up the tension level — we ask how will he ever succeed?

In most stories we see conflict developing both positively and negatively for the protagonist. In *Life Lessons*, Lionel convinces Paulette to stay, but she won't sleep with him anymore (a positive result and a negative one). Then it looks as if he's driven her away with his inability to mentor her (negative), until she reconsiders after watching him paint (positive). He tries to get her away from the young artist at the birthday party, but drives her right to him; she flaunts the younger man to Lionel by bringing him home and sleeping with him in front of Lionel (negative again).

When conflict develops positively and negatively, it makes it less likely that the audience can predict how the film is going to end. They can't assume the hero will definitely prevail in the end because his track record to that point involves obstacles that he hasn't completely hurdled. If every obstacle were easily surmounted, there'd be no real tension in your film. (Even a simple, *Forrest Gump*-type character who seems to prevail through little more than good luck must face obstacles that cause us to doubt his success.) An audience that assumes a character can deal with anything may not wait around for your climax, however nuanced it is. Negative outcomes create tension that casts doubt on whether the hero can succeed, and keep endings less predictable.

Failure as Teacher

Negative outcomes do something else in addition to creating suspense and hiding the ending. They set up incidents of failure. Failure can be a terrific teacher for your protagonist, just as it is for real-life characters. (Even business magazines like *Fortune* and *Forbes* sing the praises of those who successfully manage failure and learn from it.) Failure demands examination. If we're committed to our goals, but have trouble reaching them, we must examine everything in our lives to figure out how we can succeed — or we have to reexamine our goals. Something is going to have to give.

Your protagonist's failure to hit his goals can either defeat him or force him to change in ways that allow him to grow and succeed in his quest. How he changes — grows or disintegrates — deepens your characterization of him, as well as creating surprise twists and developing your film's theme.

Using failure to propel change or growth is commonplace in feature screenwriting. In shorts, we often see that the protagonist doesn't change: i.e., Lionel in *Life Lessons* or the brother and sister in *PEEL*. In these cases, the characters' failures force changes on others or in their situations. (And of course they bring about a change in us, the audience, as we learn about these characters.) In *Life Lessons*, Paulette changes and leaves, and Lionel's art is successful. In *PEEL*, the siblings move from driving home to being stuck on the side of the road with no compromise in sight. In other shorts, change is pronounced. In *Election Night*, Peter is completely changed by the end of the film, going from believing in change to someone who's learned it's impossible (or at least, that he won't be the one to change things). In *Franz Kafka's It's a Wonderful Life*, Kafka learns he has friends after all.

As your protagonist encounters the challenges in the story, especially the crises that don't turn his way, ask yourself how they affect him. What are the emotional consequences as well as the real world cost (i.e., affect on the plot)? Then look for ways you can *show* these results in the action of the story.

Unity of Opposites

Most films describe a conflict between characters — the protagonist and antagonist — although this is not always the case. Conflict can arise from an external situation or inner problems. But when conflict develops between a protagonist and antagonist it works best when the characters are locked together with no compromise possible between them. We refer to characters locked in a zero sum game as the unity of opposites. Such unity quite obviously helps create a strong rising conflict. The characters have purpose and strong convictions, and will fight for what they want. The more evenly matched they are, the stronger the battle and the more suspenseful the outcome.

Strong unity of opposites depends on how the characters are locked together in conflict. Characters may simply have the same goal, and only one can win. Family relationships keep conflicting characters in constant association through love, need, and geographical location. Love can also bring ostensible opposites together, until their shadow personalities emerge (*True Lies*; *I Walked With A Zombie*). Try to make the unity (what binds the characters together) as specific as possible to understand what fuels the conflict and what must give or change in the characters in order for them to find a resolution.

If the conflict of your story revolves around a situation, or the antagonist is a force and not a person, find a way to personalize the obstacle for the protagonist. A clash of man against nature can be translated into a personal conflict only if the audience understands that nature presents or objectifies a challenge the protagonist has set for himself. You need to know what the force represents to the character. It is not a conflict between man and nature or man and beast, but a struggle going on within the man himself. When the nature of the conflict is clear, a strong unity of opposites can be achieved in this situation, too.

In *The Old Man and the Sea*, adapted from the Ernest Hemingway script by Peter Viertel, the old man is striking back at the encroachments of age, and catching the fish is his only way he can. In *The Macomber Affair*, adapted from another Hemingway story by Casey Robinson and Seymour Bennett, Macomber is really fighting his own fear — not a lion. In these stories, and the films made from them, both men are fighting weaknesses within themselves. The fish and lion are creative dramatic devices for telling the story in terms of action.

Types of Conflict

In film conflict doesn't always mean physical violence. Audiences often relate far more quickly to emotional conflict than to physical violence because we've all experienced emotional friction in our own relationships. Very few adults have escaped life with no emotional scars. In the short film based on another Hemingway short story, *Hills Like White Elephants*, adapted by Joan Didion and

John Gregory Dunne and directed by Tony Richardson, from the eponymous Hemingway story, the emotional conflict escalates to a heart-wrenching recognition for the protagonists that is sure to be the source of pain for both for a long time to come, yet nothing physically untoward occurs in the film.

Obviously, physical violence makes for good drama, too, because it's a strong representation of the meeting of uncompromising positions. Film will always rely on violence to tell many stories just as dreams often use violence to get attention and illustrate their messages. In many successful feature films and shorts (*Occurrence at Owl Creek*, *The Red Balloon*, *The Appointments of Dennis Jennings*), physical violence is an intricate part of the story and its success. It is more important, though, in a short film for the violence to have a point. Because there's so little time, violence that doesn't directly serve the story will appear all the more gratuitous.

Conflict Rises in Waves

To be effective in constructing a plot, conflict needs to rise in waves. Along the way there are temporary cease-fires or "fixes," but they can't last. *Life Lessons* careens from one temporary solution to another. The first crisis arises when Paulette announces she's leaving and clearly Lionel doesn't want her to go. Lionel solves his problem, convincing Paulette to stay by swearing she won't have to sleep with him anymore. This seems to work until Lionel won't really tell her how he really feels about her own art. This sends Paulette reeling, and it looks as though she's headed for home for sure. But she gets caught up in watching him paint, and reaffirms her commitment to art.

These short-term solutions just prolong the audience's arrival at the moment of final confrontation with the antagonist. Delaying the confrontation can build tension, but also allows the writer to fill in important details about the main characters. These details help define the audience's relationship to the characters. A plot deepens and grows by including scenes that dramatize the main characters' reactions to the plot's events. As with real relationships in life, we need time to understand the allies we have and the foes we face.

Possibilities, Probabilities & Necessity

When the conflict is properly conceived and handled, the drama has a better chance of fulfilling the audience's expectations. Not because we're able to predict the outcome, but because the inevitability of the conclusion feels true to us. At the beginning of a screenplay, anything is possible. But after the first scene, the possibilities of what can happen become increasingly limited. Once the beginning defines a specific situation, group of characters and conflict, the screenwriter leaves the realm of the possible and enters the realm of the probable. The characters must follow one or more lines of probability in reaction to the conflict as the plot unfolds so that, by the end, the screenwriter is limited to only what is necessary. Because the characters have said and done specific things, there can be only one necessary resolution.

This doesn't mean the climax is inevitable from the start. A good writer constructs a plot that gets the audience asking what will happen next and what the final outcome will be. The plot must appear as though it's changing directions to keep the audience guessing. Otherwise, the audience loses interest. (How many times have you heard "predictable" as a put-down of a movie?)

As the protagonist faces obstacles and complications, he must alter his course. New characters bring new possibilities to the plot. Psychological transformations can alter the action. Missed opportunities, misunderstandings, failures — all can cast doubt on the story's outcome. Some of the best surprises in films come from the transformation of character. A character changes or grows to do something right or to do something wrong, and in so doing affects the outcome of the film. It's the screenwriter's job to incorporate and orchestrate these changes into the action of the film so the audience will accept them.

Problems with the ending of a script generally don't indicate trouble with one or two final scenes, but a plot that's disintegrated — and characters that are not logically realized — far before that. Audiences often leave a theater saying they liked a film but didn't like the ending. As screenwriters you must know how to avoid problematic endings through effective plotting long before the final scenes.

THE PRINCIPLES OF ACTION

Once conflict has been conceived, it has to be set in motion. We use the protagonist and his wants and goals to push the action forward to the climax and resolution of the story. But as the action and conflict move forward to create basic momentum and tension, a good story needs scenes that reveal why this story is happening, what's at stake for the characters, what the conflict means to them and the consequences of taking action. All this has to be orchestrated into a meaningful whole for the audience without slowing the drama.

The principles of action describe three sets of scene relationships that help us weave all these threads of the story together. All great plots are based on the laws of causality. One action causes another and this causes another and so on. The audience sees the relationships between scenes, draws conclusions about the meaning of it all, and follows along. This is what creates real narrative momentum.

Screenwriters build strong causal relationships through:

1. Cause and Effect relationships between scenes
2. Rising Conflict (attack and counterattack)
3. Foreshadowing Conflict

Cause & Effect Scene Relationships
(Action & Reaction)

Each scene should advance the action and cause a reaction in the following scene. The language of drama depends on this: that we see the cause and the effect to understand what's going on. Since the protagonist's overall story goal is not resolved until the end of the film, we are dramatizing the pursuit of that goal and what happens as a result of it along the way. The successful plot doesn't focus solely on the scenes showing the active pursuit of the goal or the points of active conflict between the antagonists. It also includes the *reaction* of the main characters, especially the protagonist, to the obstacles, complications and crises, the losses and even successes, he or she encounters. By showing characters' reactions to the conflict, the audience is better able to identify with them through their own emotional responses to what's happening.

Irwin Blacker said in *The Elements of Screenwriting*, "Plot is more than a pattern of events; it is the ordering of emotions." Cause and effect scene relationships allow you to show these emotional reactions within the parameters of the plot. Without dramatizing the emotional side of the story, films lose dimension. If a plot is all action and no emotion, it winds up melodrama, and the audience will be less likely to fully embrace it. A plot pushed by action and not by characters' emotions uses characters as puppets to be manipulated. Director Sidney Lumet said in *Making Movies*, "Drama is when characters move the plot; melodrama, when plots move characters." Cause-and-effect plotting will naturally lead you to characters moving the plot, because emotions build and force action more realistically than one arbitrary action that gives rise to another.

In *Life Lessons*, the relationship between the scenes is masterfully handled. Sequences built on actions and reactions that keep the film focused and moving ahead. Let's look at one example: after Paulette reconsiders her plan to leave New York and extracts a promise from Lionel that she won't have to sleep with him, the writer escalates the conflict again in a different manner. A new sequence begins by showing Lionel critiquing Paulette's paintings. Full of self-doubt, Paulette wants more than anything for someone, Lionel, to tell her if she is any good. The one thing Lionel is incapable of lying about is art. Art is about having to do it; it's not a choice. And she is, after all, still young. All his pussy-footing around further frustrates Paulette. As Lionel leaves the scene, he kicks himself for what he's said, showing his reaction to the increased anxiety he knows he's caused her.

The scene that follows shows Paulette's reaction: in tears, she phones her mother and asks if she can come home. We see her pain, her frustration, while in the background Lionel's music blasts Bob Dylan's "Like a Rolling Stone." The scene helps us empathize with Paulette since most of us have felt pain, frustration and self-doubt. Next, Paulette marches into the studio, angry about the music, about everything, yelling to get his attention. Lionel's unbreakable concentration at the canvas forces her to view the painting taking shape underneath his masterful brushstrokes. In her face we watch her anger melt away and awe replace it. She is not in awe of Lionel the person, but Lionel the artist.

In the film's next scene, the two of them get ready for a party, acting like an old married couple. This scene, which is the beginning of a new sequence, is also the end of the previous one. We learn here that Paulette's response to Lionel's art is to reverse herself and continue working for him. Writer Richard Price wastes no time with a separate scene for Paulette's story point. He lets the audience put two and two together, and keeps the plot moving ahead as he now gets ready for the next section of the story.

All good stories concern themselves with the characters' emotional responses to the action. Good writers know they must show this side of the story to keep the audience relating to the material. It helps us to understand the characters' motivations and to feel empathy for them. As you construct your plot, remember to incorporate scenes showing the important characters' responses to the main story points. The questions to ask yourself as you plot with a cause-and-effect approach are: what would my character feel as a result of what has just happened and, what would he do then?

Rising Conflict

Rising conflict is also based on causal scene relationships. We distinguish this type of cause-and-effect plotting from mere action and reaction by the nature of the conflict. Rising conflict entails attack and counterattack. We see this when characters battle each other, most often during the second half of the story. The attacks and counterattacks must become increasingly more serious and threatening to the protagonist as the story progresses. As the attacks and counterattacks escalate they lead directly to the last crisis and climax. Real tension results from a strong rising conflict when the antagonists are evenly matched as well as locked together.

In *PEEL*, the film begins with the sister and brother already in conflict. The sister's first line of dialogue from the back seat of the car is a subtle jab at her brother.

"If you don't want other people's opinions, don't ask for them," she says. Silence, except for the boy's bouncing of the orange off the windshield. She continues: "It was a really scrappy bit of land... that's my opinion." At first, the brother does not reply, but tension permeates the car. The boy begins peeling the orange and dropping the skin out the window. His father (the brother) responds by telling the boy not to do it. The boy ignores him and keeps dropping pieces of peel. This is still action and reaction.

The sister asks the boy for a piece of orange and he screams "NO!" He jams the orange onto his finger. This becomes too much for the father. He slams on the brakes and orders the boy out of the car to pick up every piece of peel he's dropped. The boy refuses. "We're not leaving here until you pick up every piece of peel on the highway," the father says. Father and son stubbornly stand their ground while, in the car, the sister stews because she wanted to be home by five. The father tries once more, admonishing the boy that he had better do it. Still, the boy refuses, now gesturing defiantly as if to throw the orange at his father. It's a puny attack from a pint-sized aggressor, but an attack just the same. His father angrily counterattacks by throwing the car into gear and driving straight at the boy! He stops as the bumper rubs up against his son's knees! Now the boy hurls the orange at his father. It splatters against the windshield with a smack, and the boy runs off.

Jane Campion wastes no time building the conflict. She starts in the middle of it, employing a clear attack and counterattack formula. The tension created grabs the audience and makes them pay attention.

At the beginning of the second half of *Life Lessons*, writer Price establishes Lionel's stature in the art world at the birthday party with Lionel recounting a clearly often told story about how he became an artist. As he tells the tale, he sees a young man take an interest in Paulette. Jealousy flashes as he rushes to discover who the young man is. Lionel whisks Paulette away into the bathroom. "People are laughing at you," he tells her, clearly on the attack. He lies about the young man's intentions, which only relieves Paulette's anxiety and makes her laugh. She thought he was going to tell her they were laughing at her because of her work. Lionel thinks his point is considerably worse. Stung, Paulette tries to leave, but Lionel won't let her out of the bathroom. He leaves first, and stands against the door, barring her exit. The next scene shows Lionel in a group singing "Happy Birthday" to the host as Paulette grabs the artist and flaunts her exit in Lionel's face. This is her counterattack. Lionel returns home and hears their voices ringing from her room. He turns up the stereo and plunges into his painting.

In *My Generation*, Bob goes on the attack at the midpoint when he decides to knock off his grungy hitchhiker Todd. Only Todd counters the move by revealing he has a similar agenda and he goes after Bob first. The two battle trying to kill each other until interrupted by another traveler who turns the plot in a new direction.

Foreshadowing the Conflict

To foreshadow means to show, indicate or suggest something beforehand. In film or fiction, when we foreshadow conflict, we are letting the audience know it's coming. Foreshadowing, too, is based on causality; but it's different from simple cause-and-effect scene relationships and rising conflict because the effect of the foreshadowing isn't felt until later in the film or story. Since there's little time to waste in a short film, foreshadowing isn't as readily employed as the other forms of conflict in the plot because the writer needs to pin down the problem as soon as possible.

Nevertheless, foreshadowing does appear in short films, most often in the setting up of opposing characters. At the beginning of *The Man in the Brooks Brothers Shirt*, the young writer sits in a full lounge car, reading her book and talking with other travelers. She has an amusing, cynical manner. Along comes a businessman who quickly clears the car with his clearly ribald attitude. Only the young woman remains, now happy to be alone with her book, a political treatise *The Coming Struggle*. The businessman, though, sets his sexual sights on her, and none of her sarcasm or put-downs can dissuade him from his pursuit. This foreshadows a rising conflict between the characters. It makes the audience ask, "What's going to happen next?"

At the beginning of *Words*, we meet the young orthodox priest Father Kiril with an older priest. After some initial exposition, they walk past a group of children playing war with turtles inside a ring of wood. The two priests enter their church and as they start their prayers with their brethren, writer/director Milcho Manchevski cuts back to the children lighting the ring on fire. Intercutting with the priests chanting their prayers, a child discovers a box of live ammunition and empties the shells into the flames. The kids run for cover, and we cut back to the church, waiting for the gunfire and hoping no one is hurt. This action foreshadows the anarchic world these men live in.

In *My Generation*, we know Bob is a serial killer from the start. We see his collection of hitchhiking signs from his victims in the trunk of his car. When we meet Todd and learn he's on the road following some band's tour, and then see him with his sign, we know he's Bob's next victim.

Foreshadowing can be humorous. *Anna of Milan*, written by Cesare Zavattini and Billa Billa, and directed by Vittorio De Sica, opens with a point-of-view shot through the windshield of a Rolls Royce as someone drives around the streets of Milan. We hear the driver's voice, a wealthy, married socialite wearily recounting all of her obligations for the day and week. As she drives along, she runs stops signs and stoplights, barely misses pedestrians crossing the street. She draws incredulous looks from street corners. When she makes her rendezvous with her romantic interest, a handsome writer who gets out of tiny two-door Fiat, the audience knows he's in for trouble.

Mara of Rome utilizes the same trick. It begins by contrasting the virginal young seminary student and lovely, sensual, clearly sexually active Mara.

Other ways to foreshadow conflict are to show the audience obstacles lying ahead of your hero. In *The Powder Keg*, as the driver speeds away from their pursuers, the filmmakers cut ahead to a border crossing and focus on a stop sign, clearly signaling that they will be forced to stop up ahead. This creates tension because we don't want the pursuers to catch up, and we know that Harvey is in grave danger.

Another way to foreshadow conflict is in how characters respond to events. Again from *The Powder Keg*, Harvey suddenly tells the driver he must make sure his film gets to his newspaper. When the driver refuses, saying Harvey will deliver the film himself, the photographer throws his film onto the front seat, along with dog tags for his mother. His action clearly indicates he doesn't think he's going to make it, and the seriousness of the situation elevates even more.

EXERCISES

Think of your film's story in broad blocks of movement. What is the original situation and what upsets it? How does the protagonist react? What does she decide to do? What are the consequences of the protagonist's action? How does she react? Where does this action lead? Write the sequence down in a beat sheet. (A beat is a story point made in a scene or a scene sequence that moves the plot ahead.)

Now set these main beats aside for a day or two to get some distance on them. When you come back to them, contemplate the beats in terms of the rising action, focusing on the cause and effect relationships between scenes along with the rising conflict. How does a precipitating action cause a reaction that escalates the conflict to a point where it must be resolved? Try and see a clear line of action between the inciting incident and the climax.

Now return to the exercises at the end of Chapter Three. Using these as a guide, begin to map out a broad, overall story plan. The story tools described in Chapter Three should help create this plan. A thirty-minute film will probably have a movement of seven or eight main beats from start to finish. This will translate into roughly 15 to 20 separate scenes, depending on your writing style. If, for a thirty-minute film, your outline is over 25 scenes, you probably have too much material. But don't worry about it now. As we look in greater detail at the beginning, middle and end of a short film in the next chapters, you can improve and refine your plot.

PART TWO

INTERMEDIATE STEPS

6

Fade In: Openings &
The Main Exposition

Finding the best opening for any movie can be frustrating. It must be visual, convey important information, and be interesting if not arresting. It's almost always problematic deciding how much exposition is necessary, and when and how to convey it. In a short film, with no time to waste, it can be maddening to try and get a compelling opening and then into the main exposition without squandering valuable seconds. To justify inclusion in the screenplay, every word, every image, every scene must advance the story toward its conclusion. And because of the abridged time, anything superfluous to the conflict tends to derail the film.

In my experience I find many short films suffer from an inadequate opening, getting off to a shaky start that's hard to recover from. In these cases, the filmmakers don't understand their story well enough to know how to set up a cohesive work; instead, they launch what is merely a sequence of events. Because the opening is ineffective in the script stage, the filmmakers try to address the problem in the editing room. Sometimes creative editing can save them; most of the time, however, story problems at the opening can't be resolved. What's happened is this: the filmmakers never spent enough time considering the elements — theme, conflict, wants — that needed to be set up in these beginning pages.

How do you come up with a terrific opening? Start with a problem.

THE PROBLEM

Every great film revolves around a problem for the protagonist and other characters. This problem helps define the action and framework for the story, gives it direction and unity. This problem can be subtle or overt, physically violent or emotional, but it must be apparent and affect the characters and their world. From films like *Life Lessons* to *The Lunch Date*, problems are apparent at the start and then develop with the conflict. In great films, short or long, this problem doesn't just define the action but also the theme. It's incredibly important to understand this, yet time and again writers avoid focusing on the opening problem, and the result is a story crippled from the get-go.

To create unified action the audience can follow, you must know what the *main conflict* is. Other conflict can exist in the film (and should, if the film is over six or seven minutes). But if you have several problems of equal importance in a short, your audience won't know where to focus. The main conflict needs to be apparent, and if there are other conflicts, they should play a subsidiary role.

Sometimes a writer neglects the main conflict because the protagonist's problem isn't apparent in the external action, even if there are obstacles for her to overcome. The trouble might be that the problems remain separate, discrete, and never add up to unify the action and theme. If so, the film won't satisfy the audience. This failure often occurs when writers use a protagonist's internal conflicts as the driving force (without knowing how to externalize them). You need to discover the true underlying internal problem facing your character, and find a way to illustrate and foreshadow this problem in the action so the audience can understand the meaning of the conflict.

Once you can articulate the main conflict, you know your opening must build to exposing it. The question now is how best to get there?

Every great short film is unique in how it assembles its scenes into a line of action. But understanding the function of the main exposition and inciting incident will help you master this task.

THE MAIN EXPOSITION

In Chapter 4 we defined the main exposition as whatever is primary and vital for the audience to know about the protagonist and her problem — and that can't be shown. Why can't it be shown in a short film? The main reason is time. Dramatizing the main exposition would postpone getting to the main conflict, which is what really starts the story.

A great short opens as close to the introduction of the main conflict as possible to grab the audience's attention. Frequently, good writers formulate the main exposition before choosing the opening images. But many beginning writers (of both features and shorts) feel the need to tell much more than is necessary about their protagonists before starting the story. The discipline of writing a short screenplay before a feature can help a writer avoid the common temptation to fully establish the protagonist before presenting the dramatic problem. Nothing insures an aimless feel to an opening sequence more than telling us everything about the protagonist before the conflict commences. It is the purpose of the *entire* screenplay and film to show us who the character is. At the beginning, all we need is a hint. The audience sits up to pay attention at the main conflict, not at a character biography.

The main exposition defines setting and tone, introduces the main characters and their central relationships, presents or initiates the conflict, and makes clear whatever is not self-explanatory, but necessary to understand. If there's humor in the screenplay, the exposition should be funny — aim for an out loud laugh on page one. The main exposition needs to come early and fast. If the audience isn't quickly oriented to these aspects of the film they won't be able to follow the story well. Less important details can be spread throughout the film.

Main exposition can be handled in various ways. The Greek chorus is the classic method, directly communicating to the audience the background of the story so they can follow the plot. Shakespeare occasionally employed a prologue that was read to the audience, or had a character soliloquize the exposition. The Victorian butler and maid giving us the play's main exposition at the curtain rise is now passé, but filmmakers, especially those making shorts, need the same kind of immediate exposition. If you're making a parody, you can consider using the butler and maid; otherwise consider these examples.

Narration

Voice-over narration is more common in short films than features. A narrator can express the necessary information quickly and directly. Because the film is so short, this form of exposition is more readily accepted than in a feature.

In *Ray's Male Heterosexual Dance Hall*, the protagonist is the narrator who begins the story by introducing his problem.

```
FADE IN:

BIG BAND MUSIC

CAMERA MOVES DOWN A TALL OFFICE BUILDING...

We hear the voice of Sam Logan, early thirties...

                    SAM V/O
          I used to feel I was a part of
          those office buildings. After
          all, I once had an office there.
          Okay, I didn't have an office
          with a view. But I was headed
          for a view. A good view...

AND THE CAMERA SETTLES ON A NEARBY PARK - NOON

SMALL CHILDREN play. OLD PEOPLE sit. BLUE and WHITE
COLLAR WORKERS, walk in a brisk and leisurely clip.
OTHER WORKERS sit on benches, the ground and
blankets eating their lunches.

THE CAMERA FINDS:

SAM LOGAN on a bench -- mid-thirties, a suit and
tie, feeds some peanuts to some PIGEONS. He casually
watches an ATTRACTIVE WOMAN pass.
```

```
              SAM V/O (CONT'D)
     That of course was all before
     Fabtex, the company I worked for
     became WellPeck and left me out
     of a job.
```

Out of work, Sam needs to find a good job. He starts with a problem that is clearly spelled out. With the arrival of an old friend, the story is set in motion. Sam's narration continues, providing humorous commentary on what he encounters.

On-screen narrators can also appear. Rod Serling opened *The Twilight Zone* on screen ("Consider if you will..."), disclosing fundamental information needed to understand the problem and begin the story. Serling's style of exposition was originally an inventive twist to the introductions given by off-screen announcers on many of the old anthology television series.

On screen narration is taken to its zenith in the film *The Dutch Master*. Multiple narrators tell the story on screen and off, talking directly to the audience. The film begins on a man's open mouth in a dental chair. The narration starts as the camera pans over x-rays, dental equipment in the sterile office, until it finally introduces us to Teresa, an attractive dental hygienist.

"We've known Teresa for like what, six years?" a woman says over the images.

"Longer," answers another unseen woman

"And I'm telling you, it just wasn't like her."

"Not at all."

The dialogue/narration sets up an undisclosed problem, but we know it's there. As the two women relate their story, the action shows the three friends and fellow dental hygienists doing what they usually do, getting lunch and hurrying across the street to the steps of the Metropolitan Museum of Art to eat. Then the action shifts to the two narrators, sitting on the steps of the museum and eating hot dogs. Teresa is missing. Dorothy and Kim address the audience through the camera as it hovers before them like an old friend.

"We eat here practically every day," says Dorothy, right to the camera. "Unless, of course it was raining, then we'd go back and eat in Dr. Roserman's office but he would always complain about

Teresa's chili and onions, saying the smell was bad for business. Then one day, it must have been four weeks ago, for no apparent reason, Teresa says she wants to go inside."

On screen we see Teresa enter the museum alone. She wanders about and we see her find a painting by a Dutch master that fascinates her. About three or four minutes into the movie we learn through the voiceover narration that Teresa's about to get married and is acting strangely. As the story continues, more characters are introduced, each adding his or her particular view of events. The only character who never utters a word is Teresa. By contrasting Teresa's actions with others' accounts of events, the filmmakers illustrate how little each knows or understands her. Teresa's actions are our only clue to what is going on with her.

Written Presentation

I am a personal fan of using a written presentation for all or part of the main exposition. Think of *Star Wars* without its beginning crawl about a galaxy "far, far away." What a written presentation does is immediately make your viewer an active participant with your work. The audience must sit up and *read* what's being shown on the screen. It makes them pay immediate attention to what's going on, rather than allowing them to sit back and wait for the film to engage them.

In *PEEL*, Jane Campion uses a written presentation of the main exposition. Cards appear on the screen, intercut with opening credits and shots of a highway flashing by. All are punctuated by the sound of the radio or highway noise. The first card appears:

AN EXERCISE IN DISCIPLINE

Road signs swish by, then the title flashes in big bold letters that fill up the screen.

After another flashing shot of the highway and a list of the players, a card identifying the characters and representing the relationships between them appears:

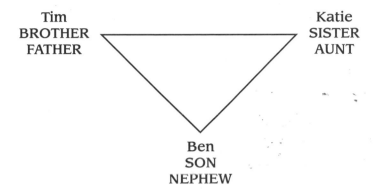

Another highway shot speeds by, and the final card comes up:

A TRUE STORY/A TRUE FAMILY

The film, which is under ten minutes, gives us the necessary information in less than a minute. Because the cards flash by so quickly, the effect is almost subliminal. But the cards waste no time, allowing the story to speed ahead into the main conflict.

Written information orients the audience to what's happening on screen quickly and efficiently. If a film isn't working because the audience is confused and can't glean necessary information about the story from the opening scenes, the judicious use of a card or two can bring everything into focus. But too often cards are used as a last resort when a production needs saving in the editing room, instead of being incorporated as a story tool at the script stage.

Visual Dramatization

Occurrence at Owl Creek beautifully presents a visual dramatization of the initial information. The film opens with the camera moving over a burnt-out landscape before dawn. It lingers for a moment on a sign hammered to a tree trunk:

> ORDER
> ANY CIVILIAN
> CAUGHT INTERFERING WITH
> THE RAILROAD BRIDGES
> TUNNELS OR TRAINS WILL BE
> SUMMARILY HANGED
> THE 4TH OF APRIL, 1862

Though a written presentation, the sign is only part of the main exposition. It serves to establish the time. A subsequent group of images establish the place.

As a low roll on a drum sounds, an owl hoots, a bugle calls, a Union officer stands on a bridge barking orders. Nearby, a sentinel watches with his rifle. This sets the film's time; it takes place during the US Civil War.

We know time and place, but the exposition is not complete. We do not yet know our protagonist or his conflict.

Union riflemen march across the bridge and come to attention before the officer. A sergeant carries a length of rope to a bearded man in civilian clothes who stands at the edge of the bridge, face beaded with sweat. His fine clothes indicate he is a gentleman. His gentle, expressive face contrasts with those of the harsh Union soldiers. Hands and feet are tied. The sergeant efficiently loops the rope into a hangman's noose and tightens the knot. Soldiers push the prisoner onto a plank suspended over a rushing river. As the sergeant secures the noose around the prisoner's neck, the man gasps and looks wildly about.

The conflict is fully established. What will happen to the man? Will he escape? Will someone come to his rescue? The entire opening gives all that is necessary to begin the thirty-minute film in less than five minutes. No names, no dialogue to speak of, only a series of powerful images, heightened by the soundtrack, that leads to the terrifying problem the condemned man faces.

The Lunch Date presents its exposition in the form of action. The first shot shows us we're in Grand Central Station and it focuses on an older woman making her way through the crowd.

Shots of the schedule board, letting us know this is about people in motion. Some homeless men are also spotlighted as part of the background. But we know nothing about the woman except her clothes and demeanor, and they say she's well to do. As she makes her way through the station, she collides with a black man and drops her bags. He tries to help her but she insists he not — which mystifies him. He tries again and she announces, "You're making me miss my train!"

This tells us exactly what she's trying to do, make a train. She finally rushes off with her hands still full and, sure enough, she misses it. While stuffing objects back in her purse she notices her wallet is missing — we only see her frantically start searching her things and realize this is what must be gone. Now the woman has a problem that will develop as the story progresses in a surprising way.

Exposition in Dialogue

Many films use scenes with dialogue to convey parts of the main exposition. The reason is obvious. Sometimes words are the best way to express what needs to be told. In *Life Lessons*, after the initial opening establishes artist and studio, the story starts with the sound of the elevator bell. In contrast to the disheveled artist we have seen, a neatly groomed man rides up in the cage. He is art dealer Philip Fowler, here to see Lionel's new work.

"There's nothing to see, it's the emperor's new clothes, I'm gonna get slaughtered," Lionel croaks, refusing to let Philip out of the elevator. Philip tries to get Lionel to come to lunch, presumably to loosen him up, but Lionel says he must pick up his assistant at the airport. "I don't know why she can't take a cab like everyone else," the artist confesses. After a pause, Philip proceeds delicately, inquiring when he will be able to return and see the work. "The show's in three weeks, you know," he says softly. Panic flares in Lionel's eyes and he hits the switch that sends Philip down the chute. "Ah, Lionel," says Philip in exasperation. "Lionel! You go through this before every show! I'm talking twenty years of this! Now get to know yourself a little better, Lionel!"

By the end of this scene, we know about the impending art show and Lionel's assistant. So far, we have half of the important information to begin the story, all given in one scene. What makes the scene work well is the conflict, already established between the two men. Their common history, including the coming exhibition, is their back-story. The art dealer who wants in the studio and the panic-stricken artist keeping him prisoner in the elevator dramatize their opposition.

The next scene reveals the second key piece of the main exposition: Lionel's assistant, with whom he has been having an affair, is leaving New York. The romance is over. Lionel doesn't want her to go. His dramatic problem is how to keep her in Manhattan and prepare for his upcoming show.

THE MAIN EXPOSITION'S RELATIONSHIP TO THE CLIMAX & THEME

The main exposition has a direct relationship to the film's climax as well as one with the film's theme. The problem posed at the beginning of the story is the one that needs to be solved or answered at the end. If Richard Price wants Lionel's loss of Paulette at the end to mean something, Lionel's total infatuation for her must be set up at the beginning, even if the author ironically undercuts the pain of Lionel's loss in the resolution.

If Mara in *Mara of Rome* is going to solve her problem with the old woman, the dispute has to be set up at the start. Even though the focus of Mara's dramatic problem changes from grandmother to grandson, the basic problem doesn't: If the grandson doesn't return to the seminary, Mara will surely be blamed. If Kafka, in *Franz Kafka's It's a Wonderful Life*, is going to finish his book, we have to know he's having trouble with it at the beginning. To initiate and maintain the tension of the chase in *Occurrence at Owl Creek* and make the climax pay off, we must establish the execution at the beginning.

If a film is about self-indulgence or delusion, or honesty and faith, or about the inability of families to communicate, this too needs to be revealed or foreshadowed for the audience at the start. Just as the audience becomes acquainted with the protagonist's problem early on, the same is true of the theme. They are going to grasp the film's intent only if the theme is introduced early.

You don't have to directly tell viewers what the film is about, but they need hints, clues. If ten people see a film and have ten different interpretations of what it was about, the film's theme couldn't have been very well developed.

Exposition, particularly in dialogue, continues without interruption until the climax of the movie, for we are always exposing characters and plot. This type of exposition also can illuminate the back-story, the action that happened before the film starts. Besides the main exposition, other information can be given, as needed, when the viewer needs it to understand what will happen next. In a short film, gratuitous information is especially problematic; it will delay action and obscure information that is truly important.

When working on the main exposition, think in terms of:

1. What is essential to be revealed?
2. What can be held back?
3. What can be implied?

Holding back or implying certain information can help to maintain tension and anticipate what will happen next. If you reveal too much, the audience can become bored. If, in *Life Lessons*, Lionel said to Paulette at the airport: "I need the friction of our crazy relationship to help me paint," the story would have been short-circuited and their subsequent fights would have lacked tension.

THE PROBLEM & THE SUB PROBLEM

A film needs a main conflict that is dramatic and has consequences for the protagonist. This is the main problem that has to be solved. If you looked at it as a question, it could be asked like this: Can Lionel hang on to Paulette? The answer will be found in the climax and resolution. We find that most effective films over six or seven minutes develop other conflicts or problems for the protagonist to face. Sometimes these are just additional obstacles or complications that help raise the tension and stakes. But some films make effective use of their sub-problems by strategically weaving them into the plot as recurring conflicts that develop and climax along with the main problem.

The sub-problem may concern the protagonist, antagonist, or another character who indirectly effects the protagonist. These are conflicts of secondary importance that impact the plot. In concept, they resemble subplots in feature length films. Both sub-plots and sub-problems start secondary story lines that are dramatized in the construction of the plot. Both give dimension to a story and add tension.

But where a subplot in a feature begins (with few exceptions) after the introduction of the main conflict and ends before the main climax, a sub-problem in a short film can effectively frame a story, starting before the main conflict and ending in the resolution. This technique allows the audience an alternate view of the conflict, by providing a last insight into the main character or story.

Using a sub-conflict as a frame does a number of things. It often provides added tension to the opening while other pieces of the main exposition are established, making scenes more exciting. It also creates a strong sense of dramatic unity to the film, bringing everything together in the resolution to show that no piece of the story has been wasted. In *Life Lessons*, the sub-problem for Lionel asks: Will he complete his paintings before his exhibition, and how will the show turn out? This question frames the action, and the answer is revealed in the resolution. *Mara of Rome* works similarly. Although we have a quick opening scene without dialogue establishing Umberto, his grandmother and Mara, the first major scene introduces Rusconi and his plan to return later for a night of love with Mara. This introduces what develops into the sub-problem: Will Rusconi ever make love with Mara? The answer comes in with the film's resolution.

But sub-problems don't have to frame action. *Franz Kafka's It's a Wonderful Life* introduces Woland the Knifeman a few scenes into the film. Woland appears again before he becomes the threat that leads to the climax of the film. Most shorts use the secondary conflict this way.

Raising more than one issue in the mind of the viewer increases the chance of greater involvement in the film. Seeking more than a single answer to a set-up means we need to see a story unfold, not a series of yes/no responses. The more complicated your set-up, the more questions it raises, the more compelling your story will be.

OPENING THE MOVIE

Good openings elicit curiosity, raising more questions than they answer. They open a doorway to a slightly different world than our own. Good openings are visual, utilizing the language of the medium — images and sounds — to conjure up feelings and carry the story's mood to the audience.

Point of Decision

Great shorts open near a point of decision or crisis, and the more dramatic they are, the better. (This crisis or decision must be connected to the main conflict.) Out of this situation, the hero's goal emerges. The best decisions or crises are life changing or significant in some way to the protagonist. This means the action is important to the character and has consequences.

Great shorts open near this point — either just before it, at it or just after it. Life changing events include:

- Starting school
- Getting a driver's license
- Graduating high school
- Starting college
- Birth
- Wedding
- Losing or quitting a job
- Divorce
- Funeral

In other words, something is about to happen, to change.

The opening of *Life Lessons* establishes the art exhibition as a life-changing situation; Lionel has nothing to show. He is understandably panicked because this could mean a blow to his career. (In the second scene, when he picks up his assistant Paulette at the airport, he learns his love affair with her is over. Lionel's day goes from bad to worse.)

In *Ray's Male Heterosexual Dance Hall*, Sam needs a job and, on a lead, goes to the dance hall. In *Some Folks Call It a Sling Blade*, Carl is about to be released and Teresa has come to interview him before he goes. In *Occurrence at Owl Creek*, the protagonist is about to be hanged. It's hard to find anything more dramatic than that.

Change in the Environment

Another strategy for starting a film may begin with a change in the environment that affects the protagonist directly or indirectly. A change in the environment can be the introduction of a new element that directly affects the protagonist. A change can be represented by war, natural disaster, or a death in a family.

The Red Balloon begins with an image of a cold and wet cobblestone courtyard dominated by large old houses. The atmosphere is gray and lonely. A young boy, Pascal, steps into frame, carrying a bookcase. He lingers at the top of a staircase to pet a cat then goes on his way until, halfway down, something catches his eye. He climbs a lamppost and retrieves a red balloon. The balloon contrasts starkly the world around him. It is large, round, bright red, the color of life. The story that follows shows Pascal struggling to keep this new element in his life.

In *Mara of Rome*, Umberto's arrival at his grandmother's indirectly creates the situation for Mara. Had he not arrived, the grandmother's disdain for Mara and her profession would not have hit the breaking point.

The Protagonist

Many films open by introducing the protagonist. As in real life, first meetings make strong impressions, so you must show the audience right up front what is important, unique and/or interesting about the protagonist, especially in relationship to the story. A good question to ask is: What's essential for the audience to know about this character at the start? This is really the beginning of his or her character arc, however small it may be in a short film. Even if the sole purpose of the film is to peel back layers like the skin on an onion and illustrate who the character really is at heart, the protagonist's outer facade must be illustrated first, so the contrast with his inner "essence" can be demonstrated.

In *Life Lessons*, the film opens with the camera zeroing in on different objects in the studio, paints, empty canvas, stereo boom-box, Napoleon cognac, and finally Lionel, alone in the big studio, disheveled and desperate. The shriek of the elevator bell introduces the conflict (with his art dealer) that is foreshadowed by the desperate look in Lionel's eyes.

You must also consider how you want to present the main character to the audience. Do you want the audience to laugh at the protagonist or pity him? Should we take him seriously or write him off? Do you want the audience to identify with the protagonist or objectify him? These questions relate to the tone of the film. If the tone is satiric or broadly humorous, the audience won't be as closely involved with the characters. A serious or ironic tone allows the audience more emotional involvement in the film. How the audience views the character depends on how you do. You need to be clear about your feelings for the protagonist in order to communicate them effectively to the audience.

Scene Considerations

There are specific considerations for the opening in terms of scene construction that can be highlighted here. Part Three covers the actual writing of scenes (craft and technique) in more depth.

Several things go into making an interesting and effective opening. First, does the scene raise a question in the minds of the viewers about what will happen in the story? If the opening scene doesn't, then where and when will it come? Bringing the dramatic question in early will help draw in the audience because they'll want to know how this problem will be resolved. The question raised in the first scene in *Life Lessons* is about his coming art exhibition: Will Lionel have any work to show? The question raised in the next scene is about his relationship with Paulette: Will she leave?

Next you want to ask: Is there action in the scene to make it interesting? Is there conflict? The opening scene in *Life Lessons*, though all exposition, is relayed through conflict between Lionel and Philip. Philip wants out of the lift, but Lionel keeps him in. This is the action that represents the conflict between them. The two men aren't yelling at each other, but each has a different scene goal. A scene goal is like a story goal; it is what a character wants to achieve with action during the scene.

Action in a scene can be physical action. Ask yourself: What's interesting that my character can do on screen? In *PEEL*, after the opening credits and exposition, the scene starts with a boy's feet propped up on the dashboard of a moving car. This may or may not be adolescent impudence, but when the boy starts bouncing an orange between his feet with a THUNK, THUNK, THUNK, throwing it against the windshield and rolling it down his legs, we know the driver of the car will start to grit his teeth.

So, even before taking a look around the car, the action has our attention. Once we've taken that look, the sound becomes more striking because it accentuates the tension existing between Tim, the boy's father, and Katie, Tim's sister. She sits sullenly in the back seat.

"If you don't want other people's opinions, don't ask for 'em," she says. Silence, except for the thunk, thunk, thunk of the boy's orange. Then: "It was a really scrappy bit of land... That's my opinion." The brother does not reply, but the tension level rises in the car.

The idea is to *show* the problem, not *tell* it. The more originally you can show it, the better. Viewers will believe the conflict much more readily if they witness the problem themselves.

Foreshadowing is a more subtle method of showing conflict and can be seen in *Mara of Rome*. After panning a plaza, the camera comes to rest on the balcony of a high-rise apartment where a young priest paces, reading his bible. Near him, an old lady feeds birds and an old man paints. Across the patio, on another high-rise balcony, a sexy woman wrapped only in a white towel emerges from her apartment. She carries two new plants to place in planters. She tosses one of the wrappers over the side before seeing the young priest watching her. Because her view is obscured, at first she doesn't realize he's a priest, and thinks he's only a young man. Gardening tool in hand, she turns the soil of the new plants and checks him out. He's clearly taken with her for she's very beautiful. From her new vantage point, she sees his collar and realizes he's a priest. She smiles at him, amused by what she sees in his face.

The contrast between the young priest and the sensual beauty creates a subtle tension in the viewer's mind, and foreshadows more conflict to come when these two characters come together. What kind of conflict we cannot predict. But in the next scene, we learn Mara is a prostitute with a high-class clientele. This serves to up the ante more, even though we aren't sure of the story's direction.

Another consideration for a strong opening is to ask if there's anything about the character we can learn now that can be utilized at the end. The earlier the writer shows us an important detail about the protagonist that affects the outcome of the story, the less contrived it feels. The first scene of *Life Lessons* accomplishes this in two ways. First it sets up the art exhibition at the end. Second, a piece of exposition shouted as Philip rides the elevator down in at the end of the scene gives us a clue what will play out at the end. Philip shouts up at him, "Ah, Lionel, Lionel! You go through this before every show! I'm talking twenty years of this! Now get to know yourself a little better, Lionel! You can pull it off. You always do!"

It's not until the very end that we understand the full implication of his statement. Lionel does "pull it off." His exhibition is a complete success. But it's not until he meets the beautiful young artist in the last scene that we can comprehend what the story means. As we watch his infatuation with this young woman, and hear him offer a job with the same lines he gave Paulette, we understand that this is Lionel's style, his technique, his *modus operandi*. He goes "through this before every show," Philip said. Lionel's declarations of love for Paulette weren't necessarily meaningless; but perhaps what he said to her in the climax was true, his art and relationships feed off each other. He needs one to fuel the other. After all, he's been married and divorced "four times" since before Paulette was born. The little piece of exposition given at the beginning, when taken in the context of the whole, helps give the final shape to the overall meaning of the film.

As a story develops, an opening image or idea that began the whole process may have to be scrapped in favor of something that gets the plot moving faster. Some screenwriters begin writing before they have thoroughly worked out their plot and story, and they fall prey to extensive rewrites once a draft is complete. A writer may discover many interesting details this way, but a lot of time can be wasted, too. You'll always need to rewrite to improve your screenplay, but you can keep it to a minimum with a good understanding of your story before starting your first draft.

EXERCISES

Consider the opening of your film. Ask:

1. What is the problem driving it?
   a. Frame it in the form of a question that conveys a sense of the main action the protagonist must take. (Will Lionel convince Paulette to stay? Will the condemned man escape?)
   b. If there is a sub-problem, pose it in the form of a question. (Will Rusconi bed Mara?)
2. Express what you think are the most important parts of the main exposition.
   a. Can this information be conveyed without dialogue?
   b. Which parts can?
   c. How can you most creatively handle this exposition?
3. If you only have one or two scenes to start your movie, what's the most dramatic (or comedic) way to open it?
   a. Is there action in the scenes?
   b. Where is the conflict coming from?
   c. Is there something going on that causes tension or gets us wondering what is going on?
   d. If your story is subtle, can you foreshadow the conflict by contrasting opposites? Is there any other way?
4. Is there something thematic, which can be dropped into the opening to hint at the direction of the film?

Now start your plot outline. Visualize the separate scenes as if you were seeing the movie. Each time you change locales, you must start a new scene. For a film thirty minutes or less, allow no more than three scenes to kick off your film. And if it is less than fifteen minutes, the very latest you must introduce the conflict is in the second scene.

The opening should poise the plot on a specific line of action that will take it to the midpoint. If you have trouble finding the best opening two or three scenes, use as many as it takes right now, with the idea that once the story gets rolling you will come back and pare it down.

7

The Middle –
Keeping the Story Alive

As in a feature, the middle section of a short film can present great difficulties. Once the story is set in motion, juggling the important plot elements — action, conflict, character and theme — so that the story keeps moving and has meaning can be frustrating. The middle is generally the longest section of a film and the hardest to keep focused. But the middle is where the battle is won or lost. If the middle wanders, doesn't move or skips over important developments, the film loses its momentum. The audience needs to move with the characters and conflict, and still be surprised and entertained.

The biggest problem most short film writers have in this section of the story is understanding how conflict informs and directs the flow of information that makes the plot. Instead of focusing on the central conflict and its effect on the main characters, and how this affects the plot, many writers veer off, develop other elements, and send the plot careening. Often they see this "development" detour as significant for characterization and theme. But it's more likely the development isn't connected in any meaningful way to the real plot action. If the threads of the main conflict are ignored, or sidelined for action that has no bearing on the main conflict, the links between the scenes break down. Momentum and meaning are lost.

The middle section must build tension to hold the audience, even in a short film. The key here is to use conflict as the guide for the plot action. Important information needs to be worked into the plot and tied to the main conflict otherwise tension dissipates. This goes back to basic cause-and-effect-plotting. The protagonist makes a move, draws conflict, and is affected, which leads to new steps and new conflicts.

This doesn't mean you have to use the same obstacle for your protagonist over and over to create dramatic continuity. In any film over five or six minutes, that would get repetitious. But the obstacles and complications your protagonist faces must reflect the main conflict on some level to be truly effective.

THE CONFRONTATION – RISING ACTION

In a story's middle, we need conflict and action to heat up. In the middle, you're dramatizing the protagonist's confrontation with problems and how they affect her. Without obstacles, complications and crises for the characters, a story stalls. I've defined these elements in Chapter 4 and can't stress enough their importance. If your story is a lot of scenes with your protagonist going places, doing things, talking with people, but no conflict develops, your script won't be very exciting. When you use the conflict effectively, you're able to build suspense and generate surprise to enhance your plot and better excite your audience. These tools will help you strengthen the middle.

SUSPENSE

According to the *Concise Dictionary of Literary Terms* suspense is a mental state of "uncertainty, excitement, or indecision." Suspense leaves the audience waiting for an outcome to the events. As the audience waits, they anticipate what will happen to the protagonist and the other main characters. "Suspense," says the *Concise Dictionary*, "is a quality of tension in a plot which sustains interest and makes the readers and viewers ask 'what happens next?'"

Tension and suspense are created in many ways. Hitchcockian suspense often lets the audience in on trouble the characters don't know about, and then exploits the audience's anticipation of how the characters will react when they find out.

The audience is always on the side of the hero, at least at the beginning. As he struggles to overcome the conflict he will gain the audience's interest and often respect. But as the story moves forward, tension and suspense need to be stoked like a fire in order to maintain them. Here are some ways.

The Antagonist

A strong antagonist contributes to creating tension and suspense. Because the antagonist best represents the hero's problem, the stronger he is, the greater the suspense as to whether or not the hero can succeed. A good rule of thumb is to bring the antagonist in at the earliest logical moment. No one sits around waiting for suspense to begin. We can only wonder what will happen once the conflict has been introduced.

In *Life Lessons, Black Rider*, and *The Appointments of Dennis Jennings*, the antagonists are introduced early and we understand their place in the plot action. Paulette arrives in the second scene and clearly establishes her desire to leave New York and Lionel. In *Black Rider*, as soon as the young black man asks the old woman about the seat on the trolley car, her ire is up and conflict is established. The opening scene of *The Appointments of Dennis Jennings* sets up Dr. Schooner's place in the story. he's running for his life as Dennis tries to shoot him.

The Dreadful Alternative

To compound suspense, put the hero in jeopardy and keep him there. Jeopardy for the protagonist can be personal, as in the risk of losing love or respect (*Life Lessons, The Man in the Brooks Brothers Shirt*). It can be physical peril (*Occurrence at Owl Creek*). An obvious negative consequence awaiting the hero if he fails to solve the story's problem adds more suspense (*Mara of Rome* and *Words*, from *Before the Rain*). Setting up a terrible fate that will befall him helps create automatic suspense from that moment on. Some presentation of this negative consequence early on will lace your story with suspense for its entire length. The price of failure for the hero must be high to generate genuine suspense.

In *Life Lessons*, the cost for Lionel if he can't convince Paulette to stay is loneliness, or so it appears. Later in the story, when she stays, her platonic presence means sexual frustration for him. But there's the problem of the art exhibition, too: should Lionel fail to paint his pictures in time his career will suffer.

In *Mara of Rome*, Mara might have to face the old lady and her petition should she fail to convince Umberto to return to the seminary. Characters lives are at stake in *Occurrence at Owl Creek* and *Words*.

Unexpected Complications

An unexpected complication adds suspense to any story. A sudden surprise, which complicates the situation or produces a new additional obstacle for the hero, can keep tension mounting. In *Life Lessons*, the performance artist Gregory Stark complicates matters for Lionel. The young "graffiti" artist Ruben Torro might also be considered a complication for Lionel, at least in the moment. How Lionel deals with Paulette and her suitor reveals a lot about his character. In general, young men clearly threaten Lionel's appetite for young women. The appearance of a young man, even Paulette's brother, always leads to real angst for Lionel.

In *Occurrence at Owl Creek*, the protagonist faces a snake in the surging river while Union soldiers shoot at him from the bridge. He dives deep to avoid this complication and is swept up in the current, complicating his escape.

TECHNIQUES FOR SUSPENSE

Two of the best techniques for creating suspense are "the ticking clock" and crosscutting. The ticking clock establishes a limited time frame for the protagonist to perform. Time is running on the protagonist's chances for success with each ticking second. In *Election Night*, Peter is fighting the clock along with the racist taxi drivers. In *The Powder Keg*, the ticking clock is Harvey's wound, which he might not survive. This technique is a standard in feature films across genres, and generally works well to heighten the tension and suspense.

Crosscutting cuts between the opposing forces of the story, generally protagonist and antagonist shows each one's progress toward their mutually exclusive goals. As one gets closer, the other is then in an inferior position. When the protagonist is worse off, suspense increases due to our worry he won't succeed. Crosscutting can also involve cutting between the protagonist and an obstacle lying ahead of his path. Showing the audience this before the character gets to it increases the tension as we anticipate what will happen when he faces it. In *The Powder Keg*, we're shown the border crossing and stop sign ahead to arouse more suspense; we know time is running out for Harvey and stopping could make it worse. This too is a tried and true practice in feature films, and a good tool for increasing suspense.

Suspense Killers

The worst enemy of suspense is predictability. If the audience easily foresees what's going to happen, and their expectations are met without surprise, they become bored. The *possibility* of imminent crises needs to be foreshadowed. But it is the possibility, not the certainty of these crises, which gives rise to suspense and anticipation. We know conflict is going to take place but if we can predict how and when it'll happen, and who gets hurt, the story loses interest, momentum and value.

A protagonist who is so strong and smart that he can solve any problem through might or intellect won't engender much suspense. The protagonist needs to be challenged. The greater the odds against the hero succeeding, the more the audience will root for him to prevail.

The early loss of the antagonist risks undercutting suspense. To keep suspense alive, the antagonist needs to be viable until the climax of the film. If he is removed from contention in the story before the final crisis and climax, momentum will be slowed and suspense lost.

SURPRISE

Surprise is a key element of successful screenwriting and filmmaking. It plays a part in maintaining suspense. It helps stimulate our curiosity regarding the story, making us ask over and again that critical question: "What's going to happen next?"

Surprise means "to take unawares or to affect with unexpected wonder." When a plot takes a sudden turn in an unexpected direction, it can surprise us. When a character behaves in a startling way or does something seemingly inexplicable, it can astonish us. As a film progresses, the audience needs to be frequently surprised by the characters and action. As the end nears, surprises must intensify. The final surprise is often the revelation or epiphany which is really the whole point of the story.

In *Life Lessons*, what's the first surprise after the initial scene establishing Lionel is a desperate man? It's in the next scene, at the airport, where he has gone to pick up Paulette. In the previous scene he tells Philip he can't go to lunch because he has to pick up his assistant. "I don't know why she can't take a cab like everyone else," he shrugs. But when we see Lionel at the airport, waiting anxiously, filmed in slow motion, emphasizing both his impatience and his total concentration on her, we realize something's not what it seems. When she gets off the plane, what he lives for has arrived. Paulette's reaction when she sees him contradicts his completely. "Oh, shit," she says.

Life Lessons constantly surprises us with Lionel's behavior, and Paulette's, too. In nearly every scene, Lionel does something startling, acting in a seemingly contradictory way, and this is one of the big reasons the film keeps our interest.

In *PEEL*, both the father and the son surprise us with their behavior. Our first surprise is when the father pushes his son out the door and tells him to go "pick up every piece of peel" he's dropped on the highway. This is a rather astonishing request, but given the circumstances, we accept it. The boy runs off in the opposite direction, to the front of the car. As his father admonishes him to obey, the boy cocks his arm defiantly, threatening to throw the orange at his father (who is behind a windshield). The boy's action surprises not only his father, but us, too. When the father responds by inching the car up against the boy's knees, his own style of threat, we are startled, if not shocked. The boy runs off and the plot now takes a new direction.

In *The Red Balloon*, the moment Pascal's mother puts the balloon out the window of their apartment is unforeseen and shocking because the action is so mean-spirited. But when the balloon waits at the window for the boy we are even more truly surprised. The boy sneaks the balloon back inside, and we, the audience, share his unexpected happiness.

In *Occurrence at Owl Creek*, the plot takes a sudden and unexpected turn when the rope breaks and the condemned man falls into the river. We are further amazed by the length of time he lasts underwater. He struggles with the ropes and finally gets them off, emerging into a startling clear perspective of life around him. After the filmmaker drives home his point, we are suddenly made aware of the Union soldiers still on the bridge. Men holler, in an audio equivalent to slow motion, gunshots ring out, and now the man is racing for his life.

In Chapter 5 we talked about probability in relationship to plot. Probability is not predictability. Whatever surprises the characters come up with, whichever direction the plot turns, surprises must be rooted in the realm of the probable. The surprises must have a reality to them, within the context of the story.

Surprise keeps us off balance, it keeps us guessing, and it helps hold our attention because we can't predict what's going to happen next. One of the strongest surprises occurring in a film is when everything seems to be headed in one direction and then something happens, and suddenly it's moving in the opposite: the reversal.

The Reversal

A reversal is an unexpected event that spins the story in the opposite direction. It causes the situation to change; good fortune changes into bad or bad into good. More often than not, the situation created is not only unanticipated but unwanted.

A reversal can be major or minor. A major reversal will force the protagonist in an entirely new and unforeseen direction. A minor reversal might cause the hero to reconsider his plan of action and discard it in favor of something else. Most feature films have at least one major reversal, usually near the end of the second act. This major reversal in a feature has dramatic implications for the protagonist and causes radical changes. Short films employ major reversals, too, but they come at a different point.

The Reversal in Relationship to the Midpoint

In a short film we find a reversal most often at the midpoint of the plot. Here, one of the main characters, the protagonist or antagonist, shifts course, and as a result the film changes direction, too. We've already discussed the reversal at the midpoint of *Life Lessons* in Chapter 4. There, Paulette is ostensibly headed home, but changes her mind when she is deeply affected while watching Lionel paint.

In *Mara of Rome*, the midpoint changes the relationship between Mara and the old grandmother from one of dreaded foes to friendship. The old woman's anguish melts Mara's anger. She goes from wanting to hurt the old woman to vowing to help her.

In *Franz Kafka's It's a Wonderful Life*, Kafka moves from writer's block to creative inspiration.

The Reversal in Relationship to the Set-Up & Climax

Sometimes we see a reversal within the set-up. In *Occurrence at Owl Creek*, the rope breaking is the catalyst of the story. Until this moment, it appears the man is going to hang. Then the rope breaks, startling us, and the film becomes one about whether or not he will escape. The reversal is used again at the climax in one of the most surprising and famous endings of a short film (and short story, on which the film is based). It's a powerful climax, again startling us, and drives home the film's theme.

Emotion & Reversals

Reversals work best when emotion connects with the action and/or consequences of the action. Emotion can fuel and cause a reversal, or can result from a change in the situation. Emotion adds depth to the reversal and enhances the drama.

In *Life Lessons*, Paulette not only reverses her decision to leave, but emotionally changes as she renews her conviction to her art.

In *Mara of Rome*, the old grandmother's despair causes Mara's anger to turn to sympathy. These moments are all emotional reversals, as well as plot reversals. They change the direction of the plot in unforeseen ways and propel the characters into the second half of the story.

THE PSEUDO-SOLUTION

Another plot strategy for the middle section might be termed the "pseudo-solution" of the story problem. Here, the initial story question or problem is answered or solved but the repercussions are more unanticipated problems. The pseudo-solution usually takes place at the plot's midpoint. The second half of the plot then shows the effect of solving the problem for the protagonist.

In *Franz Kafka's It's a Wonderful Life,* Kafka solves his writer's block, finding the inspiration when he flattens the cockroach that has crawled on his desk. But just as suddenly, he's thrown into despair when he realizes he's taken the poor bug's life. Unforeseen by Kafka or the audience is the appearance of Woland the knifeman who arrives and suspects that Kafka has had something to do with the disappearance of his pet insect. Woland threatens Kafka with torture and death if he doesn't tell him what's happened to his pet. The rest of the film deals with this new problem for Kafka.

In *The Man in the Brooks Brothers Shirt*, the plot question seems to be, will our heroine resist Gerry? When she agrees to come to his compartment for a drink, the audience knows the odds are shifting. It makes no difference that he's promised no hanky-panky. Saying no and meaning yes are employed by both sexes. The more she drinks, the less likely it seems she will be able to resist a lecherous advance. The film appears set on its course —will he or won't he bed her? Instead of waiting until the end to resolve this, it happens halfway through the film. She wakes up in his berth, with a hangover and unable to believe she has slept with him.

The real surprise comes in the second half of the film, which deals with the consequences of her actions. Gerry now tells our unnamed and hung over heroine he's in love with her; he will leave his wife and children and take care of her in New York while he seeks a divorce! All this from a man who is the antithesis of everything she believes in — a class enemy! But he offers her security, family, home — things that, as she gets older, are starting to have greater meaning. What will the worldly, unsentimental leftist do now? The plot question evolves into a new unexpected conundrum. The second half of the film answers this question, and in that answer defines her character and, ultimately, what the film is about.

When what we believe to be the main plot concern is answered at the midpoint, in a pseudo-solution, as in *The Man in the Brooks Brothers Shirt*, the story that emerges is usually more complex than one whose dramatic problem has remained unaltered. Why? Because the unsubtle problem posed in the set-up is now dispensed with and the ramifications are more complex problems (foreshadowed in the entire first half of the story). In *The Man in the Brooks Brothers Shirt* our heroine first answers a simple binary question of whether she will give in to Gerry, and now can address the more subtle aspects of her feminine character. Whether she'll put out becomes instead a story that ruminates on the possibility of emotional security with an intellectual foe.

Sometimes, as in *Twist of Fate* (a film by Douglas Kunin), the protagonist does indeed solve his problem at the midpoint. The audience follows the film to see what the protagonist will now do. The protagonist, William, is homeless and schizophrenic. Outside the posh Beverly Hills Hotel, William asks a woman with her daughter if she could "spare a little change for something to eat?" The woman ignores him, but the little girl can't. As a Rolls Royce pulls up, the little girl slips off her pearl bracelet and drops it on the ground. He picks it up and tries to give it back. But the woman, ignorant of her daughter's compassion, refuses to look at him, and they drive away.

William now has something of value, but the question is what he'll do with it. Conflict dogs him in many ways. First police appear. He's intimidated by a group of bikers. He almost gives the bracelet to a blind man. Finally, he winds up at a pawnshop, where he exchanges the bracelet for $200 and a white suit. This occurs at the midpoint. Now he has more than a little money for food, plus a white suit. The question is, what will he do with it all?

Solving the initial story problem halfway through the film can have liberating results. A plot confined by a single problem is well served by resolving the problem far before the climax; doing so can trigger new problems that intensify plot possibilities for the second half. A pseudo-solution makes a film more life-like: Often the greatest problems are posed only after we think we have gotten what we want.

EXERCISES

In the exercise at the end of Chapter 6, you focused on the beginning of the plot of your screenplay. Now it's time to juggle the rising action to keep it escalating. Though the exact number of scenes will vary with each film, the middle of a thirty-minute film (i.e., approximately a thirty-page screenplay) will be ten to thirteen scenes. In a fifteen-minute film, the middle may be five to seven scenes (and if there is one main locale such as the Lunch Date, five to seven main beats within that extended scene).

Let's start with a few questions to apply to the work you've already completed on your plot. Have you introduced the conflict clearly and strongly enough to force the protagonist to act? If so, what does he do? Will there be a serious consequence for him if he fails? In taking action, what obstacle does the protagonist encounter? Is there more than one kind? Does the protagonist face inner as well as outer obstacles? What is the best way to show this inner conflict?

Are there any complications for the protagonist (or antagonist)? Can or do the consequences pay off later in the story?

Can you envision a strong midpoint in the plot, where the action suddenly reverses direction and surprises the audience? What would happen if the plot question posed at the beginning is answered at the midpoint and the rest of the screenplay deals with the consequences? What direction would the plot take as a result? Whatever happens at the midpoint, how does this lead to the most dramatic (i.e., life changing) moment for the character within the plot? Is this a crisis or the climax of the screenplay?

Using the answers to these questions, begin to organize the material. You want to create a line of action heading first to the midpoint of the story, then on to the climax. Look for a specific midpoint, especially a reversal. The line of action, which starts at the inciting incident (the moment when the plot problem is exposed) should drive toward the midpoint, ideally creating one expectation in the mind of the audience and delivering another.

The focus of the next segment of action is the final crisis leading to a climax. The protagonist still needs complications and obstacles to face in the second half. Remember to create cause-and-effect relationships between the scenes and to orchestrate a rising conflict through an attack and counterattack strategy between the protagonist and antagonist.

Write down your scene outline, and continue to number all scenes. You may first need to write down everything that occurs to you as the protagonist moves from inciting incident toward climax. Then go back and cull through the scenes, using those that are the most effective and dramatic. You probably won't need all the material you create in the first pass. Many transitions you include won't be necessary. You may discover some scenes repeat the same dramatic information, even if locations, or characters, are different. Once you clearly perceive the main story line, strengthen connections between scenes by cutting material not relevant to the main action.

The construction of this plot outline is going to be the backbone of your work. Don't rush the process, and don't be afraid to rework the plot line you create.

8

Fade Out: Revelation, Climax & Resolution

In the final stretch of the screenplay, writers often feel energized. The words all screenwriters long to type dangle in front of them. "FADE OUT, THE END" signals the completion of the task. In the rush to get to these words, all writers, especially beginning writers, can become careless with the final section of the screenplay. Here, traditionally, the hero vanquishes the villain with "a mighty blow." But often in short screenplays, instead of being the most forceful and consequential moment of the screenplay, the climactic chase simply runs out of gas. Short films are prone to anticlimaxes because the nature of the short form (from more limited budgets to less time for building the drama) requires a more subtle resolution than long form drama. A final twist or irony or character revelation proves ideal in a short, as opposed to a feature's need for, say, triumph on the battlefield.

The ending is, of course, why we came to the party in the first place. It is the reason, the purpose, the ambition of the film. In the ending, the writer reveals what the experience has all been about. In great films, short or long, the ending gives the audience more than entertainment satisfaction. It gives them something to reflect on as the lights come up in the theater.

The same elements found in the last act of a feature are found in a short film: revelation, climax and resolution. Climax and resolution are definite terms, connected specifically to the outcome of the conflict and ending of the story. Revelation, on the other hand, is not as concrete. Though all great films and fiction employ story revelation, the level of importance and degree of insight can vary dramatically.

STORY REVELATION – CHARACTER REVELATION

Revelation means something revealed or exposed, especially a striking disclosure, of something not previously known or realized. In great films, and all great fiction, there is a moment when important information to understanding the story can't be concealed or withheld from the characters and the audience any longer. This information often comes as a shock, but always makes sense. Often it sheds light on one of the main characters and explains what's going on in the story, relating to motivations and/or back-story. Sometimes it's a sudden realization or epiphany the protagonist has about her life as a result of the events experienced in the film. Sometimes it's a realization or insight the audience has about the protagonist that she remains ignorant of.

In film and theater, this is the revelatory scene. The moment when the writer chooses to let the audience in on the secret mover or motivation behind the characters and the story. The revelatory scene is a scene or group of scenes where the truth finally comes or is forced out into the open, and the characters, especially the protagonist, must cope with it. Now, we, the audience, understand why actions were taken despite the risks, and realize what the film is really about.

In film, fiction and theater, story revelation is most often character revelation. It takes place most of the time in the second half of the work. In feature films and theater, the main revelation usually occurs near the climax of the second act, although it can come as early as the end of the first act. The film *Witness* has a shocking revelation at the end of the first act when the protagonist John Book discovers his immediate superior is part of the murder he's investigating. Many action films or thrillers employ this technique. Wherever the revelation comes, it tends to act as a catalyst and propels the plot into the next portion of the film.

The revelation almost always has consequences, frequently drastic. Sometimes the startling information causes the protagonist to doubt himself, before he finds the strength to recommit to the goal and story. Or the recognition of an overpowering truth confirms the protagonist's struggle, and then sends him and the film hurtling toward the conclusion. It's important to dramatize these responses because they allow the audience to glimpse the protagonist's true character.

In a short film, the main revelation can occur almost anywhere in the second half of the film. As in a feature, it's more powerful when linked with another element, like a reversal or crisis, climax or resolution. By definition, revelation surprises the audience. It aids in creating suspense and offers entertainment through giving crucial but unexpected answers to the characters and the audience. Revelations are most powerful when they are simple but surprising. Often the revelation is saved for the last possible moment of a short film, and is used to drive home the story's point.

Revelation & Exposition

To be truly effective, the revelation must have a direct relationship to the main exposition of the film. The problem set up at the beginning must be connected to whatever is revealed that leads to his success or failure. In a sense, the revelation can be the reason why the protagonist encounters the difficulties he does trying to achieve his goal. Once the revelation occurs, it can free the protagonist to attain his goal, or at least allow him to meet his fate more consciously. Sometimes only the audience is allowed the revelation of the story.

Again, whether the protagonist understands what the revelation reveals or it's only to help the audience sum up the depiction of the character, the revelation illustrates not just the solution to the dramatic problem, but can demonstrate why the problem took the form it did.

In *Life Lessons*, the film's final scene at Lionel's show illustrates this principle perfectly. Lionel hires a new young, pretty art groupie to be his assistant. Paulette has been forgotten. Lionel demonstrates, primarily for our benefit as opposed to his own conscious awakening, that Paulette was important for his art, not in a personal way, but to fuel his emotion, which in turn moves him to create on canvas. She was useful because she was young and pretty and interested in art — just as this new assistant is.

Writer Richard Price also illustrates the "why" of Lionel's dramatic problem. In this scene, we understand why Lionel's problem took the form it did. Why was there a question about his ability to both open the show and stay involved with Paulette? The answer is in the way he treats women. He hires them young and pretty, not to know them personally, man to woman, but to use them as emotional enzymes in his creative process. He encountered the problems he did with Paulette out of necessity. As a modern young woman, she was obviously going to rebel against a man who used her femininity exclusively as a means to paint. She objects to his refusal to engage her personally, to offer candid assessments of her work, to help her as a lover would help her.

Lionel doesn't like women, but he respects their power and needs it for his work. Long, erudite, excoriating biographies of Picasso have proclaimed the same ideas, but Richard Price's screenplay dramatizes the issues in forty-five minutes of entertainment.

Does Lionel know himself well enough to be aware of how he treats women? Yes, he comes to realize his feelings about them in the scene when Paulette finally leaves him. But he stifles his observation with a painted hand over his mouth. In the film's final scene, it is his behavior, the ultimate proof in drama, which demonstrates what he feels. He starts the cycle again with a new female factotum.

In a sense, exposition continues until the end of the film. In each new scene, the writer essentially gives the audience new information. The writer reveals, exposes certain facets of the characters and story. But the main revelation is held back until the time is ripe with dramatic possibilities to reveal it. The writer has the details the protagonist and audience need from the beginning, but holds them back for a purpose, only revealing them when the impact will be greatest and the audience truly needs them in order to follow the story. Withholding the revelation helps to maintain suspense by keeping the audience guessing about what is really going on.

Major & Minor Revelations

There are several kinds of revelation. Information about the protagonist or another major character that affects the story can cause a sudden illumination for the audience. Information the protagonist is unaware of about himself, another character, a place, object or situation directly affecting the plot-line similarly can cause a revelation for the hero and the audience. Revelations are major if they cause the action to be dramatically different than if they had never surfaced.

Minor revelations tell the audience about motivations that are not necessarily dramatic, but contribute to our understanding of the story and gain sympathy or empathy for the characters. Since a good film always surprises us, a few minor revelations should occur throughout it.

Revelation of Character

Revelation of character can proceed in a variety of ways. Information hidden from the audience, when revealed, can illuminate the character for better or worse. In *Hills Like White Elephants*, the real source of conflict between Ash and Davis is held until the film's midpoint, when it is revealed she's pregnant and he wants her to have an abortion.

Behavior is an effective way to illustrate who the character really is. In *Anna of Milan*, Anna continually says she wants to change, to run away from her life. Randall, meeting her in the light of day, riding around in her Rolls Royce, questions her sincerity. But Anna is adamant that she wants to change. Her reason is: "Inside me there is only a void, an endless void." Her desire is to fill it with Randall.

The revelation comes when Randall, in the midst of a little passionate petting while driving her car, forgets himself momentarily. He opens his eyes in time to realize he's about to hit a boy selling flowers on the roadside. He swerves, loses control of the Rolls and hits a parked truck. Anna's reaction tells the whole story. All she cares about is the car. He is an imbecile! So what if he would have hit the boy? Shaken and then angered, Randall withdraws across the road as Anna takes charge. She flags down a man in Jaguar to help her. The revelation, or the point of the story, is that no matter what Anna says, she can only be what she is — a materialist. She has no social conscience. She confuses spirituality with sexuality, blurring Randall's hope and vision of her.

The writers foreshadow her true character at the start. Her monologue, as she drives to meet Randall, numbly recounts the obligations and appointments her social position assigns her until even we, the audience, have had enough! Of course she would want to change. By hinting at her true nature in her driving, it makes the revelation of the contrast between her words and actions believable.

A protagonist's self-revelation is a powerful moment of the film. Here the protagonist experiences an epiphany about himself, especially in relationship to the conflict. The realization sends the message of the film home to the audience.

In *Hills Like White Elephants*, Ash's revelation is the climax of the film. She knows their relationship is over. Nothing will ever be the same, despite what Davis tells her. If she has the abortion he wants her to have, as she is willing to do, it will destroy her and her love for him. If she has the child, as he tells her he's willing to do, it will destroy him because he doesn't want it. It is a no-win situation that will kill the relationship. All is now inalterably changed.

In *The Man in the Brooks Brothers Shirt*, the final moment of the film is saved for the protagonist's revelation about herself. After realizing the relationship with Gerry will evaporate, she contemplates her life on the train ride back to New York. Her last line, the last line of the film, expresses her conclusions. "There has to be more to the future than Gerry Green, executive lover ... unless there's — less." This sums up her hope about her life, and her fear, and is essentially what the story is driving at: A look at the modern woman and her new role in society.

Revelation saved exclusively for the audience can be forceful and effective. We see revelation of this sort more often in novels, short stories and short films, than in features. In features, we usually find revelation that is not shared by the characters in comedies, as a last comic or ironic twist to make the audience laugh.

In *Occurrence at Owl Creek*, the last revelation is truly shocking and dramatic. The man has escaped and reaches out for his beloved when something strange happens. Using a film technique developed by Slavko Vorkapich, writer/director Robert Enrico slows and prevents the lovers from ever truly meeting. Using images of identical action filmed at slightly different angles and distances, he creates the effect of an unbridgeable chasm between husband and wife. As his love is finally within reach, the man's expression changes to horror. His body stiffens and contorts, and the film cuts back to his hanging. The revelation is the hangman's rope never broke. Our journey has not been with an escapee on the run to a woman, but one of fantasy inside a condemned man's mind. It makes a dark and powerful conclusion to the film. This technique is used in feature films, as in *Jacob's Ladder* and *The Last Temptation of Christ*.

Revelation Through Conflict

In film, new information is best revealed in action and through conflict. Revelation, too, is best when actions dramatize it or conflict forces it out into the open, and not in expository speeches or flashbacks. Think of the revelations we've discussed above as examples.

Beginning writers often use flashbacks as a way to show something from a character's past. A flashback must be essential to the whole structure and not just a means of exposition. If it is only in the film to visually tell something, and does not utilize conflict or action, it will be flat and boring, and stall the forward momentum of the screenplay.

The same is true regarding an expository speech. If the protagonist has changed or realized something important, the change must be dramatic. Having the hero say, "And then I realized..." only dulls a story. If the realization is truly a revelation for the character there'll be emotion around it. Discover the emotion and it'll help shape the scene.

Remember, we're more interested in characters who don't tell us everything, especially when it's painful. Using conflict to force the matter into the open leads to a stronger scene. Conflict necessitates more emotion in a situation.

Revelation, Action & the Climax

A film's critical revelation is often dramatized in the final action where the protagonist finally resolves the conflict. Action is always more compelling than words and if it surprises the audience it can provide a startling disclosure about the character. In *The Wedding*, from Vittorio De Sica's *Gold of Naples*, Teresa, betrayed by her bridegroom and tricked into a loveless marriage, walks out at the end. But as she heads into the night, alone, with only her sordid profession to fall back upon, she finally stops. What will she do? Will she return to prostitution or accept Don Niccola's arrangement? For a long, agonizing moment she waits, and we wait with her. Ultimately, she returns to his home, surrendering her self-respect and deciding the deal he offers is better than her difficult life on the street.

The revelatory moment or scene is an important element of the overall structure of a successful film. Revelation confers meaning to the characters and the story. It generally goes back to what the story is about. If you're stuck on the finale, especially the final revelatory scene, there are several questions to ask:

1 What is the story really about?
2 What interested you in this story at the start?
3 What is really motivating the protagonist?
4 What is the protagonist afraid of?
5 Is one of the main characters hiding something? The answers to any of these questions can provide you with a clue for finding the revelation hidden in the character's motivations or yours for writing the story. These are important questions to ask because story revelation can be a powerful moment within a screenplay and film. Without one, a film might be full of flash, but not much substance.

THE CLIMAX

The moment in a film, play or work of fiction with the greatest intensity, where the conflict is finally resolved is the climax. It's the decisive point of the plot and the most meaningful in relationship to the conflict and theme. Here, not only should the problem be solved, but the premise or theme clarified.

The climax is the key to dramatic unity. It is the culminating point for both the conflict and theme. It determines the worth and meaning of everything that has preceded it — the decisions, actions, obstacles, complications, crises. If the climax lacks power and inevitability, the theme or premise has not dictated the progression of the conflict toward it as the goal. Somewhere the meaning has become obscured to the writer. In the climax, the writer drives home the point of the story. Simply put, in the climax, *who* succeeds and *why* determine the ultimate meaning of the work.

The climax makes the theme concrete in terms of an event. By focusing the action of the film upon a definite goal, which ends at this event, the climax creates an integrated movement. In this way, the climax becomes a reference point to test the validity of every element of the structure. If a scene is not developing or leading up to this conclusion, it needs to be reworked or thrown away.

The climax isn't necessarily the final scene, but the one where the conflict reaches its final stage. A resolution often follows, but not always. In short films, falling action after the final resolution may detract from the character twist or sense of irony. In *Occurrence at Owl Creek*, climax and resolution are one.

Though it's discussed as a point in the action, the climax isn't limited to a single scene. Depending on the story, the climax may be very sudden or a complex event combining many lines of action in several scenes.

In a film, the climax must be visual and visceral, not internal. Though it doesn't have to end in screams, shoot-outs or car chases, an ending that incorporates strong actions will be more powerful and memorable than one that is restricted or confined. The protagonist's emotional response to the end of the conflict should be considered and included in the climax. It keeps the drama in human terms and makes it more understandable and satisfying to the audience.

Unity in Terms of Climax

Synthesis between action and theme is best shown in the climax of the film. Let's look at *Life Lessons* again. Chapter 4 has given us a pretty good outline of the conflict leading up to the climax of the film.

141

The climax of *Life Lessons* brings us back to Lionel's studio where he turns his confessed passion for Paulette into wonderful, powerful painting. Each time she has spurned him, he has run to his canvas. Now his obsession has pushed her to the breaking point. In her room, she turns her anger and frustration on herself; she strikes out at her own paintings. Lionel tries to stop her. "Don't do that," he says. "Are you trying to punish me?" he asks. Paulette is incredulous. "Am I punishing you? Am I punishing *you*!"

Paulette's brother is coming for her and she's leaving. Lionel again says he loves her, he'll do anything for her, but the lines sound hollow. He switches tact and asks her about her painting. Now Paulette responds: "Don't give me this shit about how real artists have no choice. What's here? Am I good? Will I ever be good? Come on, right now!" When he doesn't reply, she shouts: "Come on!"

Lionel's inability to answer is all she needs to resume packing. "I'm going home," she says. Lionel chokes out the only words he can find. "You're young yet." And when these don't get her attention, he declares his love for her once more.

"Love me?" she practically screams. "You just need me around. Sometimes I feel like a human sacrifice. I don't know, maybe if I was as good as you I wouldn't care about anybody else either, but I'm not, so good-bye."

Paulette's recognition of the truth comes here, what she has been wrestling with all along. She aspires to create good work, great work. This is what she values. She doesn't want to be just another mediocre painter. Of course, no one knows the future, and if she gives up, she'll never know. But only Paulette can find her way through this crisis. Only Paulette can determine what path she should take.

Lionel takes it personally. "Oh, so I'm the monster," he says. Then he argues insipidly about her self-image. When this fails, he changes course again.

"Okay, look, maybe it's me. No, it's me," he admits. "You know, I indulge. I indulge in love, I indulge in making my stuff and they feed off each other, you know, they come together at times, but — this is bad, this is selfish... So," he mutters huskily, "... maybe I should try and be a nice person for you. Maybe the key to that is to try and stop. You know, just to stop painting. Maybe I should — yeah, I should stop painting and be a nice person for you. Now is that what you want me to do, huh!"

Clearly, this isn't what he wants. But Lionel's confession shows us that he has some awareness of himself and his actions.

"I don't give a damn what you do," Paulette responds. "My brother's a United States Marine and I can't take this anymore. Get out of here. Get out of here! I can't take this anymore!" she screams and physically drives him from her room.

Lionel, predictably, returns to his canvas and his painting. Paulette, her brother in the background, comes in to say good-bye. Again she watches Lionel paint, awed and moved. "You know something?" she says. "If just once you came by my room and said, 'Gee, Paulette, you're a terrible painter, why don't you get a job and enjoy —'"

Lionel cuts her off, spinning from his work. "Lemme tell you something. You think I just use people, I just wring 'em out. Well, you don't know anything about me. You don't know how involved I get or how far down I go. Hell, I was married four times since before you were born, so don't you tell me." He pauses, staring at her. "So don't tell me."

With nothing left to say, Paulette leaves. Lionel angrily continues painting. His strokes are fierce, harsh. There is no doubt he's upset. He mumbles to himself. "Chippies. Know why they call 'em that? Because they like to chip away at you, man. Take a little chip at your art form, at your talent. Chip, chip, chip..." Suddenly realizing what he's said, he clamps a pigment-tainted hand over his mouth and smears paint on his face in horror.

The main conflict is now over, the story problem solved. This is where the main story has been heading since the film's midpoint. Lionel has failed to convince Paulette to stay. It was only a matter of time until he, with his jealousy and lies, drove her away. But what else do these scenes tell us about the characters and the conflict we have been watching?

The scenes sum up who the characters are, building on what we've previously seen. Lionel admits he's selfish, that he can devour relationships and feed them to his creative gods. His offer to give up painting is nothing short of disingenuous, because he can't give it up. It's what he lives for; it's who he is. On the other hand, Paulette's insecurities have driven her to an emotional brink. She wants Lionel, in the capacity of Great Artist, to reassure her about her art. She wants him to tell her she is good, she will be successful, that she is not wasting her time. Or she wants to hear she's not talented.

Art is sacred to both of them. This is what held them together in the beginning and what ultimately drives them apart. It's the only thing Lionel can't lie about, and the one thing Paulette truly values.

The second climactic scene hints at a darker aspect of Lionel's personality. He uses the derogatory term "chippie" to refer to Paulette. This is slang for a promiscuous woman or delinquent girl; originally, a prostitute. He defines the word his own way, but that it comes to his mind reveals to us, and him, his feelings about Paulette, and women in general. It shocks him. Ultimately, when we put it all together we see that Lionel can't love another person. He is in love with art. For Lionel, art requires his whole passion. This may or may not be the *sine qua non* of a true master, as Paulette recognized ("Maybe if I was as good as you I wouldn't care about anybody else either," she says), but he has little left for real people. The only honest relationship Lionel has is with his work.

These two scenes provide a strong climax to the film. The characters' emotions, attitudes and actions force the conflict to culminate. The theme is finally spelled out through the conflict, though it's been hinted at all along. Looking back, every scene contributes to the inevitability of the ending. No scene feels out of place. Thus the climax feels satisfying.

THE RESOLUTION

The events that follow the climax are a film's resolution. This is sometimes referred to as the falling action. Whatever remains unresolved at the climax, and may pose questions for the audience, must be explained here. The resolution solidifies the circumstances of the film's world as a result of the climax, fixing the fates of the main characters. The best resolution bestows one last revelation or insight into the characters or story. It comes in the last pages, and in a short film, need only be one scene.

If we left *Life Lessons* at the end of the climax, Lionel's character might be open for a wider interpretation, and the point of the story might be less specific. After all, everyone says things in anger he does not entirely mean. But because the resolution takes us to Lionel's art show, which is a big success, we gain more information.

Here Lionel meets the young artist at the bar serving drinks. From the looks they trade he shows he's as captivated by her as she is by him. Impulsively, he offers her Paulette's job, promising room, board, salary and, of course, life lessons. Watching them interact, we sense that Lionel is about to start a new cycle with this beautiful, unsuspecting fan. We know Paulette was right when she said she felt like a human sacrifice. Emotional relationships are the sacramental offering to Lionel's god, his creative process, and this new woman will become the next oblation on his artistic altar.

EXERCISES

The bulk of the work on any plot is in the middle section, but the last few scenes is where all that effort pays off. Therefore these scenes must be considered carefully.

Again, let's start with questions to help focus the work needed to be done.

Is there a story revelation you have withheld from the audience? Is it minor or major? If minor in importance, does it come sooner than the climax of the film? Is this revelation linked to the plot problem and why the protagonist is in trouble? In a sense, is it the whole reason for the screenplay? If so, is it a worthy revelation, enough to support a whole film, or can it be made stronger?

Now, how can the revelation be shown to maximize its dramatic impact? Combining it with the action of the climax is one way. Revealing it in the resolution is another.

Is the climax the peak emotional moment in the plot — where decisive action leads to a solution of the plot problem? If not, can it be strengthened? Is it the result of the orchestration of forces within the main crisis? Is the solution to the plot problem a surprise for the audience? Is the solution "proved" in the climax? Does it support your theme?

Does the resolution grow naturally out of the climax? Will the audience feel satisfied that it ties up all the loose ends? Is one last insight into the story offered in it?

Again, using the answers, organize your material. Look for ways to strengthen the drama (increase the stakes) at or before the climax. At the climax, push the forces to resolve the issues. A satisfying resolution ties up the last threads of the story.

Continue your scene outline, allotting two to five scenes to finish up your story.

Once you have a full outline, set it aside for several days or a week. Before you return to it, review this chapter, as well as Chapters 3, 5 and 6, especially the questions at the end of each one. Is the plot as original as it can be? Is it surprising as well as forceful? Are the characters pushing the action, the plot, as a result of who they are? (If not, return to Chapter 2 and the questions at the end of it for help.)

As you go over your outline, look for ways to tighten it. If you have a beginning that is two or three scenes too long, now is the time to rethink it. Look, too, for ways to increase the visual conflict. A picture *is* worth a thousand words, and should your screenplay make it to the screen, it will be greatly enhanced by how well the story is told visually, through action. Make sure the forces push against each other hard enough to drive that action.

Once you are satisfied with your scene outline, now you are ready for the fun part: Writing the actual screenplay.

PART THREE

THE STRUCTURE OF SCENES

9

Constructing the Scene

Writing the scene is considered the fun part of screenwriting, the reward after all the hard work of inventing characters and putting together a plot. Here the characters and story come alive and the screenwriter's vision is realized. It's not unusual for many writers, itching to get started on the real screenplay, to contemplate skipping over the preliminary steps and actually start scripting without a complete outline. They plan on working out the characters and the plot in the individual scenes of the screenplay.

There is no set formula for writing a screenplay. It is a mercurial process and everyone must find her own best method of working. But jumping into a scene before the characters and plot are sufficiently fleshed out can spell disaster for the beginning screenwriter. Scenes are structured action, each one advancing the development of the drama and our knowledge of the characters. If the writer does not adequately understand a character or the point of a scene, she cannot do it justice. Scenes are interconnected pieces of a greater whole. They are the links in the progression of a story. Having an overview of the complete story, and the relationships that make it work, gives cohesion to a first draft that will otherwise be missing. No matter how good a scene is, if it doesn't relate to those before and after, it cannot be considered successful in the context of the screenplay. (In interviews with writers, directors and actors you will often read how they had to drop a wonderful scene because it just did not serve the story.)

Writing a good scene, a great scene, is an art. It takes lots of practice. As in any art, there are principles of composition, technique and a craft for execution.

UNITS OF ACTION

Screenplays are constructed from scenes, building to and falling from a story climax. A scene is a unit of action. It's a single event or exchange between characters, with unity of time and place. It propels the plot forward, toward the climax and resolution. A plot can be thought of as the blueprint from which a film is designed. Scenes are the basic building blocks, and the theme is the mortar that holds everything together. But the scenes themselves should fit together so closely, and "match" the plot in your original specifications so well, that little glue is needed to insure the stability of the structure.

The organization of scenes makes the plot. The plot moves the story. As we have seen, the plot is the path the protagonist takes as he moves through the scenes toward his goal — all the time in conflict with the antagonist. Plot is *structured*, not random action. Individual scenes are structured action, too.

Throughout this book, we use action in several capacities; e.g., the rising action of the middle, the driving action of the screenplay. The action of a scene shares many ideas with these other uses of the term. Obviously, action is movement. In theater and literature, "the action" means the main subject or main conflict of a story, as distinguished from an incidental episode. It refers to an incident, event or series of events that make up the plot. The unfolding of the events in drama, according to the *Concise Dictionary of Literary Terms*, supplies an answer to the question, "What happens?" "What characters say, do, and think and what results from their saying, doing, and thinking constitute the action of all narrative literature. A planned series of related and interrelated actions, which may be physical or mental or both, make up the plot of a work of fiction or drama." A scene illustrates what characters say and do and the results of what they say and do.

The action of a scene must accomplish at least one of three goals:

1. Advance the flow of events (the plot) toward its inevitable conclusion (climax and resolution).
2. Advance the audience's understanding of the main characters by illuminating them through behavior.
3. Advance the audience's understanding of the overall story by providing expository information.

Scenes are stronger when they utilize a combination of the first two goals. As we saw in Chapter 6, providing expository information to the audience can be an awkward task. Adding conflict or physical movement to an expository scene will strengthen it. Combining exposition with either of the first two goals of a scene will make it stronger still.

All three of these scene goals relate to a film's plot directly or indirectly when the scene is properly conceived. We dramatize a story by showing our characters probing, investigating, and interacting with other forces in the film. The plot grows out of these actions. Showing something important to understanding a character and her motivation relates indirectly to the plot. The audience needs to understand or intuit motivations in order to make sense of the overall story. Finally, exposition is crucial to the plot since, by definition, the information is vital to the audience understanding the conflict or characters. Without the appropriate exposition, audiences won't be properly oriented to the film. If too many scenes fail to achieve one or more of these goals, the plot structure will crumble.

THE PRINCIPLES OF CONSTRUCTION

Above we've discussed a scene as a unit of action that advances the plot. Scene action is the movement within the scene. A character starts at a definite place or with a definite understanding of the dramatic situation. At the end of the scene, that character or another is in a slightly different place, or has furthered his understanding of the conflict. Whichever it is, by the end of the scene something has been altered.

Film Scenes vs. Theater Scenes

Films, unlike plays and sit-coms, aren't made up of fully developed scenes. Films have both more freedom and more limitation. In the theater, the proscenium separates the audience from the play. The audience will accept many theatrical conventions and contrivances, but a play succeeds primarily for two reasons. First and foremost, it succeeds to the extent that the spoken word moves the audience. And second, depending upon the relationship established between the actors and the audience, the experience can be immediate and powerful.

In a movie, the camera sits in place of the audience. Anywhere the camera can fit offers the audience a view of action it cannot otherwise have from a theater seat. The camera places the viewer inside a malfunctioning space capsule thousands of miles from earth, in the eye of a tornado or in the face of raw emotion. It can create a sense of freedom with wide-open spaces or a feeling of claustrophobia. The camera records several different characters' reactions to a brutal incident by the use of the close-up. It transcends geography by cutting from continent to continent in seconds. Because most films strive for realism, the close proximity the camera provides on the drama increases the viewer's involvement in a film. A successful film experience then, can be infinitely more intense and visceral than a theater experience because it can take you right into the heart of the drama.

But this freedom to move anywhere the production budget permits also creates certain limitations. No matter how interesting a scene is, it cannot play on and on if it does not perform any of the functions of a scene described above in a few seconds of visuals, or conform to the theme. The average length of a scene in a short film is one to three pages, although some must be longer and some shorter. What's important is that a scene fit the rhythm of the whole film.

We expect films to rely more heavily on visuals while plays and sit-coms are allowed wide latitude with dialogue. A filmmaker isn't limited only to the visual, however; what characters say and how they say it is also important. But the filmmaker's use of all his materials — space, time, color, light and sound — creates and defines the film's world. The visual and aural quality of the medium (space, color, light and sound) and its plasticity (time) can create the appearance of reality or even hyper-reality. Theater scenery and props can only suggest reality. As characters in film move through space and time, illuminated to appear saintly or satanic, they conjure up specific visual images and create the audience's experience. The more powerful these images, the greater the impact on the viewer because they appear so real and so close. Although a screenplay is more a blueprint than a completed structure, it should provide the inspiration for powerful imagery in order to successfully move the composition from the storyboard to production.

One Main Point Per Scene

Every good scene has one main point the writer wants to communicate to the audience. The point of a scene can be an incident or event in the development of the plot or an aspect of a character whose motivations the audience needs to understand. Sometimes the main point is to make the audience feel something, to empathize with a character or abhor her. The scene might dramatize the emotional impact of the preceding actions on a main character or show the results of one or more of the characters earlier efforts to achieve the goal.

Too many ideas going on in a scene will create problems for the audience. They will not know what to pay attention to and lose track of the story progression. Other ideas may be addressed in the scene, and often should, but they must complement and not obscure the main issue.

If too many scenes combine ideas of equal importance, the audience will become confused or uninterested because the film will seem unfocused. A good solution to this problem is to create separate scenes for each equally important point. Even if the characters only walk from inside a house to outside in what would seem to be a continuous movement, the mere division of the important ideas between different locations will help focus the points. *Life Lessons* illustrates this point. After Lionel critiques Paulette's work, telling her that art is about "having to do it," he walks away critical of himself and the way he sounded.

Visual Actions

It's the screenwriter's job to consider what's visually interesting and exciting in a scene. Showing characters in movement, physically doing interesting things is better than the talking actors of the stage or "talking heads" of television. Strong actions are always more dynamic than static states. The rule is: "Don't talk about it, show it!"

Throughout *Life Lessons*, Lionel's response to Paulette's denial of him is to paint. He doesn't tell us he's going to paint; he assaults his canvas. We watch him passionately slap and smear color around until his painting metamorphoses into a masterpiece. Because we see the actions for ourselves instead of hearing about them, the action has greater significance and makes it into the immediate present instead of the past.

Dramatizing a story through the characters' actions instead of through dialogue tends to deepen the audience's involvement. When we watch characters struggle to achieve what they want, it immediately involves us in an active process. We wonder: "Will they succeed?" We are asking a question that is more emotional than "what is the importance of what he is telling me with his dialogue now?" When characters do more and talk less in a scene, the audience must interpret what those actions mean. This actively includes the audience in the story. But for them to interpret effectively, the writer must provide hints to the actual motivations. It's this active participation in the story that makes a viewer more deeply feel for and identify with the characters. But when characters tell too much about themselves or the story, audiences tend to either tune them out or disbelieve them.

The Dutch Master illustrates the effectiveness of watching a character *act* rather than talk. Various narrators and commentators relate Teresa's story, but it's Teresa's actions that intrigue us most. We watch as the painting captivates her. We watch her longing grow as she searches for something more than what awaits her in marriage. When the painting comes to life, we see her shock. When the Dutchman "invites" her into the scene, we know she must accept and go, and we go along with her, willingly. Teresa never says a word, but by watching her actions we have a better understanding than those closest to her, and we're more interested in her precisely because there's yet so much to know. It's the contrast between what the other characters' say and the reality of what we see that helps keep our interest in the film. Why does the painting so fascinate her? What's happening to her? What do all her actions mean? These questions are left to the audience to sort out, after the film is done.

Where a scene plays greatly affects its mood. An open field at dawn, mid-day or sunset, during summer, winter, spring or fall yields different interpretations to a picture. A study of Impressionist Claude Monet's paintings of grainstacks at different times and seasons demonstrates the effect of light on mood.

The execution that begins *An Occurrence at Owl Creek* takes place at sunrise. The murky image of the battle-scarred landscape in the pre-dawn light casts a desolate pall over the setting and establishes a sense of foreboding. As the hangman slips the noose over the condemned man's head, the feeling of dread intensifies.

Of course, before there is a visual, words must describe it. Words are the screenwriter's first and only tools. Unlike all other steps in the production of a film, writing the screenplay is conveying the imagination in writing. The closer the words describing the images and characters' actions are to conveying the power, excitement and passion a viewer would feel watching the completed film, the more successful the screenplay will be.

Scene Progression

Just as action in a screenplay builds to the most dramatic point, the climax, the movement within a scene must build from the least important ideas to the most. If the significant point is given at the beginning of the scene, all that follows will be anticlimactic. Instead of growth, amplification or development in the drama, there will be a letdown for the audience. Once the main point is made, the scene is over.

Every good scene has a point when the substance or action of the scene begins. This is sometimes referred to as the "button." A few lines of dialogue or a few seconds of visuals may set the scene, but once hit, the action (struggle or conflict of the scene) starts. A button functions like the inciting incident in a plot; it gets things moving. It occurs within a few seconds of the scene's opening and sends the line of action toward the main point.

From the scene's introduction, a progression builds to what the point of the scene is: a plot development, character revelation or sometimes just a funny line after a piece of exposition.

The middle section usually shows the struggle or conflict involved as the main character (in the scene) attempts to achieve something important. The flow of the scene may appear to head in one direction and then as a result of new information or a surprise response, suddenly veer off on a new course, similar to the plot line of a screenplay. The action is always headed toward the climax of the scene.

Beginning and ending a scene are sometimes the most difficult part of writing it. Where it begins or ends does not usually coincide with an entrance or exit. The beginning of a scene might be built into the previous one. In *Life Lessons*, the beginning of a street scene showing Lionel and Paulette on their way to a party really occurs in the prior scene when the two are dressing for the affair.

The same is true of the scene's end that can be built into the scene following it. At the midpoint of *Life Lessons*, Paulette is ostensibly leaving New York and Lionel. In this scene, she tries to confront him, but he is lost in his painting. Unable to rouse him, she watches him paint and we watch her anger dissolve. The next scene shows Paulette getting ready to go to a party with Lionel. Clearly, sometime between the two scenes she changed her mind. We aren't told at the end of the first scene what her decision is. We're simply shown it in the context of the next, and this makes the moment more meaningful.

Sequences

Using more than one scene to illustrate a focused action like Paulette's decision to stay in New York is an example of a scene sequence. Scene sequences are groups of scenes built around a single idea, incident or event in which the locations change but the focus of the action remains the same. The group of scenes in *Life Lessons* at the party builds to the moment where Lionel forces Paulette to viciously retaliate; she leaves with another man. In the following scene, we see she has taken the man back to the studio to bed right under Lionel's nose.

Often whole sections of short films are built by the grouping of scenes around the development of a single idea that shows its progression. A look at the structure of the scenes in *Life Lessons*, *An Occurrence at Owl Creek*, *The Dutch Master*, *PEEL*, and *Mara of Rome* illustrates this. Short films usually stay closer to the characters than features that often seem to highlight hardware (car chases, alien invasions, etc.) in action sequences over characterization. In short films, the scenes are used to show the development of motivations, decisions and actions, and their consequences. If these motivations, decisions and actions are sufficiently dramatic, i.e., noteworthy, moving and vivid, they can draw the audience into the film just as effectively, sometimes even more so, than special effects.

A scene sequence in a short film is a way of avoiding an overly episodic or incidental feel to your story. Characters reveal themselves slowly over a number of scenes, which adds suspense to the delineation of their character arc. Indeed, many short films are essentially a single scene sequence ending when we have learned what we need to know about the characters. Think of *The Lunch Date*.

TECHNIQUES FOR CONSTRUCTION

Writing a great scene is a special talent, like having an ear for funny dialogue. Some screenwriters are just more naturally gifted than others. Still, few scenes come into being fully formed, like Botticelli's Venus on the half shell. Good scenes are the product of careful planning, hard work and reworking. Successful screenwriters tend to utilize particular techniques when composing their scenes. Discovering these techniques can save the beginning screenwriter lots of time and anguish.

Starting Off

Before writing a scene, spend a little time thinking about it. Clarify the topic and main point for yourself. You need to know:

1. Who is in the scene?
2. Where will it play?
3. What the characters want in the scene?

4. What do they need (the subtext) in the scene?
5. What are their attitudes?
6. Where is the conflict or tension coming from?

Clearly, who is in a scene and where it plays seem self-evident. But the screenwriter must get beyond the obvious. Often first thoughts and choices about a scene are familiar or, worse, clichéd. So it's important to take time to examine a number of questions at the onset. Not only must you know who's in the scene, but what the relationships are between the characters. Husbands and wives, siblings, employer and employee, all may have varying relationships depending on their back stories or earlier scenes in the film. Not all husbands and wives are loving, and not all employers and employees play stereotypical roles. If they do, it's usually boring in a film. Additional characters in a scene, other than the primary participants, can lend values not readily apparent. The main characters can play off minor characters for either comedic or dramatic purposes. Minor characters can provide a counterpoint to the main characters, or reinforce them.

Setting, too, can add or detract from a scene. As we have noted above, a scene's locale, including the time, season and weather contributes to creating and maintaining atmosphere. But there are far more important reasons to consider location. The skilled screenwriter often takes advantage of what's available in the setting for the characters to relate to and use. Giving the characters scenery to connect with or physical props to put into their hands, enlivens a scene and increases its level of reality. In *PEEL*, the orange is a terrific prop not only for escalating the drama, but for the rhythm and punctuation it provides before the viewer realizes its importance. Lionel's studio and loft in *Life Lessons* provide a rich setting; props abound to be exploited.

Beginning writers often don't give enough thought to the settings for their scenes. They sometimes use the first locale that occurs to them. Setting can add color to screenplays. It can enhance dramatic value by offering opportunities for the characters to engage in revealing activities. It can reflect their emotions. It is always worthwhile to consider exactly where a scene should play to maximize a location's contribution to the overall screenplay.

Goals & Objectives

Every film needs a protagonist who wants something, who has a goal. The goal directs the film. Will Lionel convince Paulette to stay? Will the condemned man escape? Will Anna sleep with Randall? The plot must stay focused on this story goal.

In every scene the characters have their scene goals or scene objectives. (Actors often write very good scenes because they understand these ideas from scene work.) These scene objectives do not have to be exactly the same as the overall story. If it is a scene goal, it is generally connected to the character's want. If it is a scene objective, it may be related to the character's need. The protagonist may want specific information to aid him in his pursuit of the goal. The information is not the goal, only connected to it. A writer sometimes offers a scene to show how a particular action or piece of information has affected a character. As a result, the character may need comfort or prodding. These scenes strengthen and deepen characterization.

The characters of main importance in a scene often have conflicting wants. The protagonist often conflicts with others besides the antagonist. These other characters provide obstacles or complications for the protagonist to overcome. The conflict creates tension that keeps everything interesting because it causes the audience to wonder how it all will turn out. In *Life Lessons*, the opening scene illustrates this point. Philip wants to enter the studio and view the paintings for the upcoming show. Lionel wants to prevent him. They both have concrete goals. Lionel controls the elevator and keeps the man out. While they are in conflict, exposition for the story is set without anyone suspecting a thing.

As discussed in Chapter 3, characters' conscious wants often conflict with their unconscious needs. It's important to discover if this is a source of conflict that can add dimension to a scene. In *PEEL*, the father says he wants his son to pick up all the orange peel thrown on the highway. What the father needs is to address his anger at his sister. He doesn't and his son runs off, creating more conflict between brother and sister. *Anna of Milan* portrays this type of conflict, too. At the beginning, Anna says she is ready for change; we see that what she wants is Randall. To her he represents change. But as the story points out, she is incapable of change. What she needs is power, to feel in control, which is probably the reason this married woman has affairs. In a number of scenes, the discrepancy between her want and need comes into play.

Scene Subtext

What the character needs in a scene usually relates to the subtext. This is what's going on beneath the surface words and actions. It is so important to understand that Chapter 11 deals exclusively with it.

Sometimes the tension in a scene comes from what precedes it. All the scenes of Lionel painting in *Life Lessons* work well only because they result from and show his response to the conflict with Paulette. "Quiet" or "happy" scenes in your story should be included only as long as the conflict is kept hanging over the characters' heads and the audience aware of it. It's paramount that the characters not escape the problem until it's solved.

The characters' attitudes can bring added tension or even comedy to a scene. Attitudes can be happy or sad, depending on what's happened to the character before the scene. The cause of these attitudes doesn't always have to be shown. Sometimes it's enough to drop in a line of dialogue to explain what's motivating the behavior. The brother and sister's attitudes in the first scene of *PEEL* are built on what's happened previous to the film opening. An impending action also might influence the behavior of a character for good or bad. A character late for a meeting might have a different attitude than one on his way to his wedding.

Think Visually

As you approach a scene one must always keep in mind how it is going to look. Think visually about the scene and the film. As it plays, try to see it in your mind's eye. What does the setting look like? What's on hand for the characters to use that will make it more interesting and more real? Mentally picture as fully as possible the action. Then think, "If I didn't have dialogue, how would I communicate the important idea of the scene?" Always try to find meaningful actions for the characters and audience.

Another question to ask is, "How have I seen this type of scene done before?" Determining this before jumping in can save time and aggravation by eliminating clichés and unconscious imitations. How many ways can a love scene play under a harvest moon? So ask, "How I can do it differently?" Try to be as original as possible. Originality and inventiveness surprise the audience and make better films than the stale and predictable.

Business

In a scene the personal actions of a character are referred to as business. These specific actions might be pouring a drink, eating an apple, fixing a meal — anything people occupy themselves with while alone or interacting with others.

Business contributes a number of valuable functions to the overall effectiveness of a film. Day-to-day activities help create a sense of reality on the screen. Seldom do people sit in head to head dialogue except in very specific situations. Even in confessionals and psychiatrists' offices, we can be distracted by the grate of the screen or a painting on the wall. Most of the time we're engaged in routine activities while talking with others, such as fixing dinner or heading to a destination. These actions also lend physical movement to a scene and keep it from becoming static. Since you want to think visually, keeping the characters' business in mind will help you.

A scene that specifically includes business that suits the character also helps define who that character is. We all know that actions speak louder than words, and audiences tend to give greater credence to what they see as opposed to what they hear. What characters do gives the audience clues about their total personality. A woman who putters at jigsaw puzzles and one who goes on wild shopping sprees make completely different comments about their respective personalities.

Because of the strong influence actions make on assessing the characters, business shouldn't be considered incidental or just as movement. Business reinforces the characterizations. If a character's business contradicts his dialogue, the scene can make a much stronger impression than a speech that tells the audience exactly what he is thinking. If a character wants to hide his emotions, but the writer wants the audience to understand and empathize with him, business can provide the telling actions. Although dialogue is extremely convenient for expressing inner thoughts and feelings, it often undermines the power of the character and the scene when it tells us too much.

Humor

Anywhere humor fits naturally into a screenplay, a writer should consider using it, regardless of genre. The humor should be organic to the situation in the scene, and not merely an excuse to be funny. Unlike some feature films, most short screenplays are better served by funny characterizations and situations rather than funny dialogue or jokes. Jokes that turn the protagonist into a stand-up comedian tend not to advance the action, but instead slow the story down. Effective comedy isn't based on quips or mechanical gimmicks. The banana peel isn't funny, it's the character who slips on it that gets you your laugh.

Even the darkest tragedies benefit from a little comic relief. In a serious or tragic work, the writer purposely uses a humorous scene, incident or remark to relieve emotional intensity and simultaneously heighten the seriousness or tragic implications of the action. Shakespeare illustrates this with the humor throughout *Hamlet*. And what would *Romeo and Juliet* be without Mercutio? Even in *Macbeth*, the episode with the drunken porter provides the much-needed comic relief to the dark portent of the tale.

Humor, of course, can be broad or realistic, light or heavy-handed. It all depends upon your story. In *Life Lessons*, Richard Price uses a light touch to add humor to an otherwise serious tale. Early in the film, Lionel shoots hoops in his studio. His basket is next to the window into Paulette's bedroom. After making several hoops, he fires off a shot that goes through Paulette's window, drawing an angry response from her and a laugh from us.

Filmmakers David Lean and Ronald Neame were partnered on a few films early in their careers. Mr. Neame, who has taught at UCLA Extension, is fond of saying that after they knew the point and the conflict of a scene, the last thing they would do is see if humor could fit into the scene organically. After all, films are entertainment.

Economy

It is an unwritten law that films must move. Every scene must advance the action; every line must keep sight of the climax. A film is always driving ahead. One of the best tools a screenwriter has to help him or her achieve this momentum is to use an economy of words. Words, description and dialogue, must be as focused as everything else in a screenplay. Random description of every detail in a scene will only derail it. Usually, when setting a scene, the scene heading provides much implied detail, for example:

```
INT. ARTIST'S STUDIO — DAY
```

A line or two of description, noting numerous blank canvases scattered around the large room or an expensive bottle of cognac lying amidst paintbrushes, will tell the reader enough to get the specific picture. Descriptions should always be kept to a minimum.

Another way to keep screenplays lean is to enter the scene at the latest possible moment. A scene that starts with the most relevant plot topic dispenses with boring or superfluous material. As soon as its goal is accomplished, the scene should end. So stay away from entrances, exits and introductions. These take up time and contribute little to the film.

EXERCISES

Take a scene from your plot outline that you feel you know well and write it. Go over it a few times in the next few days until you feel good about it. Set it aside for a week, then return to it for analysis. This exercise will work with a scene from a produced screenplay of your choice.

1. Locate the main point of the scene. What is it trying to accomplish? Is it telling us about character or conveying a plot point? Is it clear?
2. What is visually interesting in the scene? What business are the characters engaged in to enhance the visual quality of the story? What's is the mood?
3. What do the main characters want in the scene? What do they need? What are their attitudes? What are their scene objectives? Isolate the conflict.
4. How does the scene progress? Is there a specific moment where the scene takes off (hits the "button")? Is it close to

the beginning of the scene or does it come later? Are there surprises in the scene? Is it emotional? Does it make its point and end?

5. What do we learn about the characters from dialogue as well as visuals? Characterize how the scene shifts from beginning to end in terms of the relationships.

6. What is the subtext of the scene? Is there anything going on beneath the surface dialogue? If not, can the scene be improved by adding some?

Return to the scene using what you've learned and rewrite it. Save for the exercise at the end of the next chapter.

10

Dialogue: The Search for the Perfect Line

The last chapter discussed many aspects of scene construction except the most obvious: the dialogue. We think of dialogue as conversation between characters in drama or literature. But in any fictional medium, dialogue isn't conversation. It's the illusion of conversation. Real conversation is random, repetitive, and often pointless. Dramatic dialogue is ordered and purposeful.

Writing good dialogue, terrific dialogue, is like writing a great scene. It takes lots of practice. Some screenwriters have a natural gift for turning a phrase, using humor or innuendo to deepen the meaning of film conversation. A dedicated student, though, can go a long way with hard work. He can learn to actively listen to the different patterns of speech people use and develop an ear for words. Taking notes of particularly prime exchanges is another way a novice writer can grow.

THE FUNCTION OF DIALOGUE
The role of dialogue in a screenplay is to:
1. Advance the plot toward its climax
2. Advance the audience's understanding of the main characters

3. Advance the audience's understanding of the story by providing information which can't be shown
4. Set the tone for the film (especially in comedy)

Film dialogue must be crafted within the context of character and conflict. It must give the appearance that this is what a specific character would say under a specific set of circumstances. Yet it can't stray too far from the main topic of the screenplay. If a line does not serve one of these basic functions, you should consider cutting it from the page.

Advancing the Plot

The plots of films, plays and novels grow out of the interaction of conflicting characters. These exchanges between characters involve dialogue. Dialogue generally makes up the largest portion of a screenplay and a scene as well. When dialogue advances the plot, it relates directly to the conflict. This doesn't mean that the dialogue only describes specific plot-oriented details. The dialogue helps illustrate the progress of the conflict. It shows how the conflict affects the characters and what they do as a result.

Almost every scene in *Life Lessons* advances the conflict, and the dialogue reflects this. From the moment Lionel picks up Paulette at the airport until she walks out of the studio, he verbally struggles with her, trying to rekindle their relationship only to further alienate her. The dialogue reflects this. The only time the plot conflict takes a back seat is just after the midpoint when Paulette has changed her mind about leaving as the two get ready for a party they act and speak like an old married couple. The few scenes showing them on their way to and eventually arriving at the party are used to reveal Lionel's character. But by then the conflict is already locked in place, and the film can afford a short breather.

Revealing Character

What characters say and what they don't is a primary way they reveal and define themselves in life and in film. How a person speaks can be very telling about where she comes from, her level of education, and so on. Her diction or choice of words to describe her experiences provides hints to her deeper nature.

Dialogue should be thought of as a function of character. Within the context of film unity, it's an action, not merely a device to tell the story. Dialogue allows the audience to more specifically comprehend the character and distinguish her from others.

Physical action is considered the best revelation of character in a film, but sometimes only dialogue can expose real character motivations. Such dialogue should always be considered carefully. If a speech is too precise in its description of past events, it'll ring false and lose impact because in real life these disclosures are rarely made, and then usually under stress. A film character, too, then should face extraordinary circumstances when something compels him to drop his guard and reveal himself, his innermost feelings. When character revelation of this sort is properly motivated, it provides a powerful comment on the character — all the more so when it portrays him in a radically different light from what the audience expects.

Providing Information

Chapter 6 already describes the nature and importance of expository information. Generally, dialogue plays some part in conveying the main exposition. But as a film progresses, additional information is needed. Characters make discoveries about each other and the dramatic situation. Many of these discoveries are visual, but most often they need confirmation and elucidation through dialogue.

Information given in dialogue must be consequential to the story or characters. If the audience doesn't really need to know it to understand these elements, don't give it.

Setting the Tone

When dialogue helps set the tone of a film it's usually a comedy. In film, a sense of foreboding or catastrophe is best achieved through visuals and the drama, not through poetic or overly dramatic dialogue. Comedy relies on humor, funny lines, jokes and gags, visual and verbal. When dialogue crackles with quips and jokes, audiences respond with laughter. It can effectively establish a film's tone in seconds.

THE CHARACTERISTICS OF GOOD DIALOGUE

Again, dialogue isn't real conversation, but the illusion of it. As anyone who has read a court transcript or taped a college class knows, the best dialogue isn't an edited version of real speech; it's invention, contrived conversation that satisfies the demands of its scene. But it must sound real to work. If dialogue sounds stilted, false, corny, or clichéd, it can destroy a worthy story.

In a feature or short film, dialogue has the same characteristics. It's at its best when it differentiates characters, when it's clear, when it advances the tension in a scene, when it's to the point, but not "on the nose."

Voice

A character's individual voice is one of the most important ways he reveals himself. Voice is more than just how he talks. It reflects where he has come from and where he has gone. It gives an indication of how he thinks, what's important to him and what's not, and some degree of his psychology.

In Chapter 3, we mentioned a character's birthplace influences who he will become. His behavior will differ if he's born in Scarsdale or the South Bronx. Patterns of speech show where a person comes from, as do accents and dialects. Certain phrases and expressions are particular to specific ethnic backgrounds and classes. Good grammar or bad usually clues us in to someone's education. The use of special jargon characterizes occupations, and slang often identifies time and place. Understanding and using the special way people talk brings dialogue to life and makes it colorful and real.

Through dialogue you illustrate differences between people. One character can be philosophical or literal, make allusions or be direct. The owner of a racehorse sounds different from the stable hand who grooms it. Even characters of similar backgrounds often have different speech patterns, depending on their interests and the way they think. A sense of humor can define one character while the lack of one defines another.

Emotion often forces people to revive patterns of speech they believe they have left behind. A woman who has moved from Brooklyn and tried to leave every trace of it behind, may find her accent returns the moment she wishes most to hide it — when angered, for example.

To understand how different people speak, you need to develop an ear for words. As long as you work within your own scope, dialogue shouldn't be a problem. But when you introduce characters whose backgrounds diverge from yours, research becomes a true ally. Research lends authenticity to a plot and milieu, but also often produces a colorful and esoteric language that gives any screenplay authority and brings it to life.

A look at two films set in New York illustrates this point. *Life Lessons* deals with educated, artistic individuals. Their speech in the film reflects this. Except for Dr. Rosenman and the museum docent, all the characters in *The Dutch Master* are working class and sound like it.

Simplicity

In a film, dialogue needs to be understood the first time it's heard. You can't rerun a passage in a film and take time to think about it the way you can reread a book. The audience is listening to the dialogue and has to grasp its meaning before the film moves ahead. The best dialogue is usually simple. It comes in short, ordered sentences that give the illusion of real speech.

In real life, people tend to talk in short sentences or sentence fragments, with simple, direct words. They interrupt each other, repeat and overlap. Effective dialogue, however, cannot literally follow these patterns. It'll lose momentum and power if it does. You, though, can sparingly use interruptions and repetitions to emphasize what a character is saying and show another's reaction. This adds to the appearance of reality. Reality, however, can't always be the guide. For example, though realistic, you should avoid overlapping dialogue unless there are specific reasons to do it.

Poetic, flashy, and complex words and sentences generally confuse the dialogue's meaning. It makes dialogue hard to follow — whether listening and reading. This doesn't mean you can never use poetry or flashy phrases, express complex thoughts or esoteric language. A character distinguished by verbal cunning or abstract logic might use this type of language.

Progression

Just as a scene progresses to its most dramatic point, so does dialogue. Lines must build from the least significant to the most to develop the innate tension such progression contains. Whether the speech is dramatic or comedic, the principle is the same. "Jimmy fell and hit his head. He's at the hospital — In a coma."

In comedy, lines develop to a punch line, the funny twist that makes you laugh. Good writers save the joke until the end of a speech. If it comes at the beginning and the audience laughs, it can get in the way of or conceal important material that follows. Also, in comedy, jokes tend to need a line or two to set up. "It's not like I'm picky," the lady lawyer says. "All I want is a guy who's tall, dark — and has no prior felonies."

Always save the strongest lines for scene finales to maximize their impact.

Economy

Many screenplays depend too heavily on dialogue to communicate every aspect of the story. Short films tend to use even less dialogue proportionately than features. Film is a visual medium and dialogue need not tell the viewer (reader) what he'll know by watching the screen.

The best dialogue is lean. Brevity is more valuable than amplification in a screenplay, especially in dialogue. A screenwriter relies more on the visual aspects of a story than the dialogue to advance it. Because film is visual, the shorter the film segment the more its visual origins are stressed. Think of the best commercials, and the emphasis on the visual. Dialogue is used often at the end to underscore the message. Behavior and deeds are stronger indicators of a person than his words. Extraneous words, lines and even whole speeches should be cut whenever possible. As long as clarity isn't an issue, these cuts will only strengthen the dialogue, not weaken it.

Long speeches work better in novels and plays than in films. You must have a good reason to include one. Any passage running more than four or five lines should be studied carefully for trimming or complete removal. Monologues are a theatrical device, not a filmic one. If a character uses a long speech to explain how something works, it can slow the action. The writer needs to consider length and get the information across in a simpler way. A long speech used for the revelation of character is a different matter. Self-revelation can be very powerful. After all, this is sometimes the whole point of a film. The writer can take his time with the speech in order to maximize the impact of it on the audience.

"On The Nose" Dialogue

When dialogue is too direct and too clear, it often rings false, especially when the speeches involve emotional issues. In real life, most people have difficulty expressing or communicating their emotions. They tend to want to conceal or deny them. Others don't want to confront emotional issues and talk around them. Because film strives to capture the appearance of reality, real life responses are most crucial when they involve issues that the audience can identify with. Emotion is a powerful universal.

The heart of a great film is its emotional wallop. So emotion must be forced out into the open where the audience can identify with the characters feeling it. Often, beginning screenwriters will avoid emotion and conflict in their writing or are too obvious in their use. Both extremes can jeopardize whatever good will the audience may feel on behalf of the film.

The art of screenwriting is to capture characters' indirection in such a way that the audience grasps the true, deeper meaning of what's happening until the moment the characters force each other to reveal their real motivations. When viewers make the associations for themselves from their lives and backgrounds, the characters' experiences take on greater significance, and so does the film. When characters imply rather than state "on the nose" what they're feeling, it allows the audience make these associations and connect more deeply with the characters. In the next chapter on subtext, we will discuss this in more detail.

Life Lessons illustrates how the dialogue revolves around important emotional issues. In the second scene, when Paulette gets off the jet and finds Lionel waiting for her, she doesn't tell us she's angry, her attitude and actions do. In the same scene, when Lionel learns of Paulette's weekend with another man, he doesn't say he's jealous, his behavior does. He acts hurt, and then attacks the other man with sarcasm.

TECHNIQUES & TIPS

To create dialogue that sounds natural and rolls effortlessly off the actor's tongue, there are a few techniques and tips to assist the beginning writer.

Rough It Out

Once the formal idea for a scene is in mind and many, if not all, of the questions discussed in the last chapter have been satisfactorily answered, you're ready to begin writing. A good idea is to first rough out the scene, without censoring any thoughts. It doesn't matter if the speeches are long and full, if they're too flowery, too direct, or too pedantic; whether ideas are repeated, and clichés abound. Sometimes the characters just have to speak in order to really discover the heart of a scene.

Often, out of these flabby speeches, one or two lines will be real gems and say everything necessary. The rest of the speech can be red-penciled. Because of repetitions within the scene, a few lines might express an important idea better than others. Save these lines for the most significant places within the scene and cut the others.

Now look, word by word, at the dialogue and the scene. Most of the speeches should be no longer than one or two lines. (Formatting is very important here to determine the proper line length. See Appendix A.) Take out anything that sounds clichéd, looking for better ways to express your ideas. Then rewrite. Don't be afraid to juggle the beats of the scene around, using a piece of dialogue initially written for the end at the beginning to see what happens. Sometimes this will show that the whole first half of a scene is extraneous and can be dropped.

When the scene is finished, you're ready for the next step.

Read It Out Loud

Always read your dialogue out loud. The best indication of how it will sound is by how it rolls off your own tongue. We write dialogue to be spoken. It must sound natural. It's totally different than dialogue in a book, which is written to be read. Book dialogue often sounds stilted and unreal when it's read aloud. The only way to hear if dialogue sounds natural is to listen carefully to it. If the words and sentences are awkward or hard to say, then it isn't effective screenplay dialogue.

Reading the dialogue out loud will also help determine if all the characters tend to sound alike. You want to capture the different ways people talk. This can be accomplished through the use of similar phrasing for one character. One character might always use jargon, even when away from his office. Another might always use simple everyday speech, even when describing a complex medical emergency.

Depending on how good an actor you are, saying the dialogue aloud can also indicate whether or not the emotion builds through a scene. Acting out the lines can illustrate the emotional points. Listening tells you if your dialogue moves to the most dramatic point, or jumps from one emotion to another.

Nonverbal Language

Not all communication is verbal. In a scene, much can be said by the way one character looks at another, and through nonverbal reactions.

Remember, in film, the camera sits in place of the audience. By taking us right into the face of a character, it can show us with a reaction how someone feels without her uttering a word. Through the use of action, mood, music, editing, it can amplify small gestures that would be missed on stage. Nine times out of ten, the action will be stronger than dialogue. However, the description of the outward appearance and quality of the action should be succinct. It's better to suggest and imply, than to be absolute. It gives the reader an opportunity to fill in the blanks from his own imagination and the actor room for personal interpretation.

Miscellaneous Tips

Wherever possible find the specific emotions behind not only the scene, but each speech. Actors will have to do it, so you should, too. The emotion in a scene usually grows or diminishes according to what's happening. If one character tries to mollify another who's upset, the first's actions could instead actually further annoy the other. If the point of the scene is an angry explosion, the speeches as well as actions should show the progression, from bad to worse. Grounding each speech on its suitable emotional moorings will strengthen the progression of the dialogue within the scene.

Dialogue is best in face-to-face confrontation. Confrontation is conflict. Whenever characters are in conflict, emotion enters the picture. Emotion makes characters say and do things calmer heads wouldn't. Emotion always makes things more interesting because characters act (and say things) more unpredictably.

If you listen to people talk who know each other well, you'll learn several things about dialogue and interrelationships. First, when addressing each other, they rarely use the other's name. They already know who they're talking to, so what's the point of calling more attention to it? Who would they be signaling except the audience? If one person wants to emphasize an issue, he might use the other's name, but even this is the exception. When names are used in every other line of dialogue, it sounds clumsy and unnatural. If a formal situation occurs where names are used more often, then this can be accommodated in the dialogue to some extent. But each time another's name is used by a character in the situation, the character addressing the other will most likely sound obsequious. When a writer overuses the characters' names in dialogue, it's usually an indication he doesn't know his creations as well as he should.

When characters are introduced for the first time in a screenplay and film, their names do not have to be used right away in dialogue to make sure the viewer gets them. Names can be held until an appropriate moment — perhaps someone will call out one's name across the street, or it will come up naturally in the dialogue. Within the story, there will be a moment when the important characters meet and names can be exchanged at that time. You don't have to be in a rush to label all the characters. In fact, if a few lesser characters are never named, the economy of the screenplay and film will be served. Think of how many people you interact with each day whose names are unknown to you.

When several people are talking in a scene, not using names can get confusing, especially when one is speaking directly to another. Still, using a name each time a character talks to someone else sounds false. To make it simpler, use dialogue cues to indicate who the character is talking to.

```
            PHIL
         (to Ed)
     Hey, let's go!
```

Or:

```
            PHIL
        (faces Sally)
     Please, let me go.
```

These cues show the reader and actor what to do. The viewer sees the speaker turn to Ed or face Sally, and understands who is talking to whom.

The trouble with dialogue cues is that many beginning screenwriters have a tendency to overuse them. They want to direct every line of a speech. If a scene and its dialogue are well written, the emotion will flow with it. The reader will have a good idea whether one character is smiling or frowning. A good rule of thumb is to keep dialogue directions short, and only use them if they add something to the speech that's not obvious.

The words "yes" and "no" are used less than one expects in real conversation. People nod or shake their heads to answer yes or no questions. Whenever a visual reaction is possible, use it

This is true for expressing anger as well. Too often writers allow their characters to curse indiscriminately. When these words are used too frequently in dialogue, it lessens their dramatic value. It's better to find actions that express a character's anger than to call someone names. Then, when someone really wants to swear a blue streak the words will have power.

Soliloquy and asides don't work well in films. In film, people don't talk to themselves. It's very hard to pull off authentically. Most times it seems forced, unnatural. It's better if the screenwriter finds another way to get the information across to the audience. The same is true for the *non-sequitur*. These are hard to follow, reading or hearing, and so their relevance is often meaningless.

"I've loved you from the very first moment I saw you." Clichés find their way into almost everyone's speech now and then, and into almost every writer's first draft. The trouble with these hack-neyed phrases in written form is that they stand out, however mundane they are in daily speech. If you want to use them, turn them on their heads. A man might talk about being "strong-armed" by a thug. But another might describe the thug's methods as "a little strong in the arm." Not "Dead as a doornail" but, "Dead as a thumb tack." Or Daffy Duck's: "Just shows to go you!"

Always take time to make the last line of dialogue count. If the final moment is strong, when the audience leaves the film they take it with them.

EXERCISES

Take the scene you wrote and reworked at the end of the last chapter. Now go over the dialogue.

1. Do all the characters sound the same or does each one have his or her own voice? This doesn't mean you have to indicate a character has an accent, but phrasing and word choices should indicate something specific about him. Think about someone you know who is like the character and use the way he speaks as a model.

2. Do we get a sense of how each character thinks by the way he expresses himself? Is one cynical while another romantic? Is one humorous? Humor can be an important tool of the screenwriter, and if it can be worked into the dialogue organically, consider doing it. Again, draw from your own experience of people for models.

3. Is the dialogue clear the first time reading it? Does it feel real, though still convey the important information? Is it repetitive, too many lines going over the same material? Does the dialogue duplicate the visual action? Use a red-pen or marker to cut the lines which repeat, or duplicate action.

4. Do the lines in the speeches progress from the least impor-tant ones to the most? Do lines feel like they're building, or just thrown on the page? Look to organize the lines so they build to the most intense point in a speech and ulti-mately in the scene.

5. Do any of the lines seem to be "on the nose"? Can these lines be improved by finding actions to convey the points?

Have you included any non-verbal language? Look at the places where dialogue is too on the nose and try to express the character's attitude or emotions without dialogue, using the subtext as a guide. One way to achieve this is for a character to talk about something seemingly unrelated. Does this work better?

6. Do the characters use each other's names frequently? Do clichés appear in the dialogue? The obvious solution is the red pen. But with clichés, try to find more original ways of conveying the expressions.

Now rewrite the scene again. When you finish, read it out loud. Does it sound more focused? Is there a stronger progression? Can you feel the real point of the scene? If not, strengthening the subtext as described in the next chapter may help with this.

11

The Subtext of Meaning

The conspicuous results from writing a scene — the overall arrangement of action and dialogue — lead us to, perhaps, the hardest task: delineating the scene's latent meaning. Scene subtext is one of the most difficult aspects of screenwriting to grasp. It's what's going on beneath the surface, the undercurrent of emotions and thoughts that truly motivates characters to behave as they do. Most of the time subtext connects to characters' needs. It can sometimes relate to what characters consciously know and want yet can't reveal. A story's subtext answers the question why characters act and say what they do, before and after plot requirements are considered. Certain actions and dialogue must unfold for the plot to work. But the layer of meaning beneath the plot mechanics goes to the heart of who our characters really are, and why they find themselves in a particular story.

Directors and actors bring a scene to life by determining the feelings, thoughts and motives that lie beneath the actual words and actions of the characters. If the screenwriter lacks a sufficient understanding of the subtext, his scenes will be missing purpose and power. Action will all be on the surface, frustrating the director and actors' task of realizing the scenes. A screenwriter who understands subtext provides clues in the script for the director and actors dramatizing this subterranean level of the story for the audience.

Subtext isn't what you write; it's what you write around. It's the deeper level of the story that can't be told so much in words but must be shown in actions.

THE ROLE OF SUBTEXT

In real life, people rarely say what they're feeling. More often, they try to hide what bothers them, their personal weaknesses, minor transgressions. They lie about the smallest troubles and biggest problems. They may be motivated to protect ones they love or themselves, to gain power or prestige. Because motives are hidden, they often are misperceived. When this happens and problems arise, many of us find ourselves playing the episode over in our minds, trying to figure out what exactly happened and why. Why? Because we're fascinated, and usually upset, that our real desires remain so obscure that we've been so misunderstood; our words and deeds have miscommunicated our intentions. The real meaning of our actions, the subtext, has been muddled by a pattern of behavior designed to show what we want. But we're really after is to get people to give us what we need, even if we're not conscious of what that is.

In drama, where all imitates life, our aim is to show a version of reality. The ultimate goal, however, isn't to be obscure, but to be understood, to avoid the confusion between needs and wants in everyday life. The screenwriter must know his characters better than they know themselves. The writer demonstrates this knowledge of her characters through the subtext by letting the audience see what the characters really need beyond what they say they want. The easy way to understand this elusive concept of subtext is to see it as the connection between how the characters, moving according to their desires in a story, end up with what they have needed all along. Cinderella doesn't need a day off work, new slippers or to take revenge on her family. She needs a recognition that comes through love. Lionel, in *Life Lessons*, doesn't need romantic or requited love, though he talks nonstop about it. What he needs is the sexual frustration, fermented by an unstable personal life, which he channels into creative energy.

This need is revealed through subtext. It must be. Lionel himself isn't conscious of it.

The screenwriter, therefore, walks a thin line between telling too much and telling too little. Tell too much and you lose the audience's interest. Tell too little and the audience may not understand the story.

Subtext is used to reveal what can't be easily or honestly told in words. Thus, it has everything to do with needs. The need surfaces in the character in the form of feelings and thoughts that generate motives for his actions. In Chapter 3 we defined need as the unconscious motivation of a character. The protagonist has a conscious goal and an unconscious need. If a character's unconscious need contradicts his stated goal, the scene will play differently than if conscious and unconscious minds are in total agreement. Need comes from a deep part of the character's psyche of which he may well be ignorant. The character's need may be the real motivation behind everything he does in the story. But for the audience to grasp this fact, the need must be shown in a credible fashion.

Feelings, Thoughts & Motives

To understand a story, certain exposition must be overtly presented to the audience, and other pieces can be implied. Subtext compliments exposition, conveying feelings, thoughts and motivations which are too complex to tell in words, but which are crucial to understanding a story. At times, the true motives and emotions of a character are the whole point of a film. If this information is clumsily handled or just dumped in the audience's lap, viewers will doubt its veracity the same way you might be skeptical of a person who easily tells you his life story. A character's motivation carries more weight if it's closely guarded — the way true motivations in life are. When viewers have to figure out for themselves why characters do something, they become active participants in the dramatic process. When they identify with characters and feel what they're feeling, they're in an active relationship with the material, and this participation leads to a deeper involvement in the film.

Through subtext, the screenwriter allows the audience glimpses or hints of the protagonist's and other characters' true nature. Lionel tells Paulette he loves her, yet as viewers watch him over the course of the film embarrasses her, lie to her, try to control and dominate her, they wonder about his definition of love. The subtext is telling us something contrary to what the character says.

The first half of *Hills Like White Elephants* is driven by an unidentified conflict between the couple as they wait for their train. Sure, he's worried about money and she doesn't want to move again, but something much deeper than these surface concerns is fueling the friction between them. By the time the problem comes out into the open, the audience has seen Davis and Ash both say they'll do what the other wants. But by the end of the film, the audience has realized the impossibility of the situation and that what's at stake is nothing less than the couple's relationship.

Subtext & Theme

Subtext should carry a direct relationship to the film's theme. It becomes the avenue for getting the main ideas across when it wouldn't be realistic in dialogue. In *Life Lessons*, subtext defines the theme. The film isn't about love, but about how the self-absorption of the artist leads to creation. In *Mara of Rome*, the film isn't about whether or not the prostitute will corrupt the young seminarian. The real topic is the power of faith and love.

When a story's successful, audiences feel satisfied. When we feel satisfied, usually something is working on a deeper level. Even if we can't completely articulate what the story is about, it has touched us in some unaccountable way and it feels true, right. When we take the time to analyze it, to think about the characters, feelings and motives, we can make associations that allow the deeper meaning of the film to emerge.

THE EMOTION BENEATH THE LINES

Dialogue is the most obvious way to reveal emotion. "I'm really mad," one character says. "I feel sick at heart," says another. Yet dialogue is rarely the best way to express emotion unless it's forced out into open conversation.

As noted above, when characters tell too much, especially regarding difficult issues, audiences don't assign the matter the proper emotional weight. On the contrary, they tend to trivialize it. Seeing a character avoid a troubling issue or unable to find words to express his feelings engages our interest more deeply, because we do the same. Our curiosity whetted, we watch more carefully to see what the character will do.

In a scene, the emotion carrying the lines may:
1. Support the dialogue
2. Contradict the dialogue
3. Have little relationship to the dialogue.

Emotion Supporting Dialogue

When emotion supports the dialogue, the lines reflect what the characters feel. When someone is happy, it's hard to suppress. Happiness effects attitude, actions and easily filters into the conversation. In *Mara of Rome*, when Rusconi arrives at Mara's apartment, he can barely contain his joy. He acts silly and his dialogue is funny. He doesn't need to say he's happy because it's clear from his actions.

Fury also is hard to control, and it ultimately infiltrates what's said, too. After Umberto's grandmother reproaches Mara and ruins her peace of mind, Mara can't restrain her anger. She turns it on Rusconi and drives him away.

In *Life Lessons*, Lionel's depressed at the beginning of the film. He doesn't say why to Philip, he says, "I'm going to get slaughtered." When Paulette gets off the jet and sees Lionel waiting for her, she's angry. She doesn't scream and yell at him, but her anger is reflected in her attitude.

Emotional states find expression in the dialogue, but in elliptical ways. Characters talk around the cause of their emotional condition. Even though the dialogue in these scenes is an indirect indication of mood, it must still be properly motivated, usually in a progression of emotions within the scene or in the progression of scenes that builds emotion.

Emotion Contradicting Dialogue

When emotion contradicts the dialogue, it forces the character to take action contrary to what he says. He might feel fear and want to hide it. He might be angry yet be unable to show it. In *Life Lessons*, near the beginning, Lionel appears in Paulette's room, ostensibly looking for his sable brush. Paulette sees right through him: "I'm not sleeping with you," she says. He admits an impulse to kiss her foot. She recoils, causing him to let off steam about his upcoming show. Finally, he says, "I just wanted to kiss your foot. I'm sorry. It's nothing personal." Since we have heard how he says he feels about her, the lines make him sound pitiful because they deny his purported feelings.

Emotion with Little Relationship to Dialogue

Sometimes the whole point of the scene is the emotion it contains. The scene is needed to move the audience one way or another, to better identify with or oppose a character as he approaches a problem. When Paulette calls her mother to ask about coming home, most of the dialogue is incidental. What's important is that the audience witnesses the emotion and pain gripping Paulette to understand the depths of her crisis.

In *The Wedding*, during the post-nuptial party where Teresa is introduced to Don Nicola's friends and family, there's a moment when Teresa finds herself alone in the group of strangers. Everyone is curious about her, how she met Don Nicola since she's from Rome and he's from Naples, site of the story. The happy guests decide to honor her with a Roman song. One man starts the national anthem but the others find it too stuffy, so they sing a drinking tune, giving a rousing rendition. We watch as Teresa's doubt and hesitation about the marriage finally give way to happy acceptance. As she joins in singing, we feel her joy, too. The lyrics of the song, the scene's "dialogue," are meaningless to the real emotion of the scene. This happy moment makes the pain of the revelation at the end all the more poignant.

At the beginning of *Mara of Rome*, the few lines exchanged on Umberto's grandmother's patio have little value. What's important is that we see the way the young man looks at the sensual Mara clad only in a luxurious white towel prancing around her garden. When Mara catches a glimpse of him, we see her interest aroused. Then she sees his priest's collar, and her interest turns to amusement.

Remember, to the audience, your characters are initially strangers. Don't expect viewers to believe everything they say. The audience needs to see your characters in action and under pressure to discover who they really are. Only in conflict is one's true self revealed. Viewers evaluate the characters from what they do and what they say. The audience measures the truthfulness of the dialogue and weighs it against the actions characters perform to discover who each one really is.

REVEALING THE SUBTEXT

In scenes, emotions motivate characters to act as they do. The protagonist may be cool and calm, but if all the characters reflect this same indifference, the scenes won't be very interesting. In most scenes, someone's in the grip of an emotion, positive or negative, and this emotion influences the scene, how he behaves and how others interact with him. It also creates interest. It appeals to the voyeur in us as we witness a person feeling joy and making a fool of himself. Because the audience needs to become aware of the emotions and thoughts affecting the story, the screenwriter must find ways to reveal or externalize them.

Dialogue

The characteristics of good dialogue have already been discussed in Chapter 9. Asking a few questions about the characters and the emotion can help insure the dialogue strengthens the subtext of a scene. First determine:

1. What must be said in the scene?
2. What can be implied?
3. What doesn't need to be said at all?

Then ask:

4. What is the key emotion motivating the characters in this scene?
5. How would their respective emotions specifically affect the characters? What would each do? For example, would one suppress or vent his anger?
6. Would the character have a conscious or unconscious strategy for dealing with this emotion? I.e., would he use understatement or directly contradict his feelings in words?
7. Is there a progression or a shift in the emotion experienced by a character?
8. Where is the conflict or tension coming from?

Any or all of these questions should help clarify what is going on beneath the surface of the characters. Once these questions have been answered, you should have a better idea of the subtext and how a character might react to it. Dialogue may be the perfect way to bring the subtext out into the open. But if it's not, consider the following:

Physical Attitude

Physical attitude refers to a character's outward disposition or mood representing his inner emotional state. Body language, facial expressions, gestures fall under this heading. All provide hints to a character's state of mind. Film is interested in showing what a character is like as opposed to telling us what he feels, as novels or short stories do. Screenwriters can't rely on the narrative to explain complex personalities, emotions and attitudes. They must figure out ways to clue the audience in on what's really going on through the external action that can be seen and heard.

Lionel's attitude at the beginning of *Life Lessons* shows a man depressed. His whole body sags with the weight of what he is feeling inside. His appearance is a mess, clothes wrinkled, hair unkempt. When Philip mentions the upcoming show, Lionel's face conveys sheer panic. Contrast this with Lionel's demeanor in the finale, attending his exhibition. He stands erect, appearance neat, hair combed. No trace of panic remains. Above all, Lionel is supremely satisfied with his work.

The screenwriter must describe the characteristics of what the audience sees and hears in the action and the parenthetical directions. Most of the description is of an external state. In the following portion of a scene, note the words used to describe the characters' attitudes in the action and parenthetical directions.

```
EXT. TURNER HOUSE - DAY

Indignant eight year-old ALEC TURNER, dark eyes
flaring, grips the collar of his old black dog,
KING. Across the grass, towers forty-five year-old
nerd TED McCLURE. He stands over a recent brown spot
on his immaculate lawn.
```

```
              MCCLURE
          (red-faced)
      I am sick and tired of finding a
      new pile of crap on my way to
      work every morning!

              ALEC
      King didn't do it!

              MCCLURE
      Look at this!
```

He points with real emotion at the small circles of
dead grass.

"Indignant" and "dark eyes flaring," describe the eight year-
old boy Alec. He "grips" his dog by the collar as he stands against
his neighbor. Does he grip the dog to hold him back or for protec-
tion? The "nerd" McClure "towers" over brown spots on his lawn.
The parenthetical cue clues in the reader to McClure's attitude: He
is "red-faced" with anger.

This short introductory description sets the tone for the rest
of the scene. As long as the lines maintain or build on the established level of intensity, few additional cues are needed. If, however, the scene reverses and builds to apology, then cues to indicate a turnaround must be used.

Business

In Chapter 9 we discussed the business of a scene in a number of
ways. Business helps establish a sense of reality. It creates movement that makes more visually interesting images for the film.
Characters are further defined by what they do within a scene.
This business of doing relates strongly to subtext. If every action
a character takes represents a true portrait of who she is, her
action speaks more truth than the dialogue of ten characters
telling us how they feel about her.

The most important business for Lionel in *Life Lessons* is his
painting. Every time he paints, we see his total involvement in the
process, his complete commitment to the work. When he's working, not even his muse Paulette can call him away.

Lionel's use of the boom box also informs the audience
about who he is. As a tool he uses it in his creative process; the

music he plays defines his mood and serves as inspiration. But the mega-watt stereo also serves as a weapon and illustrates his self-absorption. The music blasts if Lionel is at work, regardless of the hour and who might be trying to sleep. It's a barrier protecting the artist.

Another bit of telling business is Lionel's handling of the basketball. After Lionel has convinced Paulette to stay in New York, he shoots hoops before he begins painting. One might think he's only warming up before painting, but this action shows he's in a different state. He's no longer depressed and frantic because Paulette's staying. Now he can paint, because he can play.

Actions that illustrate emotional states can be very simple. In *Occurrence at Owl Creek*, the protagonist emerges safe from the river and rapids. Though wounded by Union soldiers, he's free. He stretches his hands and grabs the sand, throwing handfuls of it over his head and into his hair, laughing, overjoyed to be alive. Then he spots one fragile flower growing from the rocks and drags himself to it just to smell. All of this underscores his joy at escaping the hangman's noose. The simplicity of these actions as expressions make them seem all the more real and poignant.

Atmosphere

Atmosphere also helps to reveal the characters' inner states by reinforcing them. Weather, time of day, nature all can contribute to creating a mood that reflects the interior world of the characters. Using the external world to mirror the inner emotions felt by the characters helps the audience share in the characters' experiences.

In *Life Lessons*, much of Lionel's painting takes place at night, when others sleep and dream. The nocturnal mood reinforces that artists are in touch with a dream-like creativity most of us every day mortals miss.

Atmosphere reflects Paulette's emotional state in *Life Lessons*, too. After the performance artist rejects her overtures, she furiously leaves the club. Lionel chases her out into the rain. He offers to kill the guy if that's what she wants. Crying, she vents her frustration and embarrassment by blaming Lionel for Stark's insensitivity. The pouring rain heightens the desolate feeling both experience because of the impossible situation between them.

A few moments later, Lionel finds Paulette at home. The tone of the film turns considerably darker as he threatens her. "I could do anything to you," he tells her. "Rape you, kill you. Because I'm nothing to you, I'm the invisible man." Playing the scene at night, in the shadowy kitchen accentuates the ominous note in his voice. She isn't safe here at the hearth; it's dark, she's alone, facing the naked rage of a man she's depersonalized.

EXERCISES

Probably one of the most important books a committed screenwriter can read is Constantin Stanislavski's *An Actor Prepares*. Not only does it give important insights into how actors work, but these same methods can be used by a writer to discover the emotions motivating characters, and thus provide a key to the subtext in a scene.

A good exercise for revealing subtext to start with is to take a character in a situation akin to the protagonist in *Occurrence at Owl Creek* when he reaches shore. How does he express his joy? He throws sand in the air and on himself as he laughs. He sees a flower and goes to smell it.

1. Create a situation where a character will experience strong emotions, i.e., joy or rage, sadness or satisfaction.
2. Characterize the feeling you choose.
3. What does the character do or say? How does he or she express these feelings?
4. Use a minimum of dialogue to express the character's inner state. Think of visual and sound effects that will help the audience to identify the current of feelings in the scene. Think of incidents and the atmosphere and how they can support the emotion.

Try this exercise with different characters and different emotions to expand the craft of your writing.

PART FOUR

KEEPING FOCUSED

12

Keeping Focused:
What Does My Protagonist
Really Want?

One of the toughest obstacles a screenwriter faces, whether beginner or veteran, is keeping the story focused. This is as true for writing a short screenplay as it is for writing a feature. But where a feature might survive an inventive interlude away from its main theme, if a short film screenplay strays from its central topic for more than a moment, it can mean failure.

There are many indications a screenplay has lost its focus. Contradictory feedback from an early draft is usually the result of an unfocused screenplay. The writer has too many ideas competing for attention, causing him to lose grip of his characters, plot and theme. Readers experience a plotless story, a loss of momentum or just a general lack of cohesion in the writing. Writer's block is another symptom of a screenplay whose purpose has become ill-defined. The imagination dries up and words won't come, often leaving the writer frustrated and depressed.

In this, the final chapter, we look at a few strategies to keep a film on track and writer's block at bay.

KEEPING ON TRACK

When a screenplay begins to wander with many ideas competing for attention, or writer's block strikes, the best way to get back on track is to return to two questions asked at the beginning:

1. What is the story about?
2. What does the protagonist really want?

What's the Story About?

Coming back to the first question can remind a writer what he originally found interesting and exciting in the material. It's inevitable that as a work-in-progress develops, it will change. A theme or controlling idea that led you to write the story may bear little resemblance to the central idea found in the finished draft. The theme may have changed without you being aware of it.

To discover what the story is really about, you have to look at the screenplay as a whole and determine what the unifying idea is. If there isn't one that's self-evident, hazard a guess as to what the screenplay suggests as its theme. Simply state it, then ask whether the material has been motivated in some way by this central idea. If you can't state your theme and you don't know what the film is really about anymore, there are a few things you can do to uncover it.

First, look at the hero. If he succeeds, what special quality enables him to succeed? If he fails to achieve his goal, what led to this failure, and what does the antagonist have that makes it possible for him to win? The answers to these questions should provide a clue to what your film is about. The fundamental qualities that lead to a protagonist's success or failure hold the answers to what you are writing about. The answers, though, have to be clear in order to help you. You can ask yourself later if a theme is valid or adequately motivated, but first you have to know what it is.

What Does My Protagonist Really Want?

The second question holds the real key to success in getting a screenplay on track. What does the protagonist really want? This is the most important question to ask. Many screenplays start to wander because writers forget what their protagonists want or need. Sometimes the protagonist's want and need are undeveloped or underemphasized, causing their importance to the screenplay to be lost and the plot to break down. In other cases, the protagonist's want or need may not be compelling enough to involve the audience, or it just may not be believable.

A protagonist must have a clear goal or need that drives the character and screenplay forward. Every scene must depend in some way on this driving action: Revealing character and information that motivate and stoke the central conflict as it rises to the crises and climax. The driving force demands that other characters react and oppose our hero. These interactions should lead to a direct cause-and-effect relationship from one scene to another that in turn keeps the plot linked. If the scenes of the plot are interdependent, that is, if one scene leads inexorably to the next, thematic problems can be more easily discerned.

The set-up of a screenplay must introduce the character's want or need. This want or need can be in place before the story opens, as in *Life Lessons,* or grow out of the opening situation, as in *The Man in the Brooks* Brothers Shirt. Many short screenplays stall right at the beginning because the protagonist's story goal doesn't emerge soon enough. Short films are just that — short — they don't have a lot of time. You must create tension in order to hook the audience. Establishing your goal as early as possible helps capture your audience by getting them to ask: Will your hero get what he wants (and/or needs)?

If the character's want or need is not compelling enough for the audience to identify with, the screenplay won't be as affecting. The protagonist's want/need must be definite and forceful to win sympathy and hold the audience's attention. And it must be important to the protagonist. Scenes that show the emotional reactions of the protagonist from actions he's taken will strengthen the audience's understanding of the want/need. In *Life Lessons,* Lionel feels guilty after fighting with Paulette. Playing these scenes gives a human dimension to the characters and conflict. Humanizing characters makes it easier for the audience to identify with them.

If a protagonist's want or need isn't believable, one that is must be found to replace it.

The Antagonist

A primary antagonist gives strength and clarity to a screenplay. As locus of the opposing force, he makes the conflict distinct and understandable. Just like the protagonist, the antagonist must have a want and need. The same questions above apply to him. What does he really want and need? Is what he wants (or needs) sufficient to drive the story to conflict with the protagonist? If it isn't, how can you make it so that it will?

A short film can survive having no main antagonist to oppose your protagonist. If so, the controlling idea or theme must be all the stronger or more clear to bind the drama together, and get the audience's attention.

These questions can serve as the basis for evaluating the comments you receive about your work. More importantly, the answers to these questions can help guide you back to the source of all satisfying drama — your characters — by insuring they have conflicting wants and needs to drive the story forward.

CONCLUSION

Writing a good screenplay, short or long, is a difficult job. There are no magic formulas that insure success other than those timeless elements of a strong premise to start from, compelling characters, a powerful story and a valid theme. Approach your material in a fresh and inventive way, and don't be afraid to rewrite, rewrite and rewrite again.

The best short films embrace complex, personal issues — themes feature films tend to back away from. Often this is the source of their success. Their plots don't have to be complicated, but their characters do. The characters' wants and needs should be strong, specific, and especially clear to drive the story. Try giving your protagonist a central problem to cope with, as well as related sub-problems, and let the plot flow from her dilemmas.

Think of the plot as the story you tell to explain how a character changes from an initial state to where we leave her at the end of the film. The focus on character pushing plot, and not the other way around, is what distinguishes all good drama and literature. While other dramatic arenas may have lost their focus on character as the defining story element, characters thrive in short films. They are why the art form exists — to explore the obvious and inner nuances of what a character thinks he wants, and really needs — and then to make visual the reconciliation between these wants and needs. Unlike features, your short film will be as complex, intriguing, exciting and, ultimately, as satisfying as your lead character.

In this book, I've attempted to outline the basic requirements of a successful short film, contrasting them with those of a feature length film, while showing that both are based the same fundamental principles. If you can write an effective short film, chances are you can write a good feature length screenplay, too. Good luck!

APPENDICES

Appendix A

Fade In to Fade Out: Proper Screenplay Format

A screenplay is a blueprint for a film. Screenplay form reflects this, having evolved over the years into a particular arrangement of styles that easily communicates the necessary information needed to produce a film. Production managers, set designers, actors, etc., all must have easy access to the information they need to do their job. Proper form indicates a film's approximate length and budget. It allows production managers to breakdown the screenplay, indicates to art directors what kinds of sets are needed, and easily identifies each actor's lines.

Most screenplays are written in master scenes. A master scene presents the action in the clearest form, <u>without</u> camera angles and few stage directions. It communicates simply what happens in the scene, letting the action be the focus and not the camera.

Scene headings, action, characters' names, parenthetical directions and dialogue are the essential styles every screenwriter must use, but there are other format characteristics the beginning screenwriter must learn as well. For example, introducing new characters, writing transitions such as "DISSOLVE TO" and even "FADE OUT" require as much adherence to format as scene headings and action. Hour long and long form teleplays (screenplays for television) are written in a similar format, though there are superficial differences. Situation comedies, on the other hand, have a formatting configuration all their own.

In this chapter, we present the fundamental aspects and jargon of screenplay formatting.

FADE IN: SCENE HEADINGS

A screenplay usually begins with FADE IN:. These words always go on the left-hand margin. Double-spaced below FADE IN is the scene heading designating the location of the first scene. The scene heading is always in capitals and always gives the same basic information in the same order. This information is:

1. INT. or EXT.
2. LOCATION
3. DAY or NIGHT

It should look like this:

```
EXT.  TURNER HOUSE  -  DAY
```

The scene heading almost always begins with INT. or EXT., indicating either interior or exterior. The abbreviation for interior or exterior is always used. INT. or EXT. is followed by the setting in which the scene takes place, and then the time of day. The setting must be the exact location of the scene. Every time the location changes, the scene heading must change. The change indicates that it is a new scene.

Time is denoted by DAY or NIGHT, though occasionally SUNRISE or SUNSET, DAWN or DUSK may be used. An exact time in the heading isn't necessary. Day or night will tell the reader all she needs to know about time. Once time has been established, it doesn't have to be repeated in each new scene heading until it changes. Often screenwriters will pick up the time again, whether it has shifted from night to day or day to night once the location of the scene changes. This is generally a good idea. Note that a dash separates the "where" from the "when" of the scene. Recently new writers have started using CONTINUOUS in the scene heading to indicate the action continues from one scene to the next. This isn't necessary, and all it does is crowd the page.

The scene heading is brief and specific. It allows the reader to quickly orient himself to the scene. It also makes essential information easily accessible for the actual production of a screenplay.

There are exceptions to every rule. Suppose a writer doesn't want to fade in on the scene, but wants to use sound to create mood before actually beginning the visual part of the film. The writer might try something like this:

```
A BLACK SCREEN

The SOUND of drums pounds in the distance.

FADE IN:

EXT. CONGO RIVER - NIGHT

The mile-wide waterway splits the jungle.
```

Here, the words fade in are not really necessary and could be dropped.

There are also exceptions to when INT. or EXT. has to be used. When an overall location serves for a series of actions remaining inside or outside, this abbreviation can be dropped from the scene heading. Note below:

```
INT. BARN - DAY

A boy runs for the ladder.

IN THE LOFT

Five kittens nuzzle next to their mother. The boy
climbs into the loft and joins cat.
```

Or:

```
EXT. CONGO RIVER - NIGHT

The sky blazes burnt-orange as smoke billows over
the trees. A small boat motors up the river.

AROUND A BEND

The boat continues toward a village afire in the
night.
```

For the examples above, each second scene could just as easily begin with INT. or EXT. and be considered correct form. These formatting rules are not absolutes that always have to be followed. The screenwriter has some leeway to describe his vision in a screenplay.

The location of the scene must be specific. If the scene takes place on a busy street, all that is really needed in the scene heading is the word STREET. That the street is in a busy city can be described in the action. The scene heading should not be cluttered. It needs to quickly orient the reader to the site of the scene.

Another description used in a scene heading is POV. POV stands for point of view. It is used to indicate what a character is seeing.

```
JOHN'S POV - THE SILVER JAGUAR

The car lies inelegantly on its side, wrapped around
a tree.
```

Or:

```
INT./EXT. BUS - JOHN'S POV

The silver Jaguar lies on its side, wrapped around a
tree.
```

Both descriptions tell us what the camera sees, but one also tells where the shot originates. The one thing to remember when using POV in a scene heading is to indicate when the shot returns to the master scene. It can be confusing to the reader if the action shifts back from a specific character's point of view to the master scene without indication.

A master scene is a specific configuration of action, information and dialogue, consisting of scene heading, a narrative description of the scene action, speaking characters' names, dialogue and parenthetical directions. It looks like this:

```
EXT. TURNER HOUSE - DAY

Indignant eight year-old ALEC TURNER, dark eyes
flaring, grips the collar of his old black dog,
KING. Across the grass, towers forty-five year-old
nerd, TED McCLURE. He stands over a recent brown
spot on his immaculate lawn.

                    MCCLURE
                 (red-faced)
          I am sick and tired of finding a
          new pile of crap on my way to
          work every morning!

                    ALEC
          King didn't do it!

                    MCCLURE
          Look at this!

He points with real emotion at the small circles of
dead grass.
```

A master scene sets the location and time, and then lets the action unfold without cluttering up the scene with camera moves and angles. It allows the characters' story to develop without the reader having to take time to put himself in place of the camera for every shot. A good screenwriter working in master scenes presents the action in such a way that the reader sees the screenplay unfold as the writer does.

Along with POV, there are a couple other descriptions that find their way into a scene heading. AERIAL VIEW indicates that we are seeing something from high above.

```
AERIAL VIEW - TOKYO - DAY

The city sprawls amorphously below rain clouds. Its
clogged expressways spiral out from the center: The
Emperor's Palace.
```

INSERT is used to draw the reader's, and audience's, attention specifically to something, as in the contents of a letter, a special insignia, detail of jewelry or anything not immediately distinguishable in the master scene.

```
INSERT - LETTER

In smudgy type:

          Dear John,
            I hope you have found the
          emerald ring and are on your way
          back home.
```

An insert shows close-up specific information needed to follow the story. It tells the reader how this information will be handled on the screen for the audience.

POV, AERIAL VIEW, INSERT should all be employed sparingly. Only when information essential to the plot can't be given any other way, or when going for a specific effect, should these techniques be used.

THE ACTION

After the scene heading comes the description of the action. The paragraphs between the scene heading and action are double-spaced. The description of the action is single-spaced. If there is more than one paragraph of action, the paragraphs are double-spaced. Action runs normal left and right margins, the same as the scene heading.

```
EXT. TURNER HOUSE - DAY

Indignant eight year-old ALEC TURNER, dark eyes
flaring, grips the collar of his old black dog,
KING.
```

The action is written in the present-tense. It isn't indented. The description of the action should be clear and to the point. Overly flowery passages can obscure what's important for the reader to understand. Still, the writer must choose his words carefully. The best style is lucid yet vivid, aspiring to scenes that come alive on the page.

When characters appear in a screenplay for the first time their names are put in ALL CAPS. For the important characters, a brief description should follow. Descriptions should supply only enough information to give a mental snapshot, not a complete biography. What characters do and say provide truer clues to their real natures. After the characters' initial introductions, their names no longer need be capitalized in the action (although whenever they have dialogue, names will again appear in capitals in the characters' names margin).

Important sound directions in the action appear in all capital letters. The door SLAMS. The tire POPS. The gun FIRES. These caps flag specific sound cues for the soundtrack.

Sometimes important props are capitalized to call attention to them. An important piece of scenery might play a significant role in the screenplay. By capitalizing it, the reader is less likely to skim over it.

CHARACTER NAMES' MARGIN

The characters names' margin runs approximately in the center of the page, but it isn't center justified. It's about two and a half to three inches from the left hand margin. The length of a character's name makes no difference; whether it is Bob or Bronowski, the names always begin at the same setting. A center justified name margin is a sure sign of an amateur screenplay.

In this margin, the characters' names are always in all capital letters. Between the description of the action and the character's name, the paragraphs are double-spaced. Occasionally, a name will be followed by one of several cues in parentheses. These can be (V.O.) for voice over, (O.S.) or (O.C.) for off screen or camera, or (CONT'D) for a continued speech which has been broken up by a page break. These parenthetical cues aren't parenthetical directions that are character directions.

PARENTHETICAL DIRECTIONS & DIALOGUE

Parenthetical directions are instructions for emotional reactions of the character who is speaking which may not be apparent. Parentheticals can also be short stage directions describing what the character is doing while speaking. Those directions should always be brief. They can be included right after the character's name or in the middle of dialogue to emphasize emotion or direct actions. Parentheticals never come at the end of a speech. If action needs to be staged or emotion emphasized when a character finishes speaking, these directions should be included as action.

Note in the scene above that the last line, which is a stage direction for McClure, returns to the action margin. It is *not* written like this:

```
                MCCLURE
        Look at this!
            (points with real
            emotion at the small
            circles of dead grass)
```

Including this much description within parenthetical directions tends to clutter the dialogue and page, and creates a clumsy look. Parenthetical margins run about two inches in from the left hand margin:

```
                ALEC
        (spins and hugs
        his mother)
    I don't want to go!
```

As with any convention, screenplay format is largely an arbitrary method designed to keep a screenplay easy to read and to present the story in visual pieces.

The lines the characters speak are the dialogue. Dialogue margins begin approximately an inch to an inch and a half in from the left hand margin of the page and an inch and a half in from the right hand margin. The left hand margin is justified, while the right margin is not. It is important not to let the dialogue spill too far past its right hand margin. If it does, it can be confused with the action.

The spacing between the character's name, the parenthetical directions and the dialogue is always single-spaced. When another character begins speaking, the spacing between the characters and their speeches is double-spaced.

When dialogue is broken up by a page break, (MORE) should appear on the last line before the break. For example:

```
                    ALEC
          Mom, could I get a raise in my
          allowance?

                    SUSAN
          A raise? How come?

                    ALEC
          I deserve one. Since I have to
                    (MORE)
```

The page break cuts the speech. At the top of the next page, the character's name should appear followed by (CONT'D) and the rest of the speech, like this:

```
                    ALEC (CONT'D)
          clean up Mr. McClure's lawn,
          too.
```

TRANSITIONS

Transitions indicate the movement or passage from one scene to the next. They can be instantaneous or gradual. All transitions except for the first FADE IN, start approximately five inches from the left hand margin. They are double-spaced below the last part of the described action. Generally, CUT TO: is not used after every scene since a cut is the normal way to move from scene to scene.

Sometimes, though, screenwriters will use "SHOCK CUT TO:" or "SMASH CUT TO:" for dramatic purposes. Usually this kind of punctuation is used to make a point or to dramatically separate scenes or scene sequences.

"DISSOLVE TO:" means one image fades away as another fades in to replace it. A dissolve usually indicates time has passed. It is used less and less frequently in the industry.

The last transition used in a screenplay is FADE OUT. it does not have to be followed by a colon, though sometimes it is. Most often, a period comes after it, denoting the end. Many screenwriters opt to follow fade out with THE END. When used, "the end" goes in the characters names' margin:

```
          THE END
```

SCREENWRITING SOFTWARE

There are many computer screenwriting software programs currently on the market that format your script as you type. Of course, it's always possible to construct a style sheet with macros and quick keys to enable you to type in screenplay format in any word processing program. But the question is, do you want to spend your time writing a screenplay or writing a program? When screenplays aren't properly formatted, everyone's job in the production of a film becomes harder. And when you graduate on to writing feature length screenplays, script formatting becomes one of the easiest ways to distinguish a pro from an amateur.

These programs are more than worth the cost, especially those which format as you type and allow changes to a script, either with automatic accommodation to the current draft or the creation of separate drafts. Stand-alone programs such as Final Draft, Movie Magic Screenwriter 2000 and Scriptware allow you to write in the correct format as soon as you start up. All now accommodate PC's and Macs.

Add-on software such as ScreenStyle, Hollywood, Script Wizard, ScriptWright and Script Werx are designed to use macro features of specific word processing programs like Microsoft Word and turn them into screenwriting programs.

The time you spend writing your own formatting program is better spent working out your story, or rewriting it. Many use computer complications as excuses not to actually write. Use a program (following the above format guidelines) to format a script, and your brain can focus on your story instead.

For reviews of screenwriting programs online, check out Neil Turitz and Jason Mann's excellent article *The Zen of Screenwriting* in Movie Maker Magazine online at <u>www.moviemaker.com/ issues/50/zen.html</u>.

Locating Screenplay Software Programs

Most screenwriting programs can be found where computer programs are sold. Some companies will send you a free demo disk or allow you to download a demo online. Following is a list of the main screenwriting programs used in Hollywood and their Web addresses if you are looking for information.

Software	Web Address
Final Draft	www.finaldraft.com
Movie Master	www.screenplay.com
Scriptware	www.scriptware.com
Hollyword	www.hollyword.com
ScriptWizard	www.warrenassoc.com
ScreenStyle	www.screenstyle.com
Script Werx	www.scriptwerx.com
ScriptWright	www.kois.com

Appendix B

Referenced Films Available on Video

The films in this list are available on video or DVD. Some can be found at the more eclectic video stores across the nation and at NetFlix or FacetsMedia. Others you can find on Amazon or through the IMDB at www.IMDB.com. Some of the specific websites are listed for harder to find films.

Life Lessons,* from *New York Stories (1989)
Writer: Richard Price
Director: Martin Scorsese
Available: DVD/VHS

Living in Oblivion (1995)
Writer/Director: Tom DiCillo
Available: DVD/VHS

Franz Kafka's It's a Wonderful Life (1993)
Writer/Director: Peter Capaldi
Available: DVD/VHS

Some Folks Call It a Sling Blade (1994)
Writer: Billy Bob Thorton
Director: George Hickenlooper
Available: DVD by itself; also on the DVD: *Short 1 - Invention* (1993)

Black Rider** (1993)
Writer/Director: Pepe Danquart
Available: DVD on *Short 1 - Invention* (1993)

405 (2000)
Written & Directed by Bruce Branit & Jeremy Hunt
Available: VHS and on the internet at iFilm.com

The Appointments of Dennis Jennings** (1988)
Writers: Steven Wright and Michael Armstrong
Director: Dean Parisot
Available: DVD; go to http://stevenwright.com/cgi-bin/
storeforgc.cgi?action=item&id-1002

The Dutch Master, from Tales Of Erotica**** (1995)
Writers: Susan Seidelman & Jonathan Brett
Director: Susan Seidelman
Available: DVD/VHS

Hire: The Powder Keg (2001)
Writer: Guillermo Arriaga, story David Carter
Director: Alejandro González Iñárritu
Available: DVD; go to www.BMWfilms.com

Hire: The Star (2001)
Writers: Guy Ritchie and Joe Sweet
Director: Guy Ritchie
Available: DVD; go to www.BMWfilms.com

---

*   Academy Award winner, Best Foreign Film
**   Academy Award winner, Best Live Action Short Film
*** Academy Award winner, Best Screenplay
**** Nominated for an Academy Award, in the Live Action Short category

Words, from Before the Rain (1994)
Writer/Director: Milcho Manchevski
Available: VHS

Gridlock (Fait d'hiver) (2001)
Writer: Johan Verschueren
Director: Dirk Beliën
Available: DVD on *75th Academy Annual Awards Short Films*

I'll Wait For The Next One (J'attendrai le suivant...) (2002)
Writers: Thomas Gaudin, Philippe Orreindy
Director: Philippe Orreindy
Available: DVD on *75th Academy Annual Awards Short Films*

This Charming Man (Der er en yndig mand) (2002)
Writers: Flemming Klem, Martin Strange-Hansen
Director: Martin Strange-Hansen
Available: DVD on *75th Academy Annual Awards Short Films*

My Generation, from Strange Frequency (2001)
Writers: Joseph Anaya, Steve Jones, Dale Kutzera and
    Dan Merchant
Directors: Mary Lambert and Bryan Spicer
Available: DVD/VHS

Occurrence at Owl Creek** (1962)
Writer/Director: Robert Enrico
Available: DVD/VHS

The Red Balloon*** (1955)
Writer/Director: Albert Lamorisse
Available: VHS

Ray's Male Heterosexual Dance Hall** (1987)
Writer/Director: Bryan Gordon
Available for rent through Facets Media, www.facets.org

PEEL, from *Short Films by Jane Campion*
Writer/Director: Jane Campion
Available for rent through Facets Media, www.facets.org

Mara of Rome, from *Yesterday, Today And Tomorrow* (1964)
Writer: Cesare Zavattini
Director: Vittorio De Sica
Available: DVD/VHS

Anna of Milan, from *Yesterday, Today And Tomorrow* (1964)
Writers: Cesare Zavattini & Billa Billa,
    short story by Alberto Moravia
Director: Vittorio De Sica
Available: DVD/VHS

**The Man in the Brooks Brothers Shirt, from *Women & Men:
Stories Of Seduction*** (HBO SHOWCASE) (1990)
Writer/Director: Frederic Rapheal, adapted from Mary McCarthy's
    short story, The Man in the Brooks Brothers Shirt
Available: VHS

**Hills Like White Elephants, from *Women & Men: Stories
Of Seduction*** (HBO SHOWCASE) (1990)
Writers: Joan Dideon & John Gregory Dunne
Director: Tony Richardson
Available: VHS

The Wedding, from *The Gold of Naples* (1954)
Writer: Cesare Zavattini
Director: Vittorio De Sica
Available: VHS

---

*   Academy Award winner, Best Foreign Film
**   Academy Award winner, Best Live Action Short Film
***   Academy Award winner, Best Screenplay
**** Nominated for an Academy Award, in the Live Action Short category

The Gambler, from The Gold of Naples (1954)
Writer: Cesare Zavattini
Director: Vittorio De Sica
Available: VHS

Twist of Fate (1993)
Writer-Director: Douglas Kunin.
Video Distributor: Threshold Films
    5919 Tuxedo Terrace Los Angeles, CA 90068
    (213) 464-4057

Facets Multimedia, in Chicago, will rent by mail from their catalogue. An annual membership costs $40, VHS/DVD rentals are
$3.50 a piece for two nights. A credit card is needed. Facets
Multimedia also has a monthly rate of $24, which gives you
unlimited rentals and no late fees. You can find them online at:
www.facets.org, or write them for a free sample catalogue at:

    FACETS MULTIMEDIA
    Rentals Department
    1517 W. Fullerton Ave.
    Chicago, IL 60614
    1-800-331-6197

A full catalogue is $7.95 plus shipping and handling.

---

*   Academy Award winner, Best Foreign Film
**   Academy Award winner, Best Live Action Short Film
*** Academy Award winner, Best Screenplay
**** Nominated for an Academy Award, in the Live Action Short category

Appendix C

General Film Index

TITLE	AUTHOR OR ADAPTOR OF SCREENPLAY
Ghost	Bruce Joel Rubin
Glengarry Glen Ross	David Mamet
Glory	Kevin Jarre
The Gold of Naples: The Gambler	Cesare Zavattini
The Gold of Naples: The Wedding	Cesare Zavattini
Gridlock (Fait d'hiver)	Johan Verschueren
Groundhog's Day	Daniel F. Rubin, Harold Ramis
Hills Like White Elephants	Joan Dideon, John Gregory Dunne
I Walked With A Zombie	Inez Wallace, Curt Siodmak, Ardel Wray
I'll Wait For The Next One (J'attendrai le suivant...)	Thomas Gaudin, Philippe Orreindy
Jurassic Park	David Koepp, Michael Crichton
Kinsey	Bill Condon
The Last Temptation of Christ	Paul Schrader
Lawrence of Arabia	Robert Bolt
Lethal Weapon	Shane Black
The Lunch Date	Adam Davidson
The Machinist	Scott Kosar
The Macomber Affair	Casey Robinson, Seymour Bennett
The Man in the Brooks Brothers Shirt	Frederic Raphael
Momento	Christopher Nolan, Jonathan Nolan
Mrs. Doubtfire	Randi Mayem Singer, Leslie Dixon
My Life as a Dog	Reidar Jönsson, Lasse Hallström, Brasse Brännström, Per Berglund
Never Cry Wolf	Curtis Hanson, Sam Hamm
New York Stories: Life Lessons	Richard Price
Norma Rae	Harriet Frank, Jr., Irving Ravetch
The Nutty Professor	David Sheffield, Barry W. Blaustein, Tom Shaydac, Steve Oedekerk
Occurrence at Owl Creek	Robert Enrico
The Old Man and the Sea	Peter Viertel
Ominbus	Sam Karmann
Peel	Jane Campion
The Piano	Jane Campion
Pirates of the Caribbean	Ted Elliott, Terry Rossio
Platoon	Oliver Stone
Pretty Woman	J. F. Lawton
Quiz Show	Paul Attanasio
Raising Arizona	Ethan Coen, Joel Coen
Rashômon	Ryunosuke Akutagawa, Akira Kurosawa, Shinobu Hashimoto

TITLE	AUTHOR OR ADAPTOR OF SCREENPLAY
Ray's Male Heterosexual Dance Hall	Bryan Gordon
Salaam Bombay!	Mira Nair, Sooni Taraporevala
Sense and Sensibility	Emma Thompson
Sideways	Alexander Payne, Jim Taylor
Sleepover	Elisa Bell
Spider	Patrick McGrath
Spiderman	David Koepp
Star Wars	George Lucas
Strange Frequency: My Generation	Joseph Anaya, Steve Jones, Dale Kutzera, Dan Merchant
The Red Balloon	Albert Lamorisse
Tales of Erotica: The Dutch Master	Susan Seidelman, Jonathan Brett
This Charming Man	Flemming Klem, Martin Strange-Hansen
Tootsie	Larry Gelbart, Murray Schisgal, Don McGuire
Trading Places	Herschel Weingrod, Timothy Harris
Trevor	James Lecesne
True Lies	Claude Zidi, Simon Mlchaël, Didier Kaminka
Twister	Michael Crichton, Anne-Marie Martin
Unforgiven	David Peoples
War of the Roses	Michael Leeson
Witness	William Kelly, Earl W. Wallace, Pamela Wallace
Yesterday, Today and Tomorrow: Anna of Milan	Cesare Zavattini
Yesterday, Today and Tomorrow: Mara of Rome	Cesare Zavattini, Billa Billa

Appendix D

The Writer's Reference Shelf

Here are more books, besides those listed in the bibliography, that can prove helpful. A few are geared to feature films, but all are valuable additions to a writer's reference shelf. Most are out in paperback and available in libraries.

THE ELEMENTS OF STYLE by Wm. Strunk, Jr. and E.B. White (MacMillian). Read this before you write another word.

THE ART OF DRAMATIC WRITING by Lajos Egri, 1960 (Simon & Schuster). Much of what Egri has to say about the dramatic form is applicable to short stories, novels, plays and screenplays, short or long. The chapter on Premise is especially important. The writing style is archaic, but if you can understand what he's talking about and apply it to your work, then this book will prove invaluable.

THE TOOLS OF SCREENWRITING: A Writer's Guide to the Craft and Elements of a Screenplay by David Howard & Edward Mably, 1993 (St. Martin's Press). A good book on the basics concepts of the craft of screenwriting. Very valuable to the short form filmmaker and the long, from start to finish.

WRITING GREAT CHARACTERS: The Psychology of Character Development in Screenplays by Michael Halperin, Ph.D., 1995 (Lone Eagle Publishing Co.). A strong examination of character from a screenwriter's viewpoint. And:

CHARACTERS & VIEWPOINT by Scott Card, 1988 (Writer's Digest Books). A good book on how to build characters and use the proper voice for your story.

HOW TO WRITE & SELL YOUR SENSE OF HUMOR by Gene Perret, 1982 (Writer's Digest Books). A good primer on humor, jokes and comedy.

MAKING A GOOD SCRIPT GREAT by Linda Seger, 1994 (Dodd, Mead & Co.). Primarily about rewriting a feature screenplay, but she has great ideas and puts dramatic concepts in easily understandable language.

THE WRITER'S JOURNEY by Christopher Vogler, 1992 (Michael Wiese Productions Book). For anyone prepared to go the distance. Also:

THE HERO WITH A THOUSAND FACES by Joseph Campbell, 1972 (Princeton University Press). A guide for living as well as writing.

THE ART AND CRAFT OF NOVEL WRITING by Oakley Hall (Writer's Digest Books). As the title indicates, this is primarily for novelists, but there is helpful information that can be applied to writing in general.

THE WRITER'S SURVIVAL GUIDE: HOW TO COPE WITH REJECTION, SUCCESS, AND 99 OTHER HANG-UPS OF THE WRITING LIFE by Jean Rosenbaum and Veryl Rosenbaum, 1982 (Writer's Digest Books). For later on, when the process of writing starts to get to you.

I CAN SEE YOU NAKED: A FEARLESS GUIDE TO MAKING GREAT PRESENTATIONS by Ron Hoff, 1988 (Andrews & McMeel). An excellent book if you have to make presentations.

HOW TO SELL YOURSELF by Joe Girard, 1979 (Warner Books). Written by a car salesman, but there is a lot of useful information on motivation, attitude, self-confidence and communication that can be applied to selling yourself to people in the film and publishing business. You can also read:

HOW TO SELL ANYTHING TO ANYBODY by Joe Girard, 1977 (Warner Books).

THE BUSINESS OF BEING A WRITER by Stephen Goldin and Kathleen Sky, 1982 (Harper and Row). Very good for the business side of writing: contracts, dealing with editors, submissions, etc.

No list would be complete without:

ADVENTURES IN THE SCREEN TRADE by William Goldman, 1983 (Warner Books) and ***WHICH LIE DID I TELL? MORE ADVENTURES IN THE SCREEN TRADE*** (Vintage). A fascinating look at the creative and critical process with great insights into the film industry.

Appendix E

Ray's Male Heterosexual Dance Hall

written by Bryan Gordon

1987

FADE IN:

BIG BAND MUSIC

CAMERA MOVES DOWN A TALL OFFICE BUILDING...

We hear the voice of Sam Logan, early thirties...

> SAM V/O
> I used to feel I was a part of
> those office buildings. After
> all, I once had an office there.
> Okay, I didn't have an office
> with a view. But I was headed
> for a view. A good view...

and the camera settles on a nearby park - noon

SMALL CHILDREN play. OLD PEOPLE sit. BLUE and WHITE
COLLAR WORKERS, walk in a brisk and leisurely clip.
OTHER WORKERS sit on benches, the ground and
blankets eating their lunches.

THE CAMERA FINDS:

SAM LOGAN on a bench — mid-thirties, a suit and tie,
feeds some peanuts to some PIGEONS. He casually
watches an ATTRACTIVE WOMAN pass.

> SAM V/O (CONT'D)
> That of course was all before
> FabTek, the company I worked for
> became WellPeck and left me out
> of a job. There I go again,
> dwelling. I just can't keep
> blaming myself for all of this.
> Fabtek merged with WellPeck. It
> happens everyday. Ah-Anyway, I
> was killing some time and
> preparing for my next job
> interview, United Cracktel, going
> over in my head why I wanted to
> work for a place like United
> Cracktel when I ran into Cal...

CAL, a clean-cut upbeat businessman in his mid-
thirties, walks briskly by. He recognizes Sam and
walks over to him.

> SAM V/O
> ... a friend of mine I worked
> with years ago. The guy had
> success written all over his
> face...

Sam and Cal warmly shake each other's hands in a
business-like manner and Cal sits down. Sam is a bit
self-conscious. They begin talking.

> SAM V/O
> I instantly plunged into my own
> saga of job interview, telling
> him that everyone tells me I
> look great on paper, decent
> resume the whole bit. Just seems
> like I don't make the right
> contacts...

> CAL
> (Self-assured)
> Contacts, Sam, that's the
> attitude.

> SAM
> Yeah, contacts, I know, but
> where, how?

> SAM V/O
> He looked at me as if I never
> participated in society.

> CAL
> I know it's tough being out of
> work, Sam.

> SAM
> Oh, very tough. Very Tough. If I
> seem overly anxious, it's...I
> am—

> CAL
> You do. It's the old cliche,
> it's who you know....

> SAM
> Why didn't I ever believe
> that?...

                        CAL
People simply kill each other...

                        SAM
I always thought the cream...

                        CAL
Would rise to the top.

                        SAM V/O
He finished my cliche. Let me
finish my cliche.

                        CAL
   (Looks at watch)
Listen, I'd love to talk to you,
but I'm on my way to find a new
position.

                        SAM
   (Surprised)
I thought you had a great
position.

                        CAL
   (Confident)
Oh, I do. But you're never
secure. I'm always looking.
You've got to constantly know
and meet the right people.

                        SAM V/O
The right people. There must be
a constant turnover of the right
people.

                        SAM
So, it's the contacts.

                        CAL
Contacts.

                        SAM V/O
Contacts

                        CAL
You're not going to find a job,
the right job, at an ordinary
job interview. I'm sorry.

>   SAM V/O
>   He's right.
>
>   SAM
>   (Pressing)
>   So where do you make the right
>   contacts?
>
>   CAL
>   (Milking)
>   Where? Lot of people ask me
>   where.
>
>   SAM
>   (impatient)
>   Yeah, Well, so, where?
>
>   CAL
>   There's only one place to meet
>   the right people, Sam.
>
>   SAM
>   (Blurting)
>   I-I—Where!
>
>   CAL
>   (Beat)
>   Sam, why don't you come with me.
>   Forget your job interview.
>   There's only one place.
>   (DIRECT)
>   Ray's Male Heterosexual Dance
>   Hall.

                                        CUT TO:

WE HEAR ANOTHER UP TEMPO — BIG BAND SOUND.

OUTDOOR SIGN: "RAY'S MALE HETEROSEXUAL DANCE HALL"

INT. RAY'S MALE HETEROSEXUAL DANCE HALL - NOON

ANOTHER SIGN: STOCK EXCHANGE QUOTES

The camera tilts down to a crowded bar, filled with
executives in suits.

Cal leads Sam through a packed, narrow bar area
filled with HETEROSEXUAL MEN all dressed in suits
and ties. A bartender's BARTENDER pours drinks.

Trophies and TV set adorn the bar. The atmosphere is
mixed with smoke, drinking, nibbling, talk, winking,
hand shakes, darting eyes, back slapping, laughter,
and distant ballroom music.

>   SAM V/O
>   This is where everybody is. No
>   wonder no one's around
>   lunchtime. They're all here.

ANGLE

Sam and Cal spring out of the packed narrow bar
area.

>   SAM V/O
>   Wow, what a place. Hey. I know
>   that guy...his secretary said he
>   was out of town.

Sam suddenly eyes the ballroom.

SAM'S POV

of the Ballroom. HETEROSEXUAL MEN dressed in Brooks
Brothers suits slow dance, not cheek to cheek,
around the Ballroom. As they dance, most talk to one
another. TWO BLACK MEN dance only with each other.
The ballroom, itself, looks like an old gentlemen's
club.

ANGLE

The sides of the ballroom. VARIOUS MEN watch other
men dance. One MAN stands whispering into another
MAN'S ear. Men, including TWO BIG EATERS, stand near
a buffet table filled with male food: Oysters and
large drum   sticks. WAITERS weave in and out
delivering drinks. A MAN checks himself out in a
mirror. Another MAN asks a MAN to dance. He nods and
the two begin to dance.

ANGLE

SAM watches the dancing.

ANGLE

A LINE OF WALL MOUNTED TELEPHONES

Various MEN talk on the phone.

> MAN ON PHONE
> Everybody stays there...the food
> is lousy, help sucks but
> everybody stays there...

> BENNY BERBEL ON PHONE
> Yeah, yeah I realize he's in a
> board of directors meeting, but
> tell him Benny Berbel is on the
> phone. I want to run something
> by him that I think he's gonna
> be interested in. I realize
> that, but uh—what's-what is your
> name? Sharon...Sharon help me
> out on this one will yeah. Get a
> message—I realize—Shar—see this
> from my point of view. Try to
> see this from my point of
> view...see everything from my
> point of view.

ANGLE

Men dancing.

REVERSE ANGLE

Cal and Sam watching dance floor.

ANGLE

A banquet table with MEN snacking food. A BIG EATER
talks to BIG EATER#2.

> BIG EATER
> Tell me something. How do you
> talk about me behind my back.
> I'm curious.

> BIG EATER #2
> Your back?

> BIG EATER
> My back.

ANGLE

THE CROWDED BAR

A well-dressed GUY AT THE BAR in his mid-thirties
finishes a martini. He talks to the BARTENDER.

               GUY AT THE BAR
      Eddie, is that clock right?

               BARTENDER
    Ah, yes, sir. It is.

               GUY AT THE BAR
        (to himself)
    Ahh—I'll give him a few more
    minutes...
        (to Bartender)
    ...better give me another one.

               BARTENDER
        (takes drink)
    Sure.

               GUY AT THE BAR
    Wait, let me have the olive.
    Thank you.

MUSIC ENDS. Some men walk off the floor. Others stay
on. Constant chatter. A DISC JOCKEY stands next to a
compact high tech turntable and places a platter.
MUSIC BEGINS. More men come on the floor with new
partners. Sam and Cal watch other Men move to floor.
Cal asks GEORGE, who looks like a banker, to dance
and the two begin to dance.

               CAL
    George.

               GEORGE
    Cal. How are you?

               CAL
    How you doing? May I have this
    dance?

               GEORGE
    Sure.

Cal and George dance.

ANGLE

On the side seated on a couple of chairs.
SCHMOOZER#1 and SCHMOOZER#2 sit and talk.

> SCHMOOZER#1
> See the game?

> SCHMOOZER#2
> Oh, good game.

> SCHMOOZER#1
> Great game.

> SCHMOOZER#2
> Great. Great game. God. Wish I
> could play like that.

> SCHMOOZER#1
> We all wish we could play like
> that.

> SCHMOOZER#2
> Yeah, I know.

> SCHMOOZER#1
> Saw the game?

> SCHMOOZER#2
> No.

> SCHMOOZER#1
> Na..me, neither.

ANGLE

Sam watches Men dance. A slick well-dressed man, RAY
PINDALLY, introduces himself to Sam. They shake and
talk into each other's ear above the music and
chatter.

> SAM V/O
> The owner, Ray Pindally, came
> over and introduced himself to
> me. Told me his place was the
> latest trendy lunchtime ballroom,
> where guys like myself,
> obviously successful, danced to
> the old tunes, all the time
> talking business. I think he
> thought I was a tourist.

                        RAY
                   (To Sam)
          The powerful usually dance in
          their own spotlight. So be
          careful.

                        SAM V/O
               Spotlight, the powerful?

Sam spots the POWERFUL MAN on dance floor.

                        SAM V/O
               Tall lean man was no question
               about it, A powerful guy.

ANGLE

Dance floor. A SPOTLIGHT follows a DISTINGUISHED-
LOOKING MAN dancing with Another Man. The other male
dancers give these men free rein and respect where
they dance.

ANGLE

SAM stands near a group of MEN. Some men have drinks
in their hands, but most look towards the dance
floor.

The Schmoozer#2 stands next to a UPTIGHT EXEC.

                        SCHMOOZER#2
               Can I use you?

                        UPTIGHT EXEC
               What for?

                        SCHMOOZER#2
               Not important. Can I use you?

                        UPTIGHT EXEC
               Of course you can use me.

ON SAM, slightly self conscious, looking around for
available men.

ANGLE

A SHORT, PUDGY MAN, quite a bit shorter than Sam,
looks at SAM from a distance and smiles.

ANGLE

SAM thinks the Short Man is looking at a man behind him.

Another MAN approaches Sam, but asks the man behind Sam to dance.

The Short Man approaches Sam and shyly asks Sam...

> SHORT MAN
> Would you like to dance?

> SAM
> (Nervous)
> Sure.

The Two walk on the dance floor.

ANGLE

Dance Floor. The Short Man takes Sam's hand and begins to lead. Sam, initially is confused by who leads, but quickly adapts. The Short Man is not a good dancer.

> SHORT MAN
> I've been coming here quite a
> long time...

> SAM V/O
> This guy was pretty upfront. He
> told me he'd been coming to
> Ray's for years and hadn't been
> asked to dance with anyone for
> months.

> SHORT MAN
> I used to ask the powerful guys
> to dance with me once in a
> while, but I'd always say the
> wrong things or step on their...

The Short Man steps on Sam's foot. Sam reacts.

> SHORT MAN (CONT)
> Sorry.

> SAM
> Uh-No, fine—it's fine.

He holds Sam's hand too tight. Sam reacts.

                    SHORT MAN (CON'T)
          I'm sorry.

                    SAM
          No, really

ANGLE

Cal, dancing with the same Partner, spots Sam and
winks.

ANGLE

Sam, self-consciously smiles back at Cal. Sam and
the Short Man dance.

                    SHORT MAN
          I'm what they call dead meat in
          this town. And most guys who are
          seen dancing with me, more than
          often, are thought less of...so,
          if you're smart, you'll stop
          dancing with me right now.

                    SAM V/O
          I felt horrible. He wasn't that
          bad a dancer. Are other guys
          going to think I'm dead meat
          because I'm dancing with dead
          meat?

ANGLE

Other Men stare at Sam as if he's "dead meat."

ANGLE

Back to Sam and the Short Man.

                    SAM V/O (CONT)
          Ah, So what? Then again, I was
          looking for a good job. This was
          not the time to make friends.
          Anyway, this guy gave me an out.

                    SAM
          Actually, I am looking for a
          good job.

>   SHORT MAN
>   (Releasing his hand)
>   Oh, well then I'll do you a
>   favor and say good-bye.

The Short Man walks away towards the bar leaving Sam
alone on the dance floor. Uncomfortable, Sam walks
off the floor.

ANOTHER BIG BAND SONG

ANGLE

Wall phones. Benny Berbel is still on the phone with
Sharon.

>   BENNY BERBEL
>   (Anxious)
>   Sharon, hel-help me on this one,
>   Sharon. You can help me. Ca-can-
>   listen I'll tell you what. Help
>   me I'll help you. What do you
>   need. What do you need? You fly?
>   I'll send you upgrades. In your
>   name. You go it. You go to the
>   theater? How bout—do you see Le
>   Miz? I'll get you Le Miz
>   tickets. Trevor is a friend of
>   mine.

ANGLE

Another MAN checks himself out in the mirror. Other
Men watch others dance.

ANGLE

Guy At The Bar is still with the Bartender.

>   GUY AT THE BAR
>   I asked you if that clock was
>   right, didn't I?

>   BARTENDER
>   Yes, sir.

>   GUY AT THE BAR
>   You haven't seen Don all day?

                         BARTENDER
              No, sir.

                         GUY AT THE BAR
              That's all right, he's gonna be
              here.

ANGLE

SCHMOOZER#1 is now at the wall of phones.

                         SCHMOOZER#1 ON PHONE
              I don't know. I-I just feel
              uptight, under a lot of strain.
              I keep repeating the same
              patterns. Emotional re-runs,
              Doctor. I-

A man approaches to use that phone.

                         SCHMOOZER#1 ON PHONE
                   (upbeat)
              Hey, how are you! I'll just be a
              minute. Okay?
                   (depressed into phone)
              Wh-where was I?

ANGLE

A HEAVY-SET EXEC and a SLENDER EXEC at the bar,
among other MEN as we hear in the b.g... a TANGO.

                         HEAVY-SET EXEC
              You think this is the era of
              style over substance?

                         SLENDER EXEC
              Yes...and we're winning.

ANGLE

On Men's feet — dancing the tango — male shoe to
male shoe.

ANGLE

Dance floor. Sam and a SMOOTH-LOOKING MAN, a good
dancer and great dresser, dance a Tango. The Smooth-
looking Man leads.

           SAM V/O
After dancing with a few other
guys, I finally got into the
swing of things.

           SAM
So, what do you do for a living?

         SMOOTH-LOOKING MAN
I'm not sure. That's not it
exactly. I mean I draw a salary.
A great salary.

           SAM
Well, if you don't want to talk
about it, it's ok....

         SMOOTH-LOOKING MAN
It's not that, quite frankly, I
don't even know what I do. You
see, my boss hired me because he
knew that others wanted me. So
to prevent others from getting
me, he hired me, now that he's
got me he doesn't know quite
what it is he wants to do with
me.
    (swings out and into Sam's
    arms)
Great benefits.

           SAM
Benefits?

smooth-looking man
Benefits are very important.

           SAM V/O
Said the man who didn't know
what he did for a living.

ANGLE

On men's feet dancing side by side.

ANOTHER BIG BAND SONG

ANGLE

Buffet table. Eaters continue to nibble over a
dwindling lunch table. A balding MAN WITH GLASSES
nibbles.

                    MAN WITH GLASSES
          I'm not in a position to say
          yes. I can only say no. In fact,
          I've never been in a position to
          say yes.

ANGLE

Schmoozer#2 and Schmoozer#1 are seated in a booth.

                    SCHMOOZER#2
          Did he mention my name?

                    SCHMOOZER#1
          What name?

                    SCHMOOZER#2
          My name.

                    SCHMOOZER#1
          No.

                    SCHMOOZER#2
          D-did you mention my name?

                    SCHMOOZER#1
          No.

                    SCHMOOZER#2
          So, then there was no mention
          really at all then?

                    SCHMOOZER#1
          Of what?

                    SCHMOOZER#2
          My name.

                    SCHMOOZER#1
          Uh...no.

ANGLE

The dance floor. The DJ puts on a very SLOW SONG.

>   SAM V/O
>   It was in the middle of a very
>   slow dance that I found out how
>   much power the powerful have.

The Powerful Guy goes to the DJ and makes him change
the record to an upbeat number. He walks back onto
the floor to resume dancing. All the other men
applaud his decision.

>   CAL
>   (passing the Powerful Guy)
>   Great choice.

>   POWERFUL GUY
>   ...thanks.

Everyone continues dancing.

ANGLE

Short Guy curses himself and his bald spot in the
mirror.

ANGLE

The wall of phones. Benny Berbel is still on the
phone.

>   BENNY BERBEL
>   Okay, do me a favor. Just get
>   him one message to him. Just get
>   one message to him...see what he
>   says. Tell him not to worry, his
>   wife and kids are okay.

ANOTHER BIG BAND SONG.

ANGLE

The dance floor. Sam and a INSECURE LOOKING EXEC
DANCE. The Nervous Exec leads. They talk.

>   SAM V/O
>   My day started to appear
>   brighter. Much brighter. I
>   danced with this man who seemed
>   very excited about working with
>   me.

                    INSECURE EXEC
          We're looking for someone. Being
          very particular. We only want
          the best. You know that. I have
          this gut feeling. I think you're
          good. Could you start, let's
          say, next week?

                    SAM
          Well, sure.

                    INSECURE EXEC
          You can?

                    SAM
          Yes, absolutely.

Insecure Exec grows even more nervous.

                    SAM V/O
          Then he confessed he had very
          little power and would have to
          confirm the offer with at least
          four executives above him. He
          apologized and promised to get
          back to me shortly.

Ray Pindally taps the Insecure Exec on the shoulder.

                    RAY PINDALLY
          Excuse me, we seem to be having
          a slight problem with your
          credit card.

                    INSECURE EXEC
          Me?

                    RAY
          Yes, sir.

The Insecure Exec, embarrassed, lets go of Sam...

                    INSECURE EXEC
          I have to take this call, excuse
          me.

And as the Exec and Ray exit...

                    RAY
          Stay out of the spot.

Sam, a tad embarrassed, stands in the middle of the dance floor surrounded by dancing Men.

                SAM V/O
        Stay out of the spot? What spot?
        I must have been ten feet from
        the spotlight.

WE HEAR ANOTHER BIG BAND TUNE.

THE BAR

Schmoozer#1 and Schmoozer#2 stand alongside with the bar tab.

              SCHMOOZER#2
        This is on me

              SCHMOOZER#1
        Oh, no, no. Don't be ridiculous—

              SCHMOOZER#2
        No, no, please. I insist. My
        turn.

              SCHMOOZER#1
        No, this is my treat really.

              SCHMOOZER#2
        No, no. Please. Your money's no
        good here.

ANGLE

Cal checks himself in the mirror.

                 CAL
         (memorizing)
        Lipton. Lipton. Jim Lipton. Big
        lips, ton of lips, ton of lips.
        Lipton. Lipton.

ANGLE

Guy at the Bar with Bartender.

             GUY AT THE BAR
        Could I have mixed up the dates?

                         BARTENDER
              It's possible.

                       GUY AT THE BAR
              Well, who—whe—I'm sure he's
              gonna reschedule, you know.

                         BARTENDER
              Oh yeah, I'm sure.

ANGLE

Schmoozer#1 and Schmoozer#2 at the bar, now dealing
with their copy of the receipt.

                         SCHMOOZER#2
              It's mine.

                         SCHMOOZER#1
              No, you take this.

                         SCHMOOZER#2
              Please, it's done.

                         SCHMOOZER#1
                  (mixing up credit card
                  and receipt)
              This is uh—

                         SCHMOOZER#2
              It's done.
                  (credit card)
              That's mine I believe.

                         SCHMOOZER#1
                  (receipt)
              Oh, then this is mine.
                  (to bartender)
              Say, George, two more. And this
              time, make sure it's my check.

                         SCHMOOZER#2
              Where were we?!

ANOTHER BIG BAND SONG - LATER

FIVE NEW MEN talk on the telephones.

ANGLE

Sam dances with a YOUNG BRIGHT EXEC, late twenties.
They trade off leading as if this is a new dance.
Sam tries to catch on to this dance. He actually
enjoys it.

>   SAM V/O
> I was then asked to take a spin
> by this executive, he had to be
> my age, who told me he was semi-
> retired. I couldn't believe it.
> He said he invented and
> successfully marketed the phrase
> "Have a Nice Day" years ago.
> Must have been so young. He was
> also testing out his new dance.

>   YOUNG BRIGHT EXEC
> You think this is a good dance?

>   SAM
> Yes, I do.

>   YOUNG BRIGHT EXEC
>   (Excited)
> Do you think I could sell this
> dance?

>   SAM
> What dance?

>   YOUNG BRIGHT EXEC
>   (More excited)
> The dance we're doing.

>   SAM
> Oh, I don't know....

>   YOUNG BRIGHT EXEC
>   (In Sam's ear)
> Keep this dance between you and
> me, I think we have a winner.

>   SAM V/O
> ...Winner.

The Young Bright Exec hurriedly leaves Sam. The
MUSIC STOPS and everyone applauds.

                        SAM V/O
          Winner....and he ran out as if
          he discovered a new vaccine.

Cal approaches Sam.

                        CAL
                   (Proudly)
          Guess what? I just got a new
          job.

                        SAM
          Congratulations. You get more
          money?

ANOTHER BIG BAND SONG. In the b.g., Men take new and
old Partners on the dance floor.

                        CAL
          Same pay. Same everything.
          Except this job is more
          geographically desirable. I just
          couldn't turn down something
          like this.
                   (Beat)
          Ask that guy right over there.

ANGLE

A rather overweight POMPOUS EXEC stands nursing a
drink, watching the floor.

                        POMPOUS EXEC.
                   (to a passing exec)
          Hey, how you doing?

ANGLE

Back to Sam and Cal.

                        SAM
             That guy?

                        CAL
          Uh-hm

                        SAM
             Really?

                          CAL
            Yes.

                                                  CUT TO:

DANCE FLOOR.

SAM and the Pompous Exec dance. Sam leads.

                          SAM V/O
            I danced with a man I normally
            would never talk to if it wasn't
            for Cal telling me he was
            important. Didn't trust his
            smile. I didn't trust his tempo.
            His attention span scaled no
            more than two seconds.

                          POMPOUS EXEC
            So, you-uh-you have a wife?

                          SAM
            No.

                          POMPOUS EXEC
            I have one.

                          SAM
            Ahh.

                          POMPOUS EXEC
            Kids?

                          SAM
            No.

                          POMPOUS EXEC
            I have a boy and girl. House?

                          SAM
            No, I rent.

                          POMPOUS EXEC
            Oh, you rent?

                          SAM
            Yeah.

                    POMPOUS EXEC
You know we have a lot in
common.

                    SAM V/O
If there was a revolution, I
would have to kill him. Any kind
of revolution. But I needed a
job.

                    SAM
Look, I'd love to talk to
you...uh-uh

                    POMPOUS EXEC
Ed....

                    SAM
I'd love to talk to you, Ed, in
your office...

                    POMPOUS EXEC
Yeah, well, none of my real
business is done in the office.
Most of my real business is done
here on the dance floor.

                    SAM
Well, let's talk right here...

                    POMPOUS EXEC
        (Letting go of his arm)
Oh, I would love to talk, but
I'm scheduled to talk to Tom
Hartlow of Hartlow International
in about—um—hoo-hoo—two minutes.
So listen, you say hello to your
good-looking family of yours.

                    SAM
I don't have a family...

                    POMPOUS EXEC
Yeah, we'll talk soon.

ANGLE

The Pompous Exec races over to HARTLOW, another
exec.

ANGLE

Sam stands alone on the floor. He looks at his
watch. Self-consciously, he walks towards the bar
area and turns around towards the dance area. Sam
recognizes Peter.

ANGLE

The POWERFUL GUY and PETER, an exec in his thirties,
dance in a spotlight.

> SAM V/O
> I was about to leave Ray's and
> make that job interview when I
> spotted Peter, my best friend
> from my last job, dancing with
> the powerful guy in the
> spotlight. The powerful guy was
> a great dancer.

The Powerful Guy spins Peter around three or four
times.

ANGLE

Sam hovers over Peter's shoulder. He taps him.

> SAM
> (Excited)
> Peter?

> PETER
> (Looks at him oddly)
> Excuse me?

> SAM
> Peter. How are you? I don't mean
> to interrupt...

> PETER
> (Covering)
> I'm sorry, my name isn't Peter.
> I think you must have me mixed
> up...

> SAM
> Mixed up? Come on, it's Sam
> Logan. Fabtek Corporation.

                    SAM V/O
          He looked at me as if I was a
          non-person, an alien, another
          species. Of course, he knew me.
          We always had lunch together. He
          always ordered meat loaf. We
          traded ball scores. We once
          dated the same secretary.

                    SAM
               (re-approaching Peter)
          Excuse me, could I talk to you
          for a second?

                    PETER
          Look, Mr. Logan, I think you
          have me mixed up with someone
          else, so if you don't mind...

Peter and the Powerful Guy quickly jettison into
another direction.

                    PETER
               (to powerful guy)
          So, I understand that your
          wife's name is Bonny also?

                    POWERFUL GUY
          That's correct, but let's talk
          business.

                    PETER
          Uh-uh. All right.

ANGLE

Sam, looking wiped out and defeated, walks slowly
towards the exit through the bar. As he is about to
exit....

                    POWERFUL GUY (O.S.)
               (calling)
          Mr. Logan?

Sam stops and turns.

ANGLE

The Powerful Guy hurries through the crowded bar
area and catches up to him. The crowd, like the sea,
parts for the Powerful Guy.

> POWERFUL GUY (CONT)
> I'm Dick Tratten of the Tratten
> Group.

> SAM V/O
> I knew the company. Great
> reputation.

> POWERFUL GUY (CONT)
> I don't know you, but I'm
> impressed with your honesty.

We hear another big band song begin.

> POWERFUL GUY (CONT)
> (milking the beat)
> Like to dance?

> SAM
> (Beat)
> Yes.

ANGLE

The Distinguished-looking Man guides Sam onto the
crowded dance floor. The other dancers APPLAUD as
the Distinguished-looking Man leads Sam under the
spotlight.. as they and everyone else dance around
the room.

> SAM V/O
> Well, I'm pleased to report, I
> danced and danced and danced
> with Dick Tratten of the Tratten
> Group. We have a lot in
> common... and the rest is
> history.

FADE OUT.

Bibliography

Aristotle, *Poetics* translated by Richard Janko. Hackett Publishing Company, Indianapolis/Cambridge. 1987.

Armer, Alan A., *Writing the* Screenplay. Wadsworth, Publishing Company, Belmont, California. 1993.

Blacker, Irwin R. *The Elements of Screenwriting*. Collier Books, MacMillan Publishers. 1986.

Lajos, Fgri, *The Art of Dramatic Writing*. Simon & Schuster, New York. 1960.

E.M. Forster, *Aspects of the Novel*. Harcourt, Brace and World, New York. 1927

Halperin, Michael, *Writing Great Characters: The Psychology of Character Development in Screenplays*. Lone Eagle Publishing Co., Los Angeles, California. 1995.

Johnson, Lincoln F., *Film: Space, Time, Light and Sound*. Holt, Rinehart and Winston, New York. 1974.

Jung, C.G., *Psychological Types,* a revision by R.F.C. Hull of the translation by H.G. Baynes. Princeton University Press, Princeton, New Jersey. 1971.

Kazan, Eli, *A Life*. Anchor Books, New York. 1989.

King, Viki, *How to Write a Movie in 21* Days. HarperPerennial, New York. 1988.

Lawson, John Howard. *Theory and Technique of Playwriting and Screenwriting*. Garland Publishers, New York. 1985.

Lucey, Paul, *Story Sense*. McGraw-Hill, New York. 1996.

Lumet, Sidney, *Making Pictures*. Knopf, New York. 1995.

McKee, Robert, *Story: Subsance, Structure, Style, and the Principles of Screenwriting*. Harper-Collins, New York. 1997.

Mehring, Margaret, *The Screenplay: A Blend of Film Form and Content*. Focal Press, Boston, Massachusetts. 1990.

Perret, Gene, *How to Write & Sell Your Sense of Humor*. Writer's Digest Books, Cincinnati, Ohio. 1982.

Seger, Linda, *Making a Good Script Great*. Dodd, Mead & Company, New York. 1987.

Shaw, Harry. *Concise Dictionary of Literary Terms*. McGraw-Hill Paperbacks, New York. 1972.

Stanislavski, Constantin, *An Actor Prepares*, translated by Elizabeth Reynolds Hapgood. Theater Arts Books, New York. 1948.

Index

PRODUCT CATALOG

FOR THE SCREENWRITER

"I LIKED IT, DIDN'T LOVE IT"
Screenplay Development from the Inside Out
by Rona Edwards and Monika Skerbelis

The most commonly used rejection line spewed by studio executive honchos when they do not buy a script is, "I liked it, didn't love it." What happens to your screenplay or novel when it leaves your hands and is submitted to a studio or production company? What happens to it after it's optioned or sold? What does "in development" really mean? Rona Edwards and Monika Skerbelis shed light on all those questions for both those who are new to the business, and those already journeying through the "storied" halls at a film studio, television network, or production company.

$18.95, ISBN 1-58065-062-7

FINAL DRAFT PRESENTS **ASK THE PROS: SCREENWRITING**
101 Questions Answered by Industry Professionals
Edited by Howard Meibach and Paul Duran

Can't sell your screenplay? Problems with your third act? No relatives in the "biz"? Then ask the pros! Final Draft screenwriting software has secured the services of top studio and television executives, literary agents, managers, script consultants, producers and produced screenwriters to answer the most important questions on the minds of developing and emerging screenwriters. Professionals from ICM, UTA, Writers & Artists Group International, DreamWorks, Paramount, and many more take the time to stop and answer your questions. Our experts will tell the reader what's right and what's wrong with a screenplay and how to fix it. They're tough and will tell you what you *need* to hear rather than what you want to hear.

$17.95, ISBN 1-58065-056-2

HOW NOT TO WRITE A SCREENPLAY
101 Common Mistakes Most Screenwriters Make
by Denny Martin Flinn

Having read tons of screenplays as an executive, Denny Martin Flinn has come to understand that while all good screenplays are unique, all bad screenplays are the same. Flinn's book will teach the reader how to avoid the pitfalls of bad screenwriting, and arrive at one's own destination intact. Every example used is gleaned from a legitimate screenplay. Flinn's advice is a no-nonsense analysis of the latest techniques for crafting first-rate screenplays that sell.

$16.95, ISBN 1580650155

THE SCREENPLAY WORKBOOK:
The Writing Before the Writing
by Jeremy Robinson and Tom Mungovan

Every time a screenwriter sits down to write a screenplay, he has to grapple with the daunting question of, "Where do I start?" The preparation time, or the writing *before* the writing, can be intimidating. *The Screenplay Workbook* is an instructional manual combined with proprietary worksheets, charts and fill-in lists designed to give screenwriters a better way to focus on the task of writing a screenplay. All of the organization is done, the right questions are asked, the important subjects are covered.

$18.95, ISBN 1580650538

FOR THE SCREENWRITER

SECRETS OF SCREENPLAY STRUCTURE
How to Recognize and Emulate the Structural Frameworks of Great Films
by Linda J. Cowgill

Linda Cowgill articulates the concepts of successful screenplay structure in a clear language, based on the study and analysis of great films from the thirties to present day. *Secrets of Screenplay Structure* helps writers understand how and why great films work, and how great form and function can combine to bring a story alive.

$16.95, ISBN 158065004X

POWER SCREENWRITING
The 12 Stages of Story Development
by Michael Chase Walker

Michael Chase Walker offers a clear and straightforward framework upon which to build story plots. Standing on the broad shoulders of Joseph Campbell, Christopher Vogler, and others who have demonstrated how mythology is used, Walker brings passion, insight and clarity to a whole new range of story traditions never before examined. Walker offers a wide variety of alternative principles and techniques that are more flexible, adaptable and relevant for the modern storyteller. This book gives insight into the art of storytelling as a way to give depth and texture to any screenplay.

$19.95, ISBN 1580650414

THE COMPLETE WRITER'S GUIDE TO HEROES & HEROINES
Sixteen Master Archetypes
by Tami D. Cowden, Caro LaFever, Sue Viders

By following the guidelines of the archetypes presented in this comprehensive reference work, writers can create extraordinarily memorable characters and elevate their writing to a higher level. The authors give examples of well-known heroes and heroines from television and film so the reader can picture the archetype in his or her mind. The core archetype tells the writer how heroes or heroines think and feel, what drives them and how they reach their goals.

$17.95, ISBN 1580650244

FROM SCRIPT TO SCREEN
The Collaborative Art of Filmmaking, 2nd Edition
by Linda Seger and Edward J. Whetmore

Join Dr. Linda Seger and Edward Whetmore as they examine recent screenplays on their perilous journey from script to screen. In addition to completely updating and revising the first edition, the authors have added a substantial new section that is an extensive case study of the Academy Award® winning film, *A Beautiful Mind*, including exclusive participation by Ron Howard. In interviews with over 70 of the top professionals in the film industry, Seger and Whetmore examine each artist's role in making a great script into a great film.

$18.95, ISBN 1580650546